A STUDENT'S GUIDE TO ESTATES IN LAND AND FUTURE INTERESTS

A STUDENT'S GUIDE TO ESTATES IN LAND AND FUTURE INTERESTS:

Text, Examples, Problems and Answers

Third Edition

Robert Laurence
The Robert A. Leflar Distinguished Professor of Law, Emeritus
The University of Arkansas

Owen L. Anderson
The Eugene Kuntz Chair in Oil, Gas & Natural Resources Law and
George Lynn Cross Research Professor
The University of Oklahoma

Pamela B. Minzner
Late Chief Justice
The Supreme Court of New Mexico
and
Professor of Law
The University of New Mexico

Original Graphics were created by:

Carolyn E. Kennedy
Graphic Artist, Placitas, New Mexico
Freedman, Boyd, Daniels, Peifer,
Hollander, Guttmann & Goldberg, P.A.
Albuquerque, New Mexico

STUDENT GUIDE SERIES

ISBN: 978–1–4224–9874–3

Library of Congress Cataloging-in-Publication Data
Laurence, Robert, 1945-

Laurence, Robert, 1945-
 A student's guide to estates in land and future interests : text, examples, problems and answers / Robert Laurence, Owen L. Anderson, Pamela B. Minzner ; original graphics were created by Carolyn E. Kennedy. -- 3rd ed.
  p. cm.
 Includes index.
 ISBN 978-1-4224-9874-3
 1. Future interests--United States--Outlines, syllabi, etc. 2. Estates (Law)--United States--Outlines, syllabi, etc. I. Anderson, Owen L. II. Minzner, Pamela B. III. Title.
 KF605.L385 2012
 346.7304'2--dc23   2012018931

NOTE TO USERS
To ensure that you are using the latest materials available in this area, please be sure to periodically check the LexisNexis Law School web site for downloadable updates and supplements at www.lexisnexis.com/lawschool.

Editorial Offices
121 Chanlon Rd., New Providence, NJ 07974 (908) 464-6800
201 Mission St., San Francisco, CA 94105-1831 (415) 908-3200
www.lexisnexis.com

MATTHEW◆BENDER

DEDICATION

The first and second editions of this book were dedicated to Frederick M. Hart, Professor and Dean Emeritus at the University of New Mexico. Fred Hart remains "teacher, colleague and friend" to us and many, many people. But we are sure that Fred Hart will agree that our dedication of this third edition must be

To
Pamela Burgy Minzner,
gone too soon.
Requiescat in pace.

R.L. and O.L.A.

PREFACE TO THE THIRD EDITION

The first edition of *A Student's Guide to Estates in Land and Future Interests* was successful in ways surprising to many, not least to Laurence and Minzner. Many thousands of students during the '80s and early '90s turned to it as a guide through what is — or can be — one of the dreary parts of the property course, a worm in the otherwise savory apple of the first year of law school. While we are hesitant to say that *A Student's Guide* made the going either easy or pleasant, it seems to have made the learning more palatable and the experience more tolerable.

Students may be interested to know the origins of this book. In a very real way it began on the floor in the living room of Anne Kass, retired now from the New Mexico trial bench, as Laurence and his study group struggled to prepare for Minzner's exam. Feeling ourselves to be the latest in the long line of American law students trying to figure out what an executory interest was, we started drawing diagrams and making charts, and things began to fall into place — we hoped. Well, we made it, and you will too.

From those early sketches, the presentation was formalized and presented to patient students at the University of New Mexico and, later, at the University of North Dakota. The presentation seemed to work, and Matthew Bender & Co. took a chance on the book, its unknown authors and its unusual format. The book did well and became the first in a series of "Student Guides" from Matthew Bender.

Laurence and Anderson were colleagues at the University of North Dakota in the early 1980s, and Anderson has recommended the book to his property students since it was first published and has occasionally corresponded with the authors about its content. His students know that estates in land, future interests, and the rule against perpetuities are among his favorite subjects. A few years ago, Minzner died and Laurence retired, and when it became time to consider a third edition, Anderson was an obvious choice to work on the new edition.

A Student's Guide never was a treatise requiring careful updating. Rather, it is a teaching and learning tool. The original and second editions of *A Student's Guide to Estates in Land and Future Interests* have been too successful and well received by students to make us eager to make sweeping changes. On each page is the imprint of a student like yourself trying to learn a mysterious and difficult subject.

We've discovered over the years a few pedagogic changes that we think should be made, and we admit that technology has caught up with us. The original diagrams were painstakingly drawn by hand by Carol Kennedy, a New Mexican graphic artist. She used a computer to draw the diagrams for the second edition. The diagrams in this addition, which are patterned after Kennedy's work, were prepared on a computer by the staff at Lexis.

One final point to both teachers and students: we continue to believe that students have the most difficulty distinguishing among contingent remainders, executory interests, and vested remainders subject to divestment. In a large measure, the goal of this book, with its constant emphasis on the year 1536, is to make these distinctions understandable. This year 1536 is not used as a historic landmark, although it is, but as a marker to indicate the need for students to use a slightly more complicated formula to classify interests properly. Note that we write usually in the present tense, though we describe a system of estates in land that never really existed in fact. Later in the presentation we modify the system with statutory law until it becomes the modern law of estates in land. We intentionally do not cover modern law in detail, as the variations from state to state are far too great for our purpose, which is to provide students with a workable means of learning the common law of estates in land and future interests in England in about 1700. We use the present tense to describe this artificially simplified system so students will not be tempted to ask: When and in what order and which came first? As always, we appreciate suggestions of both students and teachers about improving the presentation.

We are grateful to those who helped develop the first edition. Lynn Cianci Eby, New Mexico '78, put together an original outline, problem set, and answers from which chapter seven and the second appendix still heavily draw. Alice E. Herter, New Mexico '79, developed a series of slide presentations which improved the original presentation and influenced the textual treatment in this manuscript. Claudette Abel, Cory Carlson, Richard Gleason, and Karen Johnson, all North Dakota '81, provided valuable assistance by researching the property law of the several states. Ms. Johnson deserves special mention for her efficient and professional direction of the first editorial process. Ms.

PREFACE TO THE THIRD EDITION

Adele Hunter, formerly of the University of New Mexico School of Law staff, typed all of the drafts when such a task was far more demanding than it is today.

Since the original appearance of the first edition of *A Student's Guide,* we have had valuable advice from many, many people. Much of that advice came from our students who used the text with varying degrees of enthusiasm at the New Mexico, North Dakota, Arkansas, Florida State, and Oklahoma law schools. Teachers and colleagues from those institutions and from around the country have offered suggestions. Though too numerous to be listed here, we thank them all, even while admitting that we haven't always followed their advice. Also, the geometric properties of the system will be obvious and, hence, some credit must go to Laurence's former patient high school math students in DeWitt, New York; Andover, Massachusetts; and Moriarty, New Mexico.

For this new edition, Dr. Kathie Anderson read and edited the manuscript. Professor Anderson's colleagues at the University of Oklahoma, Professors Katheleen Guzman and Taiawagi Helton, offered their suggestions, and Professor Helton test drove the manuscript in his property class.

Robert Laurence
Hindsville, Arkansas

Owen L. Anderson
Norman, Oklahoma

September 2011

INTRODUCTION

The American legal system is part of the common law family of legal systems. The common law brought to America by English colonists survived both the American Revolution and an effort by some reformers to adopt a civil law system. Louisiana, a former French colony, follows civil law. The significance of English common law, of course, has lessened with the modern emphasis on legislative innovation, in particular such important legislative events as the Uniform Commercial Code and the Uniform Probate Code. Nevertheless, the English common law influence remains, even in the twenty-first century, in the particular — some would say peculiar — set of concepts and a good deal of vocabulary for the law of real property.

A traditional introduction to the law of real property has been a sketchy survey of the period between 1066 and 1290, from which flows a good bit of the intellectual heritage of property law. During this period, for example, the concepts of alienability by gift or sale and inheritability by intestate succession became associated with an individual's interests in real property. During this period, additionally, a range of interests in land of a rather different sort was recognized. One could acquire and hold interests measured in terms of time, for example, for one's life or for the life of one's bloodline as represented by direct descendants, and for other time periods.

During the era of Norman feudalism in England between 1066 and 1290, a system of property developed that proved better and stronger than its feudal beginnings. While the so-called English common law system of estates in land, which evolved as the English common law itself emerged, may not have been a direct or necessary result of the feudal times that fostered both, the English common law system of estates and associated doctrines were at least an indirect result of the economic aspects of the feudalism, which William the Conqueror introduced and strengthened beginning in 1066.

The property law that emerged in the English feudal era seems to have been a reasonable response to contemporary societal and economic conditions. More importantly, however, that same set of feudal ideas still influences modern property law. In this book, in order to emphasize the practical significance of English real property law, we have de-emphasized English legal history.

We have tried to isolate those concepts basic to a beginning American law student's understanding of estates and future interests and to clarify the relationships among those concepts. A relatively coherent and conceptual system can be extracted from the English common law of real property, and we offer that system as an effective introduction for beginning law students.

This book is not a treatise. That is not to say that we have not given the book a great deal of thought. We have, but this is not a scholarly treatment of the law of estates in land and future interests. This book is a learning tool, a presentation of the material covered in a first-year property course in a way that makes sense to us and has made sense to our students.

We believe our presentation is special in three ways. Firstly, the text will introduce you, in a formalistic, even mechanistic, and certainly oversimplified form, to a system of estates in land that never existed. History takes second place to logic, detail to broad outline, and practical importance to chronology. We have found that this presentation provides a firm base on which to build other discussions of the topic, discussions that will be led by your property professor. Furthermore, we think that other approaches obscure the essential legacy of English common law and equity, which is to provide a set of concepts and a technical vocabulary to express those concepts.

Secondly, the graphic illustrations that symbolize the various interests in real property are intended to make the sometimes slippery distinction among the various interests less slippery, although we decline to say "easy to grasp." We have developed the symbols and the graphic illustration into their current form, but we make no claim that we were the first to put pencil to paper in an attempt to draw a contingent remainder.

Finally, the presentation includes extensive review problems with answers and explanations. The problems have been answered as they would have been at English common law, which we fix somewhat arbitrarily at about 1700.

INTRODUCTION

At the end of the presentation, problems are answered as they would be affected by modern statutes, such as those included in Appendix III, representing in 2011 the states of California, Illinois, Minnesota, New Mexico, and North Dakota. We hope you will find your state or a state with statutes similar to yours on that list. To begin, you are invited to learn the common law, the first step to learning the modern departures from common law by particular states.

As with prior editions, we begin with the definition of five present estates in real property and how they are created.

TABLE OF CONTENTS

TABLE OF CONTENTS

TABLE OF CONTENTS

Chapter 1

THE BASIC PRESENT ESTATES

A. BLACKACRE

Observe the estate of Blackacre, the traditional metaphor for an interest in real property:

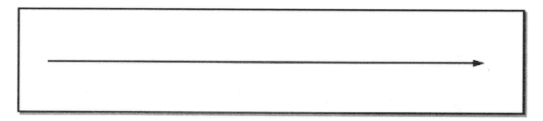

That's right. For the purposes of this presentation, we describe no green hills, gurgling streams, quietly lowing cows, or honking geese. We include no strong-backed farmers working the field, stately baronial mansions, and stone and rail fences older than memory. We ask that you consider merely a ray, a graphical representation of the traditional Blackacre.

Yet much symbolism is tied to that ray. For one thing, the arrow represents infinitely long duration. The ray represents the endlessness of time. By representing time, the ray suggests that interests in Blackacre may be divided between current or "present" interests and future interests. Indeed they may. More, much more, will be said later of this particular legacy from the English law of property.

Briefly consider a cross-sectional look at the ray representing Blackacre:

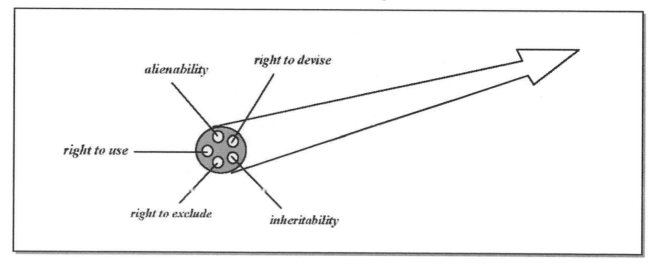

Voilà! A bundle of rights. We leave to your property professor a closer inspection of each of these rights and the limitations on these rights. We focus on the time or durational dimension. Our task is to illustrate the ways in which Blackacre may be divided among those having present rights to present possession and those having present rights to future possession. This possibility of division between present and future interests is a special legacy of the English common law system of estates. Hence, again, Blackacre through time:

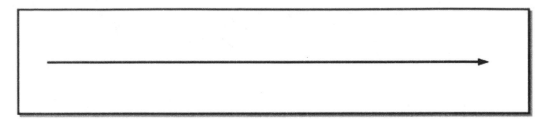

B. FOUR PRESENT ESTATES

English common law lawyers developed a few basic forms of present possessory ownership of Blackacre. We begin with four: the fee simple absolute, the fee tail, the life estate, and the fee simple determinable. As you will learn, we will give each interest a symbol and we will illustrate each one graphically, using Blackacre's ray.

1. The Fee Simple Absolute, a/k/a/ Fee Simple or Fee

If X owns a *Fee Simple Absolute* interest in Blackacre, then:

(a)   X is entitled to the present possession of Blackacre;

(b)   X is entitled to the future possession of Blackacre until X dies;

(c)   X's heir, as determined by the Canons of Descent, is entitled to possession of Blackacre immediately upon X's death;

> The principal English Canon of Descent was that people of closer consanguinity to X took the property over those of more distant relationship. When two or more people had equal relationship to the deceased owner of Blackacre (1) males took over females and (2) the elder male took over the younger male. Females shared equally if there were no males. With the exception of this last rule, royal succession to the British Crown is governed by the Canons. Due to sweeping statutory reforms, few other matters are governed by the Canons of Descent. When this edition went to press, the tectonic plates of the unwritten British Constitution seemed to be moving, and the passage of the British Crown may soon go to males and females equally. Perhaps.

(d)   the heir of X's heir, as likewise determined, is entitled to the possession of Blackacre immediately upon the death of X's heir;

(e)   and so on, through an indefinite succession of heirs; however,

(f)   notwithstanding (c), (d) and (e), X or anyone who inherited Blackacre from X or X's heirs may, at any time and without the consent of anyone who might later inherit Blackacre, "alienate" (transfer) all or part of Blackacre during his lifetime (inter vivos) or by will (devise).

We illustrate X's fee simple absolute as:

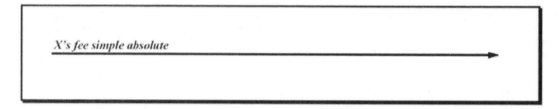

The fee simple absolute is the most complete form of ownership recognized at common law. No conditions on possession, inheritance, or survivorship limit a fee simple absolute. A fee simple continues forever. Is it absolute ownership? No. Don't forget the "power" dimension: it may still be illegal to build a rendering plant outside your neighbor's breakfast nook. What we mean by "most complete" will become clearer as we consider less complete ownership, but a few characteristics may be mentioned here in the context of X's fee simple absolute in Blackacre:

a.   X's possession of Blackacre is conditioned only by the restrictions that society places legitimately on private property rights. For examples of these restrictions, see *State v. Shack*, 58 N.J. 297, 277 A.2d 369 (1971) (restricting the right to exclude), or *Reid v. Architectural Board*, 119 Ohio App. 67, 192 N.E.2d 74 (1963) (allowing land-use restrictions).

b.   X's estate in fee simple is indefinitely *inheritable*. At classic common law, inheritance reflected the principle of Primogeniture (the second Canon of Descent was called the Rule of Primogeniture); the inheritance rules were complex, male-dominated, and yet functional. The system tended to send property to one person rather than divide it up among several heirs. Today, statutes that vary to some extent from state to state dictate how property is transferred at death. For example, these statutes might dictate a transfer of at least a portion of the property to decedent's surviving spouse with the balance being shared by the closest surviving heirs based on degrees of kinship. Heirs of the same degree would typically receive equal shares without regard to gender. For example, if X died unmarried and "intestate" (without leaving a will), survived by one son and two grandchildren of a deceased daughter, then these statutes might transfer an "undivided" one-half of X's fee simple absolute to the son and undivided one-fourth to each of the grandchildren. Thus, these intestacy statutes dictate the "heirs" (people) who "inherit" (succeed to) the property of a person who dies "intestate" (without a will). In these materials, we use the word "inheritable" to describe the right to let intestacy statutes transfer property at death to one's heirs absent a will.

c.   X's estate in fee simple is indefinitely *devisable*. Today, statutes govern an owner's right to "devise" (transfer) property by a written document called a "will." A will transfers property at death, not at the time the will is prepared. But X's lawful devise of Blackacre by will defeats X's heirs' inheritance of Blackacre. In these materials, we use the word "devisable" to describe the right to transfer property at death by will. In England, the right to transfer certain property interests by will was not firmly established until 1540 when Parliament enacted the Statute of Wills, but, for our purposes, we will assume that certain interests were devisable before that date.

d.   X's estate in fee simple is freely *alienable* (transferable) "inter vivos" (between the living). This means that the property can be sold or given away by its owner during the owner's lifetime. An inter vivos transfer defeats both devisees and heirs. Thus, if X alienates the entire fee simple while alive, then X's heirs will no longer inherit Blackacre and X's devisees will no longer take Blackacre under a will in which X purported to devise Blackacre. In these materials, we use the word "alienable" to describe the right to transfer property while alive.

We illustrate the fee simple once more for emphasis:

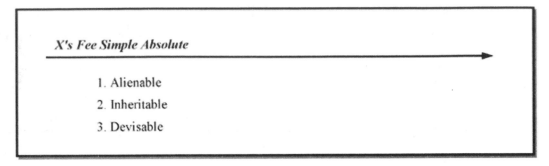

2. Fee Tail (from "tailler," Norman French for "to cut" or "to carve") or Entailed Estate

If X owns a Fee Tail interest in Blackacre, then:

(a)   X is entitled to the present possession of Blackacre;

(b)   X is entitled to the future possession of Blackacre until X dies;

(c)   upon X's death, only X's children and other direct "lineal" descendants are entitled to inherit (among these direct lineal descendants, the Canons of Descent apply; upon the death of a child of X, that deceased child's children are entitled to inherit);

(d)   and so on, through an indefinite succession of lineal descendants of X ("Lineal descendants" are sons, daughters, grandchildren, great-grandchildren, etc. Cousins, nieces, nephews, uncles, aunts are called "collateral heirs." "Lineal ancestors" are parents, grandparents, and great-grandparents. But all of these are "heirs." The closest heir would inherit X's fee simple absolute, but only lineal descendants may inherit a fee tail);

(f)   X or any of X's lineal descendants who inherit Blackacre may <u>not</u> devise it; and finally,

(g)   X or any of X's lineal descendants may not alienate the entire fee tail, but X or a lineal descendant may alienate only the right to possession of Blackacre until death. At the time of X's death, regardless of who is in possession of Blackacre, the estate passes to X's lineal descendant, as described above.

We illustrate the fee tail as follows:

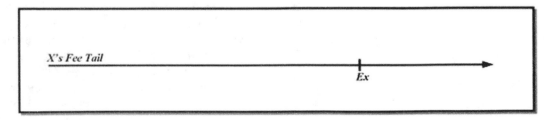

Since the fee tail will pass only to the lineal descendants of X, at some point in time, no one may be eligible to own Blackacre — *i.e.*, when X's direct line dies out. We call this event "***Expiration***," denoted in the diagram by ***Ex***. Be aware that many writers and courts do not use this word as narrowly as we do. The word "expire" or "expiration" in this guide means the natural termination of the fee tail or the life estate at death.

Note that a fee simple absolute does ***not*** expire. While X's direct line may die out, we should theoretically always be able to find an heir of X. More on this later!

> The fee tail probably was the most significant estate planning device in the years between 1285 and 1472. In 1472 a technique called "common recovery" allowed the interests of the lineal descendants to be frustrated. The details of this remedy are beyond the scope of this presentation, but the popularity of the fee tail and its eventual demise are evidence of the relationship between social history and the evolution of legal concepts.

The chief characteristics of X's fee tail in Blackacre are as follows:

a. As with the fee simple, X's possession of Blackacre is without condition, other than those restrictions that society might place on private property rights.

b. X's fee tail in Blackacre is inheritable only by the direct lineal descendants of the original owner, X.

c. X's fee tail in Blackacre is not freely alienable or devisable. The only thing that any owner may alienate is the right to possession for the life of that owner; on the owner's death the property passes automatically to that owner's direct lineal descendant.

We illustrate the fee tail once more for emphasis:

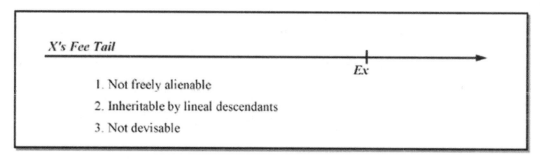

Note the words given above: "The only thing that any owner may alienate is the right to possession for that owner's lifetime." Does your new-to-the-law mind question the notion that property ownership means ***more*** than the right to possess property during one's lifetime? To achieve a proper understanding of estates in land and especially of future interests, you must accept the notion that ***full*** ownership of property is much more than a lifetime of possessory rights. The land will still exist after the owner dies; thus, ***full*** ownership of property during life includes the right to specify its disposition upon death.

You should now understand the major difference between the fee simple and the fee tail. The fee simple owner controls disposition; the fee tail owner does not. For example, if X owns a fee tail, then X's children or their children will secure possession irrespective of X's desires. X has no power to devise Blackacre and only the right to alienate Blackacre for life. In contrast, if X owns a fee simple absolute, then X can freely alienate or devise Blackacre to anyone.

In the next estate, the life estate, the owner has no control over the disposition of the property at death and the children of the life tenant are ***not*** entitled to future possession.

3. Life Estate; Estate for Life

If X owns a **_Life Estate_** interest in Blackacre, then:

(a)   X is entitled to the present possession of Blackacre;

(b)   X is entitled to the future possession of Blackacre until X's death;

(c)   X's heirs are entitled to inherit nothing by way of X's ownership of Blackacre; and

(d)   X may alienate only the right to possession of Blackacre during X's life.

We illustrate the life estate as follows:

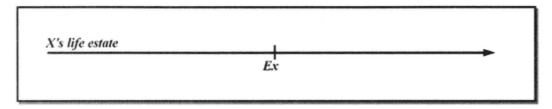

A life estate "expires" upon X's death.

a.   Possession is without condition, but possession is only of the life estate — X's life. The life tenant has no right to possess something belonging to a future tenant. This limitation presents some problems. For example, how can a life tenant enjoy a heavily wooded Blackacre if he or she wants to build a factory and the future tenant is an ardent environmentalist? The problem of balancing the interests of a life tenant and a future tenant was resolved at English common law by the doctrine of waste. The doctrine of waste limits the life tenant's use of the land, but the doctrine is flexible and permits a court to balance the competing interests. Thus, we characterize the life estate, as well as the fee tail, as an unconditional possessory interest.

b.   The basic life estate is not inheritable or devisable. It expires with X, leaving nothing for X's heirs to inherit.

c.   The life estate is freely alienable, but expiration still occurs on X's death. If X sells to Y, then Y holds a life estate that expires on X's death — a so-called life estate **_pur autre vie_** ("for the life of another"). This modification of the life estate is not essentially different from the basic form except that a life estate **_pur autre vie_** is inheritable and devisable. Thus, if X sells to Y, then Y has an interest in Blackacre measured by the life of X. If Y predeceases X, then Y's heir or devisee may possess Blackacre until the death of X.

We illustrate the life estate once more for emphasis:

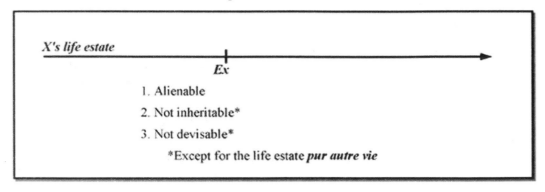

4. Fee Simple Determinable, Determinable Fee

If X owns a *Fee Simple Determinable* interest in Blackacre, then:

(a)   X is entitled to the present possession of Blackacre;

(b)   X is entitled to the future possession of Blackacre until X dies;

(c)   X's heir, as determined by the Canons of Descent, is entitled to possession of Blackacre immediately upon X's death;

(d)   the heir of X's heir, as likewise determined, is entitled to the possession of Blackacre immediately upon the death of X's heir;

(e)   and so on, through an indefinite succession of heirs; however,

(f)   notwithstanding (c), (d) and (e), X or anyone who inherited Blackacre from X or X's heirs may, at any time and without the consent of anyone who might later inherit Blackacre, "alienate" (transfer) all or part of Blackacre inter vivos or by devise (will); and

(g)   all of the above is exactly as in the definition of a fee simple absolute, subject to a self-executing condition that, if broken, automatically ends X's or X's successors' right to possess Blackacre.

We illustrate the fee simple determinable as follows:

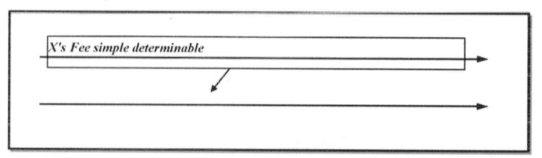

The fee simple determinable, you will note, does not expire; however:

a.   Possession is conditional — for example, Blackacre may always have to be farmed or always used for church purposes.

b.   Blackacre is indefinitely inheritable.

c.   Blackacre is freely alienable.

d.   Blackacre is devisable.

Points (b), (c) and (d) ought not surprise you, because this estate, as the name suggests, is a type of *fee simple.*

The fee simple determinable was not nearly as important at English common law as the first three estates you learned. This estate may have served at an early time as a device to secure the repayment of a loan; *i.e.,* a mortgage. For example, early forms of mortgages may have resembled conditional conveyances: O might convey to his creditor as long as a sum of money remained owed to that creditor. The fee simple determinable was not used frequently in England; however, in the United States the fee simple determinable occurred with greater frequency. The fee simple determinable has been used in conveyances to charities, in conveyances that restrict land use, and in conveyances to railroads for rights-of-way. In Texas and some other states, the typical "oil and gas lease" is classified as a fee simple determinable; yes, this is so, even though the parties called the instrument a lease.

A fifth present possessory interest, the fee simple on condition subsequent, will be easier to grasp if we introduce some other ideas first.

Some questions may have been nagging at you for a page or two: Who says possession is conditional in the fee simple determinable? Who limits the fee tail? How does X know what he or she has? Who decides? To answer these questions, we now consider the creation of estates.

C.   CREATING THE ESTATES AND THE ART OF CONVEYANCING

Meet the famous O, well known throughout property law casebooks. Suppose O owns a fee simple absolute. Do not worry about how O got it. Just assume that O owns Blackacre in fee simple absolute.

> An early eastern religion pictured the world supported on the backs of three elephants. The elephants stood on the backs of two turtles. It was considered improper to ask on what the turtles stood.

O may create a fee simple absolute in A with the following grant:

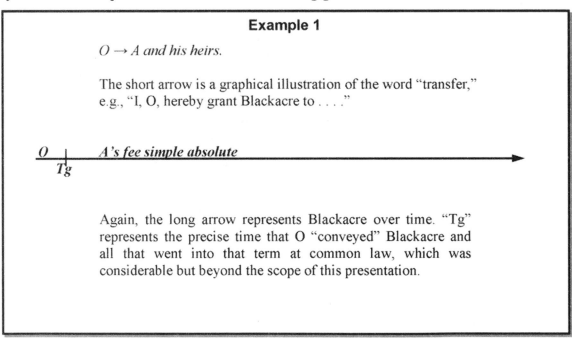

Example 1

$O \rightarrow A$ *and his heirs.*

The short arrow is a graphical illustration of the word "transfer," e.g., "I, O, hereby grant Blackacre to . . . ."

O | A's *fee simple absolute* $\longrightarrow$
Tg

Again, the long arrow represents Blackacre over time. "Tg" represents the precise time that O "conveyed" Blackacre and all that went into that term at common law, which was considerable but beyond the scope of this presentation.

The common law was very specific about how to create a fee simple absolute. These words, **and no others,** would do. Today, because modern caselaw and statutes favor the creation of the fee simple absolute, the fee simple absolute is the default estate. That is, courts will generally presume that O intended to create a fee simple absolute if O's intent is unclear based on the words O used when making the grant. But for now, let's assume that O used "and his heirs." Whether at common law or today, by using the words "and his heirs," O granted a fee simple absolute.

Observe that O owns Blackacre until the time of the grant (*Tg*), at which point A becomes the owner. Thereafter, A's interest in Blackacre is as complete as the law recognizes. The entire time dimension is occupied by A's interest; no one else has an interest in the property. O is merely a former owner.

What about A's heirs? The conveyance was, after all, to "A and his heirs." While A is alive, A's heirs are unidentifiable, that is, they are only potential heirs. A's heirs can be determined only upon A's death because a living person has no heirs, only potential heirs. Under the Canons of Descent, A's eldest son has the most likely chance of inheritance, but the eldest son won't be A's heir unless he is still living at A's death. Nonetheless, even if A has no *close* relatives, then that doesn't mean he won't have an heir when he dies. For example, a complete stranger — perhaps a distant cousin in another country — might become A's heir. Such a distant relative might be a so-called "laughing" heir because he or she may have no remorse over A's death and might actually rejoice in inheriting Blackacre! If A and all of A's direct descendants die in a common accident, for example, then a collateral heir would inherit under the Canons of Descent. So, *no* living person has an heir, but *every* deceased person is presumed to have an heir.

Of course, it is possible for someone to die without an heir. An heir is determined by intestacy statutes, which generally specify a limit on eligible heirship. If A dies without an heir, then A's estate "escheats." Today, A's estate would escheat to the state government where Blackacre is located. In feudal England, A's estate would escheat to A's overlord. Because escheat rarely occurs, A's fee simple absolute is regarded as indefinitely inheritable and thus non-expirable.

Common law courts long ago decided that the words "and his heirs" gave nothing to A's heirs and were not, hence, words of purchase. The only word that describes the recipient and thus the only word of purchase in the grant "to A and his heirs" is the word "A." A is the "purchaser," which meant at common law that O either gave or sold Blackacre to A.

The words "and his heirs" are words of limitation; that is to say, they indicate the estate that has been created, the fee simple absolute. We know, practically speaking, that the fee simple is without limitation. You will encounter some words of limitation shortly that condition the use of the estate A has been given. The point here is that words of limitation "limit," or describe, the grantee's estate, but do not give rights in the estate to anyone other than A.

To summarize, A is the grantee, and the word "A" is also the word of purchase. The words "and his heirs" are words of limitation (in the case of a fee simple absolute, essentially words of non-limitation). The essential words of conveyance are called the words of grant, which might have been: "I, O, grant Blackacre to A and his heirs."

O may grant a fee tail to A with the following conveyance:

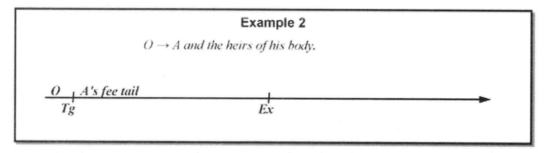

Example 2

O → A and the heirs of his body.

O | A's fee tail
Tg   *Ex*

Notice that we have not accounted for the entire time dimension of Blackacre. We have, as yet, no ownership assigned to the time beyond expiration (*Ex*); that is, the time after A's direct line ends. Be patient; we will address this "future interest" in good time.

In Example 2, the "grant" is from O to "A and the heirs of his body." "A" is the word of purchase and "and the heirs of his body" are the words of limitation. These latter words limit the estate that A receives. We will not know which heir of A's body (that is, which of the children or perhaps grandchildren or even great-grandchildren) will inherit until A dies. Therefore, no one takes anything at the time of the grant except A. Just as in the fee simple absolute, there are no words of purchase except "A" in the grant.

The fee tail may come in special forms.

Example 3

O → A and the heirs of his body by W.

This grant creates a "fee tail special," and only lineal descendants of both A and W are eligible to inherit. Why would O make such a grant? Perhaps W is O's daughter. He is pleased to gift Blackacre to A but wants to make sure that W's children will inherit Blackacre, not other children of A by an earlier or later spouse.

Examples 4 and 5

O → A and the male heirs of his body.

O → A and the female heirs of his body.

Respectively, the "fee tail male" and the "fee tail female" are self-explanatory. Apparently, no one ever thought to try:

Example 6

O → A and the basketball-playing heirs of his body.

However, it's hard to believe that no one tried:

Example 7

O → A and the Harvard-educated heirs of his body.

In any case, we recognize only the basic fee tail and the three special forms discussed above.

O may grant a life estate to A as follows:

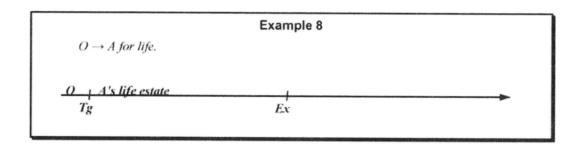

The life estate was the preferred estate at common law. That is, the law presumed that a life estate was created by any grant that did not fit one of the other estates. As Littleton wrote late in the fifteenth century: "For a man purchase lands by the words, 'To have and to hold to him for ever'. . . he hath but an estate for term of life, for that there lack these words, 'his heirs,' which words only make an estate of inheritance in all feoffments and grants." *Littleton's Tenures* § 1 (Wambaugh ed., 1903). The common law's preference for the life estate has now been generally abandoned in the United States by statute. Thus, as previously stated, the fee simple absolute is now generally preferred.

Each of the following examples creates a life estate in A at traditional common law and fee simple absolute at modern law:

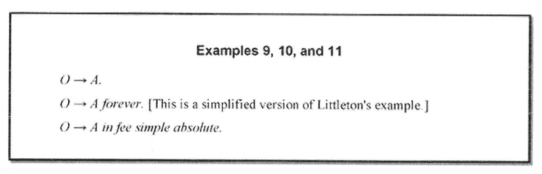

Finally, O may grant a fee simple determinable to A:

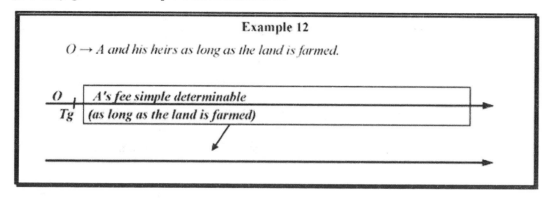

The common law was not so strict about the wording of this grant, although the words "and his heirs" were still required to create a ***fee simple*** determinable. As previously mentioned, modern law presumes that O intended to convey a fee simple interest unless words of limitation indicate otherwise. Thus, a conveyance "to A for so long as the land as farmed," would most likely be construed as a fee simple determinable.

Examples 13 and 14

O → A and his heirs **until** *the land is no longer farmed.*

O → A and his heirs **while** *the land is farmed.*

A has a fee simple determinable.

Here we have used one condition — that the land be farmed. Almost any condition will do. O decides. Of course, public policy limitations will limit what conditions will be enforceable. Sometimes statutes reflect public policy limitations; sometimes courts announce limitations when called on to interpret or construe deeds or wills. As you might expect, statutes and decided cases are easier to take into account in drafting documents than issues that have never been litigated or anticipated by legislators.

The illustration for the fee simple determinable indicates that if the land is not farmed, then A will lose his estate and someone else will take possession. Who? This "future interest" will be discussed shortly.

D. FEE SIMPLE ON CONDITION SUBSEQUENT

We now consider one more present possessory interest, the fee simple on condition subsequent.

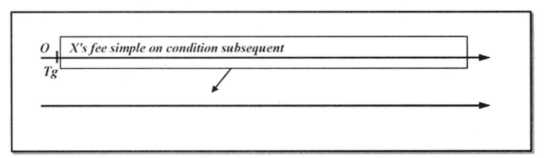

X is said to own a *Fee Simple on Condition Subsequent* interest in Blackacre if:

(a)   X is entitled to the present possession of Blackacre;

(b)   X is entitled to the future possession of Blackacre until X dies;

(c)   X's heir, as determined by the Canons of Descent, is entitled to possession of Blackacre immediately upon X's death;

(d)   the heir of X's heir, as likewise determined, is entitled to the possession of Blackacre immediately upon the death of X's heir;

(e)   and so on, through an indefinite succession of heirs; however,

(f)   notwithstanding (c), (d) and (e), X or anyone who inherited Blackacre from X or X's heirs may, at any time and without the consent of anyone who might later inherit Blackacre, "alienate" (transfer) all or part of Blackacre inter vivos or by devise (will);

(g)   All of the above is exactly as in the definition of a fee simple absolute, *subject to* a condition that, if broken, allows the creator of the estate (the grantor) to end X's right or X's successors' right to possess Blackacre by entering and reclaiming it. This right to enter and reclaim is passed from the grantor to her heirs. However, for simplicity, we will say that the grantor may enter when we really mean that the grantor or those who succeed the grantor at death may enter. Later, we will add more about this right to enter and reclaim.

We illustrate a fee simple on condition subsequent with the following conveyance:

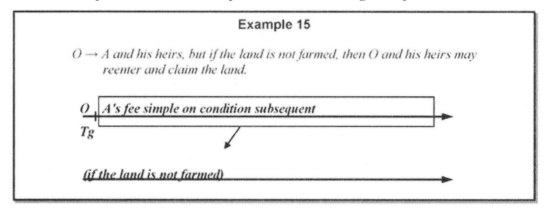

Once again, as with the fee simple determinable, other wordings are acceptable. You may substitute "provided that if . . . then" or "on the condition that if . . . then" for "but if . . . then." The grantor may be described as able to "reenter and claim," or to "enter and reclaim," or to "reenter and reclaim" the land. "And his heirs" is required at common law, but modern law presumes that O intended to convey a fee simple interest unless the words of limitation indicate otherwise. If A (or a successor to A's interest) breaks the condition after O's death, then the land could be reclaimed by O's heirs.

The graphic illustration in Example 15 suggests that this grant is very much like the fee simple determinable (see Example 12), and it is. The only difference is that the condition limiting the duration of the fee simple determinable is self-executing, while the fee simple on condition subsequent requires O to enter and reclaim Blackacre. Who cares? Well, for example, a statute of limitations for adverse possession might begin to run the instant that a condition for a determinable fee is broken; however, the statute of limitations for adverse possession of land subject to a condition subsequent might not begin to run until the right to enter and reclaim has been demanded. Do you understand why?

The requisite period for adverse possession is measured from the time a cause of action in ejectment accrues. When O has created a fee simple determinable, O's cause of action arguably accrues the moment the condition is broken, thereby giving O the immediate right to possession. Hence, the statute of limitations governing ejectment would begin to run automatically when the condition was broken.

However, when O creates a fee simple on condition subsequent, he is not entitled to possession until he demands possession. Arguably then, O has no cause of action in ejectment until he has demanded reentry. Only then does the statute of limitations for adverse possession begin to run.

A statute of limitation restricts the period of time during which O might make a valid demand. The words of the statute might treat the optional right to make a demand to reenter in the same manner as the self-executing condition in a fee simple determinable. And a court of equity might well apply the doctrine of laches to a long-unexercised right of entry.

These, then, are five basic present possessory estates in land. Master them. You must be able to classify an unambiguous present estate with only a glance at a conveyance. Otherwise, what follows in this guide will become unmanageable. Outside of a few "hybrid" estates, you have only one more present estate to master.

> Please forgive the redundancy of "present possessory interest" this one time. We address estates in land and future interests. All present estates are possessory by nature and all future interests that become present estates will then become possessory.

E.   REVIEW PROBLEMS (BEFORE 1536)

Answer the problems using what you have learned so far. So, if you are working through this guide for the first time, then consider only the preceding materials. In chapter four, you will learn that the law of estates in land and future interests was affected by the Statute of Uses enacted by Parliament in 1536. If you have already worked through the book, then you may wish to answer these problems based on the entire book.

1.   O wants to give his land to his only child, but O wants the land to stay in the family forever. How should he proceed?

2.   O wants to sell her property for the highest possible price. How should she proceed?

3.   O wants to give his land to A, but he wants the land back if it is used for commercial purposes. Can he do so? How?

4.   O wants to give her land to her church as long as the land is used for church purposes, but if the land ceases to be used for church purposes, then O wants to be able to take back the property. Can she do so? How?

5.   O wants to give her land to her husband until he dies. Can she do so? How?

Answers to Review Problems

1.   O wants to give his land to his only child, but O wants the land to stay in the family forever. How should he proceed?

    He should create a fee tail:

    O →   *Child and the heirs of his body.*

2.   O wants to sell her property for the highest possible price. How should she proceed?

    She should create a fee simple absolute:

    O →   *Purchaser and his heirs.*

3.   O wants to give his land to A, but he wants the land back if the land is used for commercial purposes.

    Can he do so? Yes.

    How?

    He might create a fee simple determinable:

    O →   *A and his heirs as long as the land is never used for commercial purposes.*

    Or, he might create a fee simple on condition subsequent:

    O →   *A and his heirs, but if the land is ever used for commercial purposes, then O and his heirs shall have the right to reenter and reclaim the land.*

> The fee simple determinable and the fee simple on condition subsequent are not interchangeable methods of conveying property. In addition to your client's wishes, governing statutes and controlling cases will be relevant in determining which estate to create.

4.   O wants to give her land to her church as long as it is used for church purposes, but if the land ceases to be used for church purposes, then O wants to be able to take back the property.
        Can she do so? Yes.
        How?

> She may do so by creating a fee simple subject to condition subsequent:
>
> *O →   The Church, its successors and assigns, but if the land ceases to be used for church purposes, O or her heirs may reenter and reclaim the land.*

> The Church has no "heirs." With corporate entities, use instead the words "its successors and assigns."

5.   O wants to give her land to her husband until he dies.
        Can she do so? Yes.
        How?

> She may do so by simply creating a life estate:
>
> *O →   Husband for life.*

Chapter 2

FUTURE INTERESTS BEFORE 1536

From studying the diagrams in the prior chapter, you have observed that all of the illustrations of the Blackacre ray, except those illustrating the fee simple absolute, leave space along the ray for additional interests. In other words, in these illustrations, we assume that O begins with a fee simple absolute. Where X or A have a fee simple absolute, no space is left for any additional future interest because the fee simple absolute is the largest possible interest — the full interest. All of the illustrations that indicate something less than the full fee simple absolute leave space for additional interests. These additional interests are called "future interests." Thus, no future interests follow a fee simple absolute, but a future interest or interests must follow anything less than a fee simple absolute.

Specifically, a future interest or interests must follow the life estate, the fee tail, the fee simple determinable, and the fee simple upon condition subsequent. Why? Because we must account for the full fee simple absolute. The common law courts were strict about this matter. The state of the title to Blackacre must be identified in terms of both present and future interests that together make up the fee simple absolute. Mathematically speaking, the sum of the present and any future interests must equal the fee simple absolute.

At some point, the future interest or interests will, or at least may, become possessory. Upon the expiration of the life estate or the fee tail, upon the breaking of the condition in the fee simple determinable, or upon the demand to reenter after the breaking of the condition in a fee simple on condition subsequent, a future interest will become a present estate.

These as-yet unassigned parts of Blackacre are not, of course, physical "parts" of the land, but rather they are "interests" that are, in some sense, future. They are *future* interests in the sense that they will not become *possessory* interests, if ever, until some future time. But you know from your property course that "ownership" of property does not require actual possession. These "future interests" are presently protected property rights in land, but actual possession of the land itself is delayed.

For now, recognize two broad categories of future interests, future interests retained by the grantor and future interests conveyed to additional grantees. The first category, and the easier to master, identifies future interests retained by the grantor, O.

A. FUTURE INTERESTS IN THE GRANTOR

Throughout this text, we will assume O owns a fee simple absolute unless the discussion or the problem indicates otherwise. Thus, when O conveys to A a fee simple absolute, O grants to A all that O owns, no future interest is created, and O retains no interest in Blackacre.

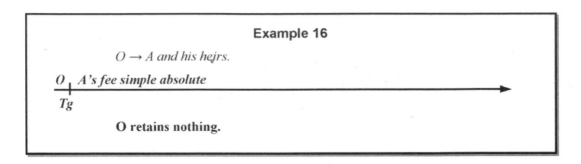

Example 16

$O \rightarrow A$ *and his heirs.*

O A's *fee simple absolute*

Tg

O retains nothing.

In each of the other four present estates previously discussed, the common law courts determined that, with no further words than the grants you have already studied, O retains a future interest. O, in other words, owns a present right to future possession of the land. Your major task is to learn the vocabulary.

With two of the four estates, if O says nothing further, then O retains the future interest known as a reversion.

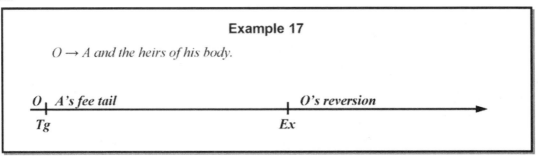

Example 17

$O \rightarrow A$ *and the heirs of his body.*

O A's *fee tail* O's *reversion*

Tg Ex

Those readers who are fans of Jane Austen are now in position to understand what was going on in *Pride and Prejudice*. Mr. Bennett held Longbourn in fee tail male, and Mr. Collins held the reversion. Mr. and Mrs. Bennett having produced only daughters, Mr. Bennett's estate was set to expire on his death, putting Mr. Collins into possession. The possibility, indeed certainty, of her eviction from the estate on her husband's death was very stressful on Mrs. Bennett's nerves, and added additional pressure on the daughters to marry soon, and well. Since we know that Mr. Collins and the Misses Bennett were distant cousins, we can surmise that some generations back a grantor whom we would call "O" created the fee tail male in one of his collateral heirs, say a nephew, keeping the reversion to himself. That reversion has now descended to Mr. Collins, and the fee tail male to Mr. Bennett. Luckily, of course, Jane marries well, and Lizzie exceedingly well, so all is saved, though admittedly we wonder what holiday family get-togethers will be like.

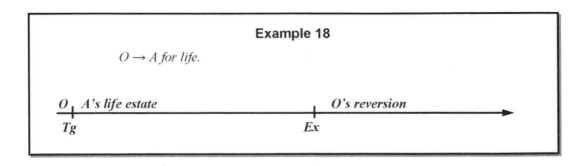

Example 18

$O \rightarrow A$ *for life.*

O A's *life estate* O's *reversion*

Tg Ex

In Examples 17 and 18, O has an interest that is present in the sense that O can sell it, give it away, or devise it. Further, if O dies without a will, then the reversionary interest will pass to O's heirs. Thus, in both examples, O's interest is presently alienable, inheritable, and devisable. O's interest is future in the sense that O is entitled to possession at a future point in time — the expiration of the prior estate. Should O enter Blackacre, O would be a trespasser; however, O does have the right to protect Blackacre from waste by A.

In Example 17, if A dies survived by a son (S), then S will inherit the fee tail. O will continue to own the reversion. If O dies leaving a will in favor of a child (C), then C will hold the reversion. Absent a contrary agreement between C and S, the relationship between C and S respecting Blackacre will be governed by the law of waste.

Admittedly, it is far easier to appreciate the presence of a reversion when only a life estate is created in the grantee. The reversion present when only a fee tail is created, however, was apparently just as real at early common law. At that time, the dying out of a direct line occurred often enough to make the reversion after a fee tail an important future interest. A reversion was considered a substantial interest at common law. Hence, a reversion was alienable inter vivos, devisable and inheritable.

If O says nothing extra in creating the other two present estates, then two similar but differently named future interests arise in O.

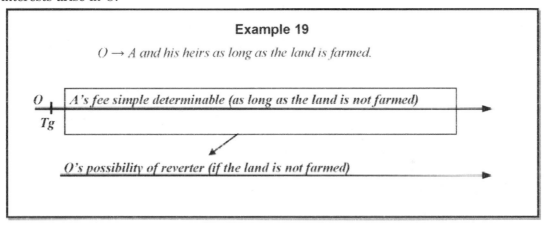

Example 19

$O \rightarrow A$ and his heirs as long as the land is farmed.

O
Tg
A's fee simple determinable (as long as the land is not farmed)

O's possibility of reverter (if the land is not farmed)

Don't be tempted to say "possibility of reversion." You must be able to distinguish reversions from possibilities of reverter and use the correct terminology when identifying each present estate and future interest.

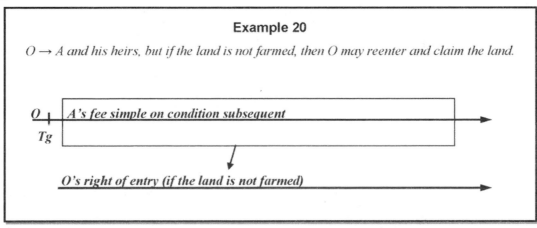

Example 20

$O \rightarrow A$ and his heirs, but if the land is not farmed, then O may reenter and claim the land.

O
Tg
A's fee simple on condition subsequent

O's right of entry (if the land is not farmed)

O's right of entry or re-entry is also called a "power of termination." This future interest will become a present interest only if the land is not farmed and O exercises his right of entry.

The possibility of reverter and the right of entry are classified as "future interests" because O has no present right to possession of Blackacre as a result of having created such an interest. Again, the right to **possess** property is only one of the strands in the "bundle of rights" that we call Blackacre. Your understanding of property is by now sophisticated enough to appreciate that possession, while a very important strand in some cases, is not all you need to know about property ownership. O owns a valuable, albeit presently nonpossessory, property interest that gives O a present right to future possession. In modern terms, you might think of O's right as similar to a landlord's right to re-take possession of the property in the future at the expiration of a lease or perhaps upon breach of a condition in the lease. In fact, for this reason, your landlord's interest is sometimes today called a "reversionary" interest or even a right of entry.

Summary of Transferability (Future Interests in the Grantor)

Three future interests are possible in the grantor: the reversion, the possibility of reverter, and right of entry. They are created automatically upon creation of four of the five present estates. If the grantor created a life estate or a fee tail, then the grantor retained a reversion. If the grantor created a fee simple determinable, then the grantor retained a possibility of reverter. If the grantor created a fee simple on condition subsequent, then the grantor retained a right of entry. The transferability of the possibility of reverter and the right of entry were restricted at common law. The following chart compares and contrasts the three future interests that may be created in the grantor.

Future Interests in the Grantor Before 1536

	Reversion	Possibility of Reverter	Right of Entry
How created?	When O conveys an expirable estate, *i.e.*, a fee tail or a life estate.	When O conveys a fee simple determinable.	When O conveys a fee simple on condition subsequent.
Alienable inter vivos?	Yes	No	No
Devisable?	Yes	Probably not	No
Inheritable?	Yes	Yes	Yes

> Most of these restrictions on alienation have been removed by statute, but for the purposes of this presentation, we will consider both the possibility of reverter and the right of entry to be <u>inalienable</u>. Whether a possibility of reverter was devisable depends on an interpretation of the Statute of Wills (1540), as amended in 1542, which provided for the devise of estates "in possession, reversion or remainder." Judicial opinion indicated that the statute did not include rights of entry. A scholarly dispute continues about the effect of the statute on possibilities of reverter. Some modern statutes appear to be attempts to clarify the common law rules; others are more straightforward. Whether the law of waste protected O's future interest in the case of a possibility of reverter or a right of entry is unclear. Why? Because the preceding present estate is in "fee simple." Should it perhaps depend on how certain the "condition" is likely to occur or be broken?

Remember these three future interests in the grantor. We will add details later, but what you have learned so far is what you need to know for now about the reversion, the possibility of reverter, and the right of entry.

Obviously, these interests have other legal aspects. For example, if the language employed in a deed is not clear, then uncertainties arise regarding the interest(s) created, perhaps necessitating an action to try title to resolve them. Such interests may have estate tax consequences. Advanced property courses and advanced tax courses will involve practical problems in which the technical vocabulary you are acquiring will prove helpful. For our purposes, all you need to learn now are the concepts, the primary language by which such interests are created, and their significance within the general system of estates in land.

B.   FUTURE INTERESTS IN A GRANTEE

You know that O may convey Blackacre to A and retain one of the future interests discussed above. The common law also allowed O, if O was careful to follow the rules, to convey a future interest to some third party, whom, for the moment, we shall call "B." Those common law rules, which developed early, were strict. If the rules were broken during the early common law period, then the conveyance of the future interest was ineffective, and O ended up retaining, rather than conveying, a future interest.

We make two points before we lay out these rules. First, the bad news is that these rules, though older than old — remember that we are still talking about times *before* 1536 — are still important today. The classification of an interest has, or at least, may have, crucial consequences. While both case law and statutory principles governing construction of language in documents have become more flexible than they were before 1536, the rules discussed next still influence the case law and thus are significant when classifying interests.

Second, the good news — sort of — is that these rules are rules of law, not rules of construction. Thus, they are not rules to aid you in deciding the grantor's intent. Indeed, these rules, if not followed, may frustrate the grantor's intent because these rules of law must be followed for the future interests to be valid.

Three rules were relevant to creating future interests in a grantee before 1536:

Rule 1. Only expirable estates could be followed by a future interest in a grantee.

Hence, to be valid, a future interest in a grantee had to follow either a fee tail or a life estate. That's not hard to remember, since in those two cases, O has a reversion if the deed or will contains nothing extra. In other words, the common law permitted, all in one grant, the "replacement" of an alienable reversion in the grantor by a future interest in a third party. This seems reasonable, doesn't it? After all, if O conveys a life estate to A, then O keeps a reversion that he can then alienate to B. Thus, Rule 1 allows O to convey both a life estate in A and the remainder of his interest to B in one deed. The only detail — perhaps a mildly annoying one — is that the future interest that follows these rules is called a "remainder," not a reversion. The person in whom the interest is created traditionally has been called a "remainderman," regardless of gender.

On the other hand, Rule 1 implicitly provides that a future interest in a grantee could not follow a fee simple determinable or a fee simple on condition subsequent, as these interests are not "expirable." This too seems reasonable. After creating a fee simple determinable or a fee simple on condition subsequent, O retains a future interest that O may not subsequently alienate to B or anyone else. Thus, the law reasonably prohibits O from doing so in one grant.

Finally, the fee simple absolute is never followed by any future interest. If O retains no interest after conveying a fee simple absolute to A, then O has nothing left to transfer to any other grantee.

This is all quite simple and logical, isn't it?

Rule 2. The future interest created in B must be capable of taking effect (become a present possessory interest) immediately upon expiration of the preceding estate.

Consider the following simple example:

Example 21

O → A for life, then to B and his heirs.

A has a life estate; B has a remainder.

No graphic illustration is given for this grant, because the illustration depends on the classification of the remainder, which we have not yet discussed.

Here are two examples of future interests in B that do not satisfy this requirement:

Examples 22 and 23

O → A for life, and one year later to B and his heirs.

O → A for life, then to B ten years after A's death if B is still solvent.

Notice that in Examples 22 and 23, the future interest will not be ready to take effect (to become a present estate) at expiration, A's death. Hence, in both cases, the future interest in B is invalid before 1536. The state of the title, then, is that A has a life estate and O has a reversion. B has nothing. O clearly conveyed only a life estate to A. So O, having failed to properly transfer the remainder of his interest, keeps what is left — a reversion.

Here are two examples that satisfy the requirement that the future interest is capable of taking effect (becoming present possessory) immediately upon the expiration of the preceding estate:

Examples 24 and 25

O → A for life, then if B survives A, to B and his heirs.

O → A for life, then if B has married C, to B and his heirs.

In both cases, B's future interest is ready to take effect (that is, the condition is ready to be tested and possibly become present possessory) upon A's death. B has a remainder in both cases.

How about:

Example 26

O → A for life, then if B marries C either before or after A's death, to B and his heirs.

This future interest is not valid under the common law rules before 1536, because the condition is not verifiable at the expiration of A's life estate. Thus, A has a life estate, B has nothing, and O has a reversion.

Well, how about:

Example 27

O → A for life, then if B marries C, to B and his heirs.

Depending on how the condition is read, this conveyance is similar to either Example 26 (hence invalid) or Example 25 (hence valid). How do we resolve this dilemma? The common law judges held that a condition that **could** be read to be verifiable at A's death **should** be read that way. *Purefoy v. Rogers*, 2 Wm. Saund. 380, 85 Eng. Rep. 1181 (1690). Thus, Example 27 creates a valid remainder in B because the condition is capable of being tested at A's death. If B has not married C by that time, then B will not take possession of Blackacre; B's future interest will never become a present possessory interest unless B marries C before A dies. This result involves the doctrine of destructibility of contingent remainders, discussed in detail later.

Is this rule of *Purefoy v. Rogers* a rule of law or a rule of construction? The court is setting forth a rule to aid in finding O's intent. The court is presuming that O intended to create a valid interest. Hence, this rule is a rule of construction, which validates O's grant to B in Example 27. But rules of construction go only so far. Courts will not reform an instrument where O's intent is unambiguous. Thus, the future interest in Example 26 is void because the court will not simply ignore the words "or after." However, the courts only invalidate that portion of the grant that runs afoul of Rule 2. So, A's life estate is valid and not affected by the invalid grant to B.

Rule 3. The future interest created in B must not take effect before the expiration of the preceding estate.

This third pre-1536 rule for a future interest in a grantee is similar to the second. Consider:

Example 27 (again)

O → A for life, then if B marries C, to B and his heirs.

Here, B has a remainder. But compare:

Example 28

O → A for life, then if B marries C while A is living, immediately to B and his heirs.

In Example 28, as construed by the early common law cases, the condition takes effect before A's death — the instant B marries C — cutting short A's life estate, an impermissible grant before 1536. Since the grant cannot take effect as written, A has a life estate, B has nothing, and O has a reversion.

At this point, we must emphasize that the phrase "but if" seemed to signal an impermissible "cutoff," whereas the word "if" received a radically different construction. "If" is construed as not cutting short the preceding interest; thus, the condition is tested at the expiration of the prior estate and is therefore valid. But now consider:

Example 29

O → A for life, but if B ever becomes President, then to B and his heirs.

Since the condition might be met before, at, or after A's death, you might argue that the *Purefoy* case referred to above requires that we test the condition on expiration and preserve B's remainder. You would lose that argument to the heavy hand of grammar. The common law courts decreed that "but if" indicates an intention to cut short A's life estate if B became President before A died, even though, as the facts actually develop, B may not become President until after A's death. B does not have a remainder. O has a reversion. [Incidentally, thanks for ignoring the anachronism. For the sake of variety, we will occasionally slip in grants involving people or institutions that didn't exist during the time period we are discussing.]

Here are some additional examples:

Example 30.   *O → A for life, then to B and his heirs.*
              B has a remainder.
Example 31.   *O → A and the heirs of his body, remainder to B and his heirs.*
              B has a remainder. Note, however, that using the word "remainder" makes the future
              interest neither more nor less than a remainder.
Example 32.   *O → A and his heirs as long as A farms the land, then to B and his heirs.*
              B's interest follows a fee simple determinable, which does not expire. Thus B's interest is
              not a remainder and is void before 1536. B has nothing, A has a fee simple determinable,
              and O has a possibility of reverter. Remember, because O has an inalienable possibility of
              reverter, even if O later realizes his error, O cannot correct the error by transferring his
              possibility of reverter to B and his heirs.
Example 33.   *O → A for life and one year after A's death to B and his heirs.*
              The one-year wait is improper before 1536. The "remainder" is void, B has nothing, and
              O has a reversion. In this example, if O had realized his error, then he could transfer his
              reversion to B and his heirs, but the reversion becomes effective (present possessory) the
              instant A dies, not one year later.

Example 34.   *O → A for life, remainder one year after A's death to B and his heirs.*
                The word "remainder" is improperly used and does not save the grant. As above, the one-year wait voids the interest following the life estate. Thus, O has a reversion.

Example 35.   *O → A for life, then if B has married W, to B and his heirs.*
                B's interest is ready to take effect — *i.e.*, the condition is ready to be tested — at A's death. B has a remainder.

Example 36.   *O → A for life, but if B marries W, then to B and his heirs.*
                Here, B's interest does not take effect at expiration; therefore, no remainder. O has a reversion. Notice the importance of the precise wording when this example is compared to Example 35. In other words, the sole difference between these two examples lies in the common law sense of "cutoff" suggested by the "but if" in Example 36.

Example 37.   *O → A for life, but if A should become an attorney, then to B and his heirs.*
                As in Example 29, the attempt to cut short A's life estate is improper before 1536. The "remainder" is void, B has nothing and O has a reversion.

Example 38.   *O → A for life, then to whoever owns the Dodgers and that owner's heirs.*
                That future owner of the Dodgers — the owner at A's death — has a remainder even though the actual person to whom the remainder belongs is not identifiable at the time of the grant or even during A's lifetime. Why? Because the time of A's death is uncertain. At the instant of A's death, the remainder will become present possessory and Blackacre will belong to whoever is then the owner of the Dodgers. If the Dodgers no longer exist at the death of A, then the property will revert to O.

Example 39.   *O → A for life, then if B has reached age 21, to B and his heirs.*
                B's interest follows A's expirable estate and doesn't cut it short, and the condition is ready to be tested at the expiration of A's life estate. Therefore, B has a remainder.

Example 40.   *O → A for life, remainder to A's heir and his heirs.*
                A's heir, unidentifiable so long as A is alive, has a remainder. The instant A dies, her heir or heirs will be identifiable. A may leave more than one heir entitled to share Blackacre. For example, A may die, survived by three daughters.

Compare Example 40 with "O → A and his heirs." Can you see the difference between the two conveyances? What may A sell in this example and in Example 40? These two conveyances, which you have just found to be not equivalent, are made equivalent by the venerable **Rule in *Shelley's Case***, discussed in chapter six. However, in chapter seven you will learn that the **Rule in *Shelly's Case*** has been altered in some states. Stay tuned.

Before proceeding to the next tasks, recall that you have just learned how to determine whether a particular future interest in a grantee is a remainder and thus valid at pre-1536 common law. If the interest is not valid because the interest is not a remainder, then O retains what she purported to grant to the grantee. Of course, you must then determine the particular future interest that O has kept: a reversion, a possibility of reverter, or right of entry.

If the future interest is valid as a remainder, then you have two more tasks. First you must decide what ***present*** estate the remainder will become if it ever becomes ***possessory.*** That is, if B has a future interest in Blackacre, which of the five present estates will B have if and when he is able to possess Blackacre? For example:

Example 41.   *O → A for life, then to B for life.*
                B has a remainder in a life estate.

Example 42.   *O → A for life, then to B and his heirs.*
              B has a remainder in fee simple.
Example 43.   *O → A for life, then to B and his heirs as long as B remains unmarried.*
              B has a remainder in fee simple determinable.

That is easy enough. Look for the same clues in classifying the remainder as in classifying a present estate.

The second task is to classify the remainder. Two primary categories of remainders were recognized at common law: vested remainders and contingent remainders. We discuss vested remainders first.

1. Vested Remainders

X's remainder is a vested remainder if:

(a)   X is a person born and ascertainable, and

(b)   no condition other than expiration of the preceding estate must be met before X's interest becomes present possessory.

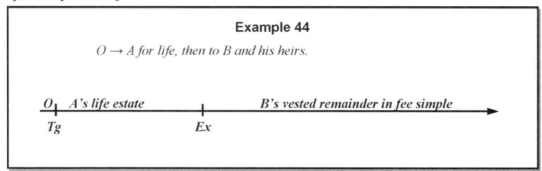

For now at least, you should proceed in small steps. You should satisfy yourself that the illustration above is accurately classified: (1) that B's future interest is, indeed, a remainder; (2) that B's remainder is in fee simple; and (3) that B's remainder is vested.

Compare the next two examples, which illustrate vested and non-vested remainders:

Example 45.   *O →   A for life, then to A's youngest child living at the time of A's death and that child's heirs.*
              The grant to A's youngest child living at the time of A's death grant is (1) a remainder, (2) in fee simple, but, until A dies you cannot determine who will be A's youngest child then living. Therefore, although there may be a very likely candidate (suppose A is 92 at the time of grant and has a youngest child, age 55), the actual taker cannot yet be ascertained (because that child may die before A dies). Hence the remainder is not vested.
Example 46.   *O →   A for life, then to B and his heirs.*
              No problem. The grant to B is (1) a remainder, (2) in fee simple, and (3) vested. B has a vested remainder in fee simple.

In this guide — and probably in your class — when a letter is used to indicate a person, assume the designated person is born and ascertainable. When a letter is not used to designate a person, assume that person is not born and ascertainable. When we want to indicate otherwise, we will provide more information.

Example 47. $O \rightarrow$ *A for life, then to the very first child born in New York City on the day of A's death and that child's heirs.*

The second grant is (1) a remainder, (2) in fee simple, but (3) the child is unborn and therefore the remainder is not vested.

Example 48. $O \rightarrow$ *A and the heirs of his body, then to B's heir and his heirs.* Assume B is living.

The second grant is (1) a remainder, (2) in fee simple, but (3) a living person has no heir, only ***potential*** heirs, so B's heir is unascertained and the remainder is not vested. As to whether the interest is a remainder at all, notice that it does not violate Rule 2 above. Why? Because B may die before the prior estate ends, in which case, B's heir would be capable of being determined in time. [If B dies before A, leaving S as his heir, then S would have vested remainder. Okay, we are getting ahead of ourselves here. We will explain this later.]

Example 49. $O \rightarrow$ *A for life, then to B and his heirs as long as the land is farmed.*

The second grant is (1) a remainder because the condition is understood to apply to B's possession. A does not have to farm; thus, the condition to the second grant will not cut short A's life estate because it does not apply to A. The remainder is (2) in fee simple determinable, and (3) the remainder is vested because no condition must be satisfied for B to come into possession. Therefore, B has a vested remainder in fee simple determinable.

Example 50. $O \rightarrow$ *A for life, then if B has agreed to farm the land, to B and his heirs.*

The second grant is (1) a remainder because the condition can be construed under the Rule of *Purefoy v. Rogers* as not allowing B to agree to farm after A has died and because it also is construed as not cutting short A's life estate. (2) The remainder is in fee simple. But (3), comparing this to the example immediately above, we do not know whether B will or will not consent in time. Thus, the remainder is not vested.

A vested remainder was considered a substantial interest at common law. Hence, a vested remainder was alienable inter vivos, inheritable, and devisable.

2. Contingent Remainders

A remainder that is not vested is called contingent. X's remainder is a contingent remainder if:

(a) X is unborn or unascertainable, or

(b) A condition must be satisfied before X may come into possession. Such a condition is called a "condition precedent." Since X has a remainder, we know that the condition precedent must be able to be tested at or before the expiration of the preceding estate. See Rules 2 and 3, above.

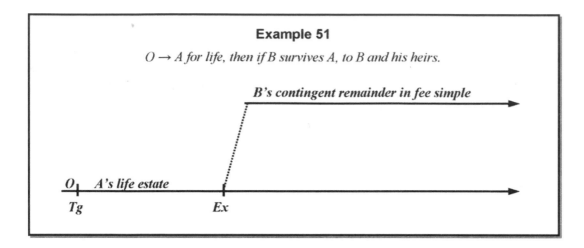

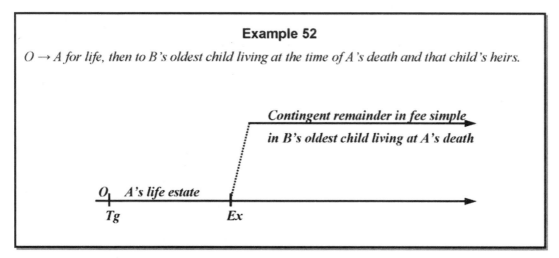

We experienced some difficulty in attributing ownership of the contingent remainder in Example 52 because the remainderman is unascertainable, which is exactly the reason the remainder is contingent. Suppose B's oldest child at *Tg* is S. Does S have a contingent remainder? No, S has merely an expectation — a *hope*, really — of meeting the condition imposed by O. When a remainderman is unascertainable, any person who might become the remainderman has an **expectancy,** not a contingent remainder. Because the remainder "belongs" to an as-yet unascertainable person, perhaps you will find it easier to characterize the owner by using the description contained in the document. In Example 52, then, O has created a contingent remainder in favor of "B's oldest child living at A's death."

You noticed, we hope, the unassigned chunk of Blackacre in both the diagrams in Examples 51 and 52. This too is a future interest — one that becomes possessory if the contingent remainder does not — and it is a reversion. In other words, if the condition is not met, or if the remainderman is not born or ascertainable when A dies and A's life estate expires, then O regains the land. Thus, the complete illustration:

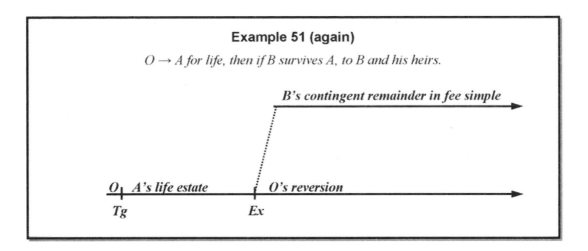

Just as with the reversions that you have already learned, these reversions arise without additional language by O. They arise by implication because O has not accounted for the full fee simple, the interest that we presume O holds at the time of the grant. Thus, if O fails to account for the full fee simple absolute in the grant, then O will retain a reversion following a contingent remainder.

> As your property class progresses (or may have already progressed), O may not necessarily own the full fee simple. O's interest may be burdened with liens, easements or other servitudes, an oil and gas lease, a landlord-tenant lease, etc. In general, O's grantees take subject to these burdens. In nearly all states, a donee takes subject to these burdens in all circumstances, but purchasers take subject to them only if they have actual, constructive, or inquiry notice of them as determined by recording acts and case law. These important topics are beyond the scope of this guide.

Here are some other examples of contingent remainders:

Example 53.   *O → A for life, then if B has married C, to B and his heirs.*
               B has a contingent remainder in fee simple. O has a reversion.

Example 54.   *O → A for life, then to A's firstborn child and that child's heirs.*
               If A has children, then the remainderman is known and the remainder is vested. If A has no children, then O has created a contingent remainder in fee simple in favor of A's unborn "first born." O has a reversion.

To classify the remainder in Example 54 properly, you must know whether A has any children — something that cannot be ascertained from the language of the grant. Additional facts are often needed in real life as well as in this guide and in class. In this guide, we will give you the information that you need. Your teacher may do so too, or perhaps let you wrestle with the need for more information. Note, too, that because the classification depends on facts outside the grant, and because those facts are inherently subject to change, the classification of the estates in a grant is subject to change over time. Here, for example, if A has no children, the remainder is contingent, but the remainder will change from contingent to vested upon the birth of A's first child. As our presentation continues, we will give you practice at repeatedly classifying estates as the facts change.

Example 55. $O \rightarrow A$ *for life, but if A's firstborn is male, then to that child and his heirs.*
                 Careful! A's firstborn doesn't have a remainder. The "but if" language seeks to cut short A's life estate if A's firstborn is a male. Thus, there is ***no remainder at all***: no vested remainder, no contingent remainder. Before 1536, the interest in A's firstborn is void and O has a reversion. Thus, remember the process. First determine whether the interest is a remainder by applying Rules 1, 2, and 3, above. If not, then the interest is void prior to 1536. If the interest is a remainder, then next determine what the interest will be if it becomes a present estate (*e.g.*, in fee simple, in fee tail, in a life estate, in fee simple determinable, or in fee simple on condition subsequent). Then determine whether the remainder is vested or contingent. If the remainder is contingent, then consider whether O has accounted for the full fee simple. If not, O has kept a reversion.

Now let's consider a special type of contingent remainder called the alternative (or alternate) contingent remainder. X and Y have alternative contingent remainders if:

(a)   X has a contingent remainder, and

(b)   X's remainder is followed immediately by Y's future interest, which is also a remainder and one that becomes present possessory in exactly those circumstances in which X's remainder will not become present possessory.

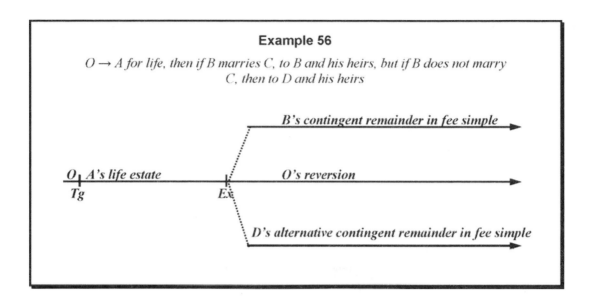

Notice those words "but if" that you may have begun to regard as an indicator of a non-remainder. That is good thinking, but this is an exception to that otherwise sound rule. "But if" means non-remainder (and void before 1536) **unless** it introduces a condition precedent that is the opposite of the earlier condition precedent. In this latter case, you have alternative contingent remainders.

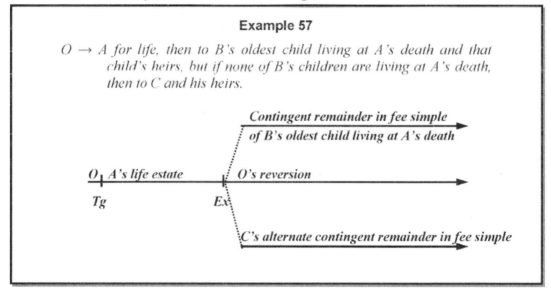

You may be confused by O's reversion following the alternative contingent remainders. O appears to have accounted for the full fee simple in the grant. Since either one condition or the other must be met, you may believe that O can never get Blackacre back. This is not strictly true, because, for reasons discussed in chapter three, A's life estate might end as a matter of law before the life estate expires (that is, before A dies). The simplest example of this is if A refuses the life estate. A beneficiary of a gift may refuse to accept it — whether the gift is by deed, will, or delivery of possession. If A refuses the life estate (perhaps the land is more of a liability than an asset) and because the conditions on the alternative contingent remainders are to be tested only at expiration of A's life estate (at the death of A), then neither contingent remainder is ready to take effect. Thus, O implicitly keeps a reversion — that is, without express language in the grant — and ends up with a fee simple due to A's refusal to accept a life estate. But why this particular result? For purposes of this guide, the short answer is that the common law courts said so!

A contingent remainder was not considered a very substantial interest at common law. Hence, a contingent remainder was not alienable inter vivos, but was inheritable and devisable.

In review:

1. Whether a remainder is contingent or vested often depends on information not included in the grant. For example, consider:

Example 58

O → A for life, then if B has married C, to B and his heirs.

The classification of B's remainder depends on B's marital status. If B has married C, then we know that when A dies, the condition will be met. Hence, if A is alive and B has married C, then B's remainder is vested. On the other hand, if B and C are not married, then B's remainder is contingent. Note the precise language of the grant, the condition "if B has married C." So long as they marry before A dies, the condition is met. With this particular grant language, they do not have to *still* be married when A dies. Thus, if B marries C during A's lifetime, then the remainder becomes vested. If A dies before B and C marry, then O's reversion becomes a present estate. If B marries C after A dies, then the marriage comes too late for B's remainder to be become present possessory. Why? Rule 2, above. A remainder may change from contingent to vested (but not from vested to contingent) due to facts that are set forth in the grant. Later on, we will give you some problems involving such changing conditions. In the meantime, we will give you all the relevant facts as of the time of the grant and ask for analysis under only one set of facts.

2. Remember, before classifying the remainder, make sure the future interest *is* a remainder. If it is not, then the interest is void. If it is a remainder, then determine what the interest will be if it becomes a present estate.

    [We are sorry if our harping on this methodical approach is starting to annoy you, but we want you to be methodical. If you are methodical about this, then you are less likely to err. Thus, we choose to err on the side of repetition.]

3. Make sure you have accounted for all future interests in any grant. A grant may include more than one future interest. Consider:

Example 59

O → A for life, then to B for life, then to C for life.

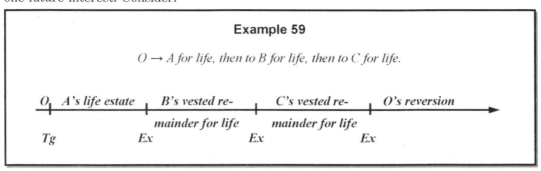

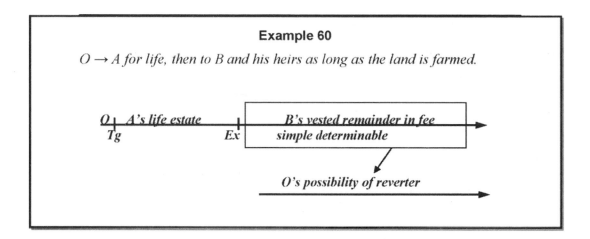

Example 60

O → A for life, then to B and his heirs as long as the land is farmed.

What has been described thus far is a system that emerged over at least several hundred years. The rules governing the definition of a remainder and distinguishing vested and contingent remainders actually represent the three conveyancing rules that property lawyers observed at common law.

We intentionally do not explore the feudal economic and social structure that led to the common law rules of conveyancing. We present basic common law rules of conveyancing without attempting to answer why they were so formulated. The answers would require a much longer book and would detract from our objective, which is to provide a methodical approach to determining the state of title. We leave the "whys" to legal history scholars.

In these first two chapters, we have presented a system of five present interests and five future interests permitted by the common law courts before 1536. These interests are summarized in the following charts. After you have looked over these charts, try your new intellectual equipment on the review problems, using our analytical approach, which is summarized following the charts. The answers to the review problems immediately follow. You will meet in subsequent chapters one more present-possessory interest and one more future interest, for a final total of a dozen.

C. REVIEW MATERIALS

1. Summary of present and future interests before 1536

PRESENT POSSESSORY ESTATE	*FUTURE ESTATE*	
	Grantor	*Grantee*
Fee Simple Absolute	NONE	NONE
Fee Tail	Reversion	Remainder
Life Estate	Reversion	Remainder
Fee Simple Determinable	Possibility of Reverter	NONE
Fee Simple on Condition Subsequent	Right of Entry (Power of Termination)	NONE

2. Summary of transferability

[Strictly speaking, land could generally not be devised until after the Statute of Wills was enacted in 1540. The "Devisable" column below gives the rules for the post-1540 devise of the pre-1536 interests. Remember, we are intentionally avoiding historical accuracy in favor of what we believe is a useful approach to learning about the present law of estates in land and future interests.]

Present Interests	*Alienable*	*Devisable*	*Inheritable*
Fee Simple Absolute	Yes	Yes	Yes
Fee Tail	Limited	No	Modified
Life Estate (other than life estate *pur autre vie*)	Yes	No	No
Fee Simple Determinable	Yes	Yes	Yes
Fee Simple on Condition Subsequent	Yes	Yes	Yes

Future Interests	*Alienable*	*Devisable*	*Inheritable*
Reversion	Yes	Yes	Yes
Possibility of Reverter	No	Probably not*	Yes
Right of Entry	No	No	Yes
Remainder —			
Vested	Yes	Yes	Yes
Contingent	No	Yes	Yes
* The answer here depends on an interpretation of the original English Statute of Wills (1540), as amended in 1542. The Statute provided for the devise of estates "in possession, reversion or remainder." Whether the possibility of reverter, like the right of entry, was not within the 1542 amendment is still debated. *See* John A. Borron, Jr., *Simes & Smith, The Law of Future Interests* § 1901, at 200 (3d ed. 2011).			

D. OUR SUGGESTED ANALYTICAL APPROACH (BEFORE 1536)

We urge you to use this step-by-step approach — at least until you master the following problems. If you do, then you are less likely to err.

First Determinations:

1. What did O have before making the grant?

    Assume O begins with a fee simple absolute unless otherwise stated.

2. What does A have?

    Fee simple absolute?

    Fee tail?

    Life estate?

    Fee simple determinable?

    Fee simple on condition subsequent?

3. If there are no further grants, what has O retained, if anything?

    Nothing if A has a fee simple absolute.

    Reversion if A has a life estate or a fee tail.

    Possibility of reverter if A has a fee simple determinable.

    Right of entry if A has a fee simple on condition subsequent.

Second Determinations:

If there are further grants, then ask, as to each one:

4. Is the interest a remainder?

    a. [Rule 1] Does the interest follow an expirable estate?

        i. If no, then the interest is not a remainder. Strike the interest (it is void prior to 1536) and determine what is left in O, if anything, under First Determinations, question 3, above.

        ii. If yes, then the interest may be a remainder. Proceed to b, immediately below.

    b. [Rule 2] Will the interest take effect immediately upon the expiration of the preceding estate?

        i. If no, then the interest is not a remainder. Strike the interest (it is void prior to 1536) and determine what is left in O, if anything, under First Determinations, question 3, above.

        ii. If yes, then the interest may be a remainder. Proceed to c, immediately below.

    c. [Rule 3] Can the interest take effect before the expiration of the preceding estate?

        i. If yes, then the interest is not a remainder. Strike the interest (it is void prior to 1536) and determine what is left in O, if anything, under First Determinations, question 3, above.

        ii. If no, then the interest is a remainder. Proceed to 5, immediately below.

5. Since the interest is a remainder, what will the remainder be when it becomes possessory?

    Fee simple absolute?

    Fee tail?

Life estate?

Fee simple determinable?

Fee simple on condition subsequent?

6.   Is the remainder vested or contingent?

     a.   Is the holder of the remainder born and ascertainable?

         i.   If yes, then the remainder may be vested.

         ii.   If no, then the remainder is contingent, unless some extraneous facts show that the remainder has become vested.

         iii.   In either case, proceed to b. immediately below.

     b.   Is there a condition precedent to possession other than the expiration of the preceding interest?

         i.   If no (and if the holder of the remainder is born and ascertainable — answered under 6.a., above), then the remainder is vested.

         ii.   If yes (or if the holder of the remainder is unborn or unascertainable — answered under 6.a., above), then the remainder is contingent.

     c.   Note: If a contingent remainder in one party (*e.g.*, B) is immediately followed by another remainder in another party (*e.g.*, C) that can become possessory only in exactly those circumstances in which the first party's (B's) remainder cannot, then both parties (B and C) have alternative contingent remainders.

7.   If the remainder is contingent, does O retain a reversion?

Yes, unless O has otherwise accounted for the full fee simple absolute.

E. REVIEW PROBLEMS

1.   Give the "state of the title" for each of the grants below. That is, what present or future interest in Blackacre is conveyed to each of the parties at Tg, before 1536?

> **HINT**: Although we have listed O first, you may find it easier to name the other interests first, before deciding what, if anything, O has retained.

a. $O \rightarrow$ A.

O has _____

A has _____

b. $O \rightarrow$ A in fee simple absolute.

O has _____

A has _____

c. $O \rightarrow$ A and the male heirs of his body.

O has _____

A has _____

d. $O \rightarrow$ A for life, then to B and his heirs.

O has _____

A has _____

B has _____

e. $O \rightarrow$ A for life, then if A dies unmarried, to B and his heirs, otherwise to W for life.

O has _____

A has _____

B has _____

W has _____

2. In each case below, what is B's interest? The time of the grant is 1530.

    a. O → *B and his heirs.*

    b. O → *B and his heirs as long as the fences stay in good repair.*

    c. O → *B and his heirs, but if a Democrat is ever elected President, O may reenter and reclaim the land.*

    d. O → *B and the heirs of his body.*

    e. O → *A and his heirs.* [B is A's oldest boy, alive and well at *Tg.*]

    f. O → *A for life, then if B marries C, to C and her heirs.*

    g. O → *A for life, then if B marries C, to B and his heirs.*

    h. O → *A and his heirs, but if the land is ever used for commercial purposes, to B and his heirs.*

    i. O → *A for life, then to W for life, then, if Z is still alive, to C for life, otherwise to B and his heirs.*

3. In each case below, O is your client. If possible, construct a grant that will dispose of her property in the way she desires. If it can't be done, then explain why.

    a. O wants her friend A to have a fee simple absolute.

    b. O wants A to have a fee simple — "almost"; *i.e.,* she never wants the land to be used for commercial purposes.

    c. O wants A to have a fee simple, unless and until B returns from Rome, in which case she wants B to have a fee simple.

    d. O wants her son, S, to have the land until he dies and afterwards she wants the land to return to her, unless she is dead, in which case she wants the land to go to her heirs.

    e. O would like to let A have the land while A is alive. After A dies, O wants the land to go to the first to marry of B or C.

    f. O wants her friend A to have the land for A's lifetime and then she wants the land to go to her friend B's youngest son, but only if B marries C. If B doesn't marry C, then O wants the land to go to her church, but only for as long as the land is used for church purposes.

    g. O wants the land to go to A and stay in A's direct family line.

4. Classify the first future interest in each of the conveyances below as one of the following:

(1)   None; the future interest is illegal, void, or meaningless before 1536

(2)   Vested remainder

(3)   Contingent remainder

(4)   Alternative contingent remainder

      a. _____   O →   *A for life, then to B and his heirs.*
                              [B is alive and well.]

      b. _____   O →   *A and his heirs then to B and his heirs.*
                              [B is alive and well.]

      c. _____   O →   *A for life, then to B's oldest child living at A's death.*

      d. _____   O →   *A and his heirs, but if the land is not farmed, to B and his heirs.*

      e. _____   O →   *A for life, then if X has married Y, to C and his heirs, but if X has not married Y, then to B and his heirs.*

Answers to Review Problems

> Although we urge you to use the step-by-step approach outlined just prior to the review problems, to conserve space, we do not walk you through that analysis with each answer. If some of your answers do not agree with ours, we suggest that you reconsider your answers in light of the above approach.

1. Give the "state of the title" for each of the grants below. That is, what present or future interest in Blackacre is converyed to each of the parties at *Tg*, before 1536?

   a.   O →   A.

   This problem invites you consider what the common law courts would hold that O created when imprecise words of grant are used. At "old" common law, O has a reversion and A has a life estate because the magic words "and his heirs" were required to create a fee simple absolute. However, at modern law, largely statutory, A has a fee simple absolute and thus, O has nothing. Although applying modern law to pre-1536 grants is not historically accurate, we suggest that you apply this modern rule as an exception because we believe that the "default" estate is now the fee simple absolute in every jurisdiction. For example, consider the following California statute: "Unless a different purpose appears by express words or by necessary inference, every estate in land created by deed or will, without words of inheritance, shall be deemed an estate in fee simple." CAL. CIV. CODE § 1105 (1982).

   Of course, modern courts are not as exacting as the courts were long ago, so courts will try to construe ambiguous grants consistent with what they believe O would have intended. In so doing, they are aided by various court-made rules of construction. Thus, the modern preference for a fee simple absolute is not always trump. For example, if O conveyed to "A until he dies," then most courts would likely conclude that O conveyed a life estate and thus kept a reversion.

   b.   O →   *A in fee simple absolute.*

   At "old" common law, A has a life estate, and O has a reversion. Remember, the magic words "and his heirs" were required at common law. At modern law, A has a fee simple absolute, and O has nothing.

   c.   O →   *A and the male heirs of his body.*

   O has a reversion.

   A has a fee tail male.

   d.   O →   *A for life, then to B and his heirs.*

   O has nothing.

   A has a life estate.

   B has a vested remainder in fee simple.

   e.   O →   *A for life, then if A dies unmarried, to B and his heirs, otherwise to W for life.*

   O has a reversion.

   A has a life estate.

   B has a contingent remainder in fee simple.

   W has an alternative contingent remainder in a life estate.

2. In each case below, what is B's interest? The time of the grant is before 1536.

   a.   O →   *B and his heirs.*

   B has a fee simple.

   b.   O →   *B and his heirs as long as the fences stay in good repair.*

   B has a fee simple determinable.

   c.   O →   *B and his heirs, but if a Democrat is ever elected President, O may reenter and reclaim the land.*

B has a fee simple on condition subsequent. Once again, it was friendly of you to avoid comment on the anachronism.

d.   O → *B and the heirs of his body.*

B has a fee tail.

e.   O → *A and his heirs.* [B is A's oldest boy, alive and well at **Tg**.]

B has nothing. B has only an expectancy (not a property interest) that he will be entitled to receive the property when A dies.

f.   O → *A for life, then if B marries C, to C and her heirs.*

B has nothing. This might properly be called a "trick question." Note that there is no **grant** at all to B. We did not mean for you to wonder about any property rights that B gets by being C's husband.

g.   O → *A for life, then if B marries C, to B and his heirs.*

B's interest depends on B's marital status. Assuming that B is unmarried, B has a contingent remainder in fee simple. If B is married to C, then the remainder is vested. If B has married someone else, then the remainder is contingent, as B might still divorce that person and marry C.

h.   O → *A and his heirs, but if the land is ever used for commercial purposes, to B and his heirs.*

B has nothing. The "but if" language purports to cut short A's interest, so the interest O attempted to give B is void before 1536.

i.   O → *A for life, then to W for life, then, if Z is still alive, to C for life, otherwise to B and his heirs.*

B has an alternative contingent remainder in fee simple.

> Think carefully. If Z is still alive after A and W die, then C will take for life, but then when C dies, who will take? We think O. B takes only if Z fails to survive A and W.

---

3.   In each case below, O is your client. If possible, construct a grant that will dispose of her property in the way she desires. If it can't be done, then explain why.

a.   O wants her friend A to have a fee simple absolute.

O → *A and her heirs*

b.   O wants A to have a fee simple — "almost"; *i.e.*, she never wants the land to be used for commercial purposes.

O → *A and his heirs as long as the land is not used for commercial purposes.*

c.   O wants A to have a fee simple, unless and until B returns from Rome, in which case she wants B to have a fee simple.

This is not possible at common law before 1536.

d.   O wants her son, S, to have the land until he dies and afterwards she wants the land to return to her, unless she is dead, in which case she wants the land to go to her heirs.

O → *S for life.*

e.   O would like A to have the land while A is alive. After A dies, O wants the land to go to the first to marry of B or C.

O → *A for life, and then to the first of B and C to marry and that person's heirs.*

We guess that you might have tried this, which would have done just as well:

O → *A for life, then to B and his heirs, if B marries before C does, but if C marries first, then to C and his heirs.*

> Note that in both cases, O has a reversion, which will become possessory if neither B nor C has married at the time of A's death. But also note that O has a reversion because A and B each have an alternative contingent remainder. Saying that O has a reversion is sufficient; you should not say that O has two reversions.

    f.   O wants her friend A to have the land for A's lifetime and then she wants the land to go to her friend B's youngest son, but only if B marries C. If B doesn't marry C, then O wants the land to go to her church, but only for as long as the land is used for church purposes.

            O →   *A for life, then if B marries C, to B's youngest son, but if B doesn't marry C, to the Church as long as the land is used for church purposes.*

    g.   O wants the land to go to A and stay in A's direct family line.

            O →   *A and the heirs of his body.*

4.   Classify the first future interest in each of the conveyances below as one of the following:

(1)   None; the future interest is illegal, void, or meaningless before 1536

(2)   Vested remainder

(3)   Contingent remainder

(4)   Alternative contingent remainder

    a. 2   O →   *A for life, then to B and his heirs.*
                      [B is alive and well.]

    b. 1   O →   *A and his heirs then to B and his heirs.*
                      [B is alive and well.]

    c. 3   O →   *A for life, then to B's oldest child living at A's death*

    d. 1   O →   *A and his heirs, but if the land is not farmed, to B and his heirs.*

    e. 4   O →   *A for life, then if X has married Y, to C and his heirs, but if X has not married Y, then to B and his heirs.*

Chapter 3

THE FAMILY OF REMAINDERS

To this point you have learned several new concepts, including the general concept of a remainder, which is the subject of further exploration in this chapter. The word "remainder" refers to a future interest created in a grantee after an expirable estate in compliance with the rules discussed in Chapter 2.

You also learned in the previous chapter that remainders are of two basic types: vested and contingent. For reasons similar to those that restricted the evolution of the concept of a remainder, the evolution of the two types of remainders was slow. The contingent remainder was recognized much later than the vested remainder. Further, as indicated earlier, the contingent remainder was considered inalienable inter vivos; perhaps the factors that influenced its late recognition influenced the concept that it was inalienable. Finally, the contingent remainder had a very special attribute: it was a "destructible" interest. The doctrine of destructibility of contingent remainders reflects the special, congenital disability shared by all contingent remainders at common law — a disability that was not present in vested remainders.

A. THE DOCTRINE OF DESTRUCTIBILITY OF CONTINGENT REMAINDERS

The general property of destructibility shared by all contingent remainders is as follows:

A contingent remainder is destroyed unless it vests at or before the expiration of the preceding estate. If a contingent remainder is destroyed, then, at the expiration of preceding estate, the next vested estate comes into possession, which is often a reversion.

This is easier to illustrate by example than by statement. Consider:

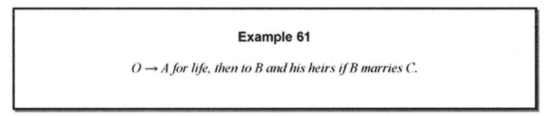

Example 61

O → A for life, then to B and his heirs if B marries C.

We sketch this as follows:

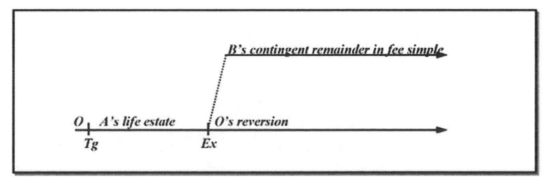

43

Now, suppose that B dies unmarried. B can no longer marry and thus can no longer satisfy the marriage condition. In this example, you can easily determine that the contingent aspect of B's gift prevents B or anyone claiming through B (*e.g.*, B's immediate heir who could have been identified when B died) from having any claim to Blackacre. The state of the title after B's death is: A has a life estate and O has a reversion. B's contingent remainder has been eliminated ("destroyed") by failing to satisfy the contingency on which it was dependent. Our illustration is:

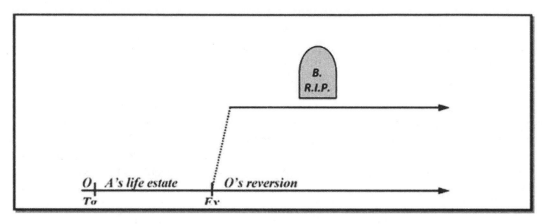

Or, more simply:

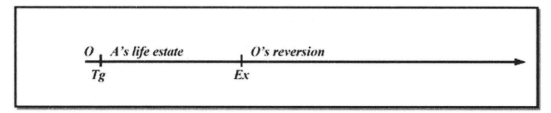

Although contingent remainders are generally devisable and inheritable, some conditions will impose an express or implied condition of survivorship. When this happens, the contingent remainder is neither devisable nor inheritable because the remainder is contingent on the remainderman not dying (in this example, not dying before marrying), an event indispensable to B's valid disposition by will of Blackacre or the succession of B's heir to Blackacre. Conditions of survivorship are not the primary focus of this chapter. However, another example may be useful: "**O → A for life, then to B and his heirs if B reaches age 21.**" Here, B has an interest that is subject to an implied condition of survivorship. If B dies at age 10, then his contingent remainder is destroyed because the condition can no longer be met by B or by anyone else.

Probably for reasons associated with the same rules that generally restricted the meaning of a remainder, the common law courts found destruction had occurred in other instances not quite so easy to understand. Consider:

Example 61 (again)

O → A for life, then to B and his heirs if B marries C.

We sketch this as follows:

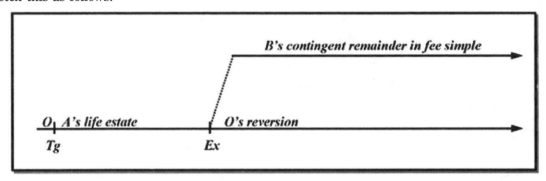

Suppose, however, that A dies and B is still living and unmarried. In this instance, B's contingent remainder was destroyed at common law because it "failed to vest" before the expiration of the prior estate. A contingent remainder required the continuation of a preceding expirable estate, such as a life estate or a fee tail (in this example, until B married). That is, the contingent remainder condition must have been met or be instantaneously met when the preceding estate expired. If the condition was not so met, then the contingent remainder was destroyed.

> Do not confuse this with Rule 2, discussed in section B of chapter two. Rule 2 is considered in testing whether the future interest qualifies as any sort of a remainder. If it was not a remainder, then the interest is void prior to 1536. Here, the test is whether an interest that is a remainder, specifically, a contingent remainder, will vest in time — that is, at or before the expiration of the preceding estate.

As suggested by the prior example, if B's interest disappeared, then O's reversion is all that is left. Thus, if B has not married C by the time A dies, then O's reversion will become possessory and O will have a fee simple absolute. B will never take, even if he subsequently marries C. Our illustration is:

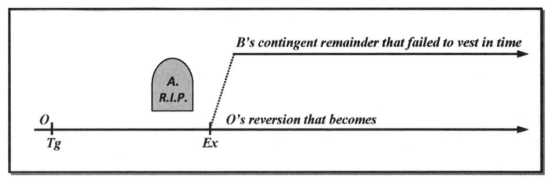

Or:

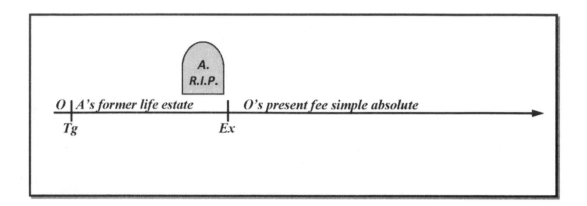

Let's use the same example for yet a third set of facts: Suppose that B marries C while A is living. Now the graph changes dramatically:

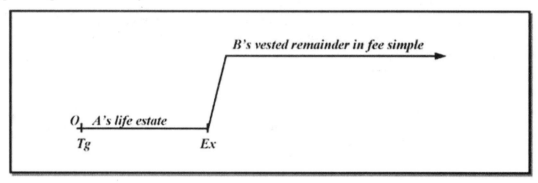

Or, more simply:

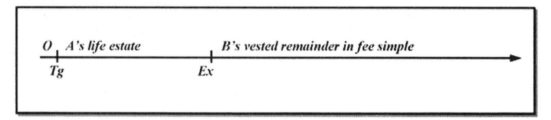

Vested remainders are indestructible. Why? Because the remainderman is born and identifiable and because no condition precedent exists that may prevent the remainderman from taking. While O's reversion disappears, it is not "destroyed" — legally speaking — because reversions are not destructible; however, they may disappear for purposes of stating the title because the facts establish that the reversion cannot become possessory. Or to put it another way, the reversion is no longer needed to account for the full fee simple absolute.

You might say, in reaction to these observations, "Suppose the vested remainderman dies before the expiration of the preceding estate." You might observe that B will never come into possession of the land. OK, let's try one:

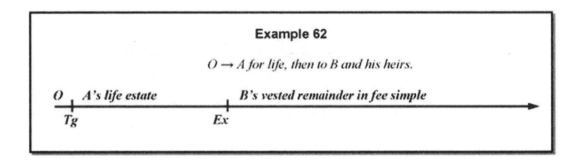

Now, suppose B dies, leaving H as his heir. Substitute H for B.

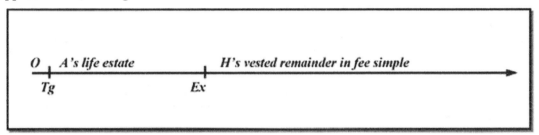

A still has a life estate, and H has a vested remainder in fee simple. You were right in your observation that B never took ***possession*** of the property, but it is clear that B had an inheritable interest in the property — the right to take possession at A's death, a right that H inherits. We can say that B ***owned*** the vested remainder that was inherited by B's heir along with all the rest of B's property, assuming B had no will. Of course, if B had a will that devised Blackacre to D, then D, rather than H, would receive B's remainder.

In chapter two, we made the point, without amplification, that a vested remainder could never become contingent, although a transformation from contingent to vested was both possible and common. Do you understand why? Consider this conveyance:

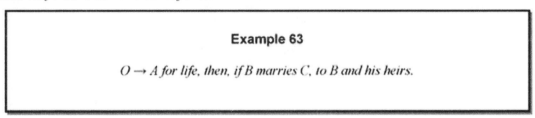

If B is unmarried and A is alive, then the diagram looks like this:

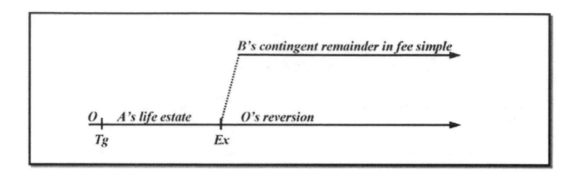

Now, suppose B marries C while A is alive. The contingent remainder vests and O's reversion disappears because it can no longer become possessory:

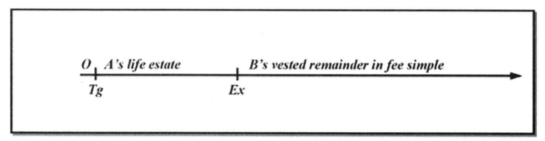

Now, you might be thinking, suppose B divorces C while A is still alive — putting aside how difficult it was to get divorced back in the days we're talking about. Or suppose B or C dies after they marry while A is still alive. Does the vested remainder "unvest" and become contingent? No. In O's original grant, O did not require that B **remain** married to C or still be married to C at the time of A's death. So, B has met the condition and the remainder is vested for all time.

Now, suppose that O had put the more detailed condition on B's remainder:

Example 64

O → A for life, then, if B marries and is still married to C on A's death, to B and his heirs.

Upon B's marriage to C, the remainder still does **not** vest because the condition cannot be tested until A dies. But because the condition can be tested at the instant A dies, B's interest is a remainder, although a contingent one. This remainder will instantaneously vest when A dies if B is still married to C. If B is not still married to C, then the contingent remainder will be destroyed. Hence:

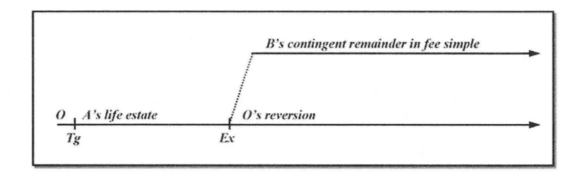

But now suppose that B married C **before** A died but then B divorces C **after** A dies. Well, when A died, B received a fee simple. B's then present fee simple estate is not subject to any conditions. Thus, B would still have a fee simple absolute.

In summary, a contingent remainder has a deadline because it is "destructible." The contingent remainder must become a vested remainder at or before the expiration of the interest that precedes and supports it.

> A remainder may vest *at* expiration. For example, consider **O → A for life, then if B survives A, to B and his heirs**. Thus, to say that a remainder must vest *before* expiration is incorrect. It may vest "at or before" expiration. If B is alive when A dies, B will have a fee simple absolute. So far, so good, but we now add further qualifications.

The estate that precedes and supports a contingent remainder will be a life estate or a fee tail. As you will now learn, either estate may end in one of three ways: expiration, merger, or forfeiture. You will also learn that, if the supporting estate ends before the contingent remainder vests, then the contingent remainder is destroyed.

1.   Destruction of a Contingent Remainder at the Expiration of the Prior Estate

Consider:

Example 65

O → A for life, then to the first son of A who reaches age 21 and his heirs.

Suppose further that A dies leaving a son, age 16. The contingent remainder is destroyed. O's reversion becomes possessory. If A dies leaving only a minor son, then the state of the title is that O has a fee simple absolute.

As a review of the idea that a contingent remainder must vest in a timely manner and as a review of other attributes of a contingent remainder, consider this example, a conveyance that creates a life estate followed by alternative contingent remainders in fee:

Example 66

O → S for life, then to A and his heirs if A marries S and, if A fails to marry S,
then to B and his heirs.

First, let's assume that O, S, A, and B are all living.

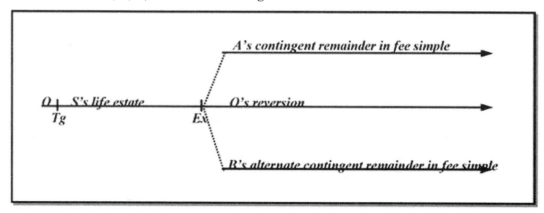

Next consider the following additional fact: B dies, without a will, leaving D as his heir. The answer is illustrated by substituting "D" for "B," because B's contingent remainder is inheritable. Note that the condition does not require B to do anything, so no implied condition requires that B must survive A.

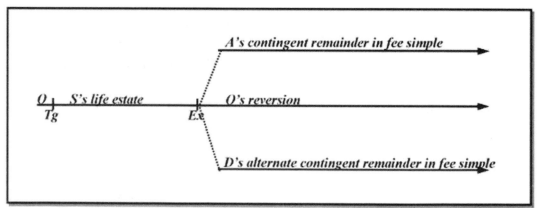

Next consider this additional fact: A marries S. Now the graph changes radically:

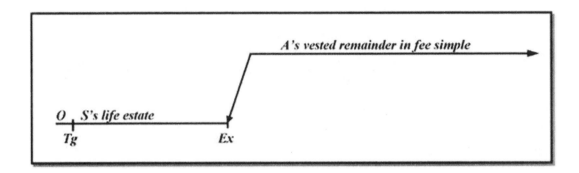

Finally, S dies, and the graph changes again:

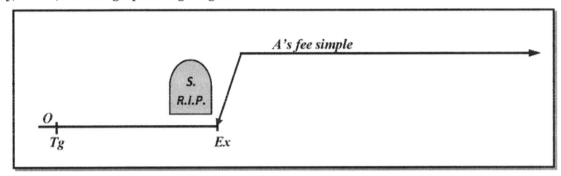

Or:

Here we eliminate the history of Blackacre, because it is no longer necessary to the "present" state of the title. As you will learn in your property class, past history may be essential to fully account for the state of the title, which could be burdened by various interests that were created in the past, including easements, restrictive covenants, and many other interests. In this book, we assume no burdens or interests beyond present possessory estates and future interests that may or will become present possessory estates.

2. Destruction of a Contingent Remainder at the Termination of the Prior, Supporting Estate by Merger

The concept of merger in property law, which you may not yet have studied, has broader application than its contribution to the law of contingent remainders. As a general principle, in some factual circumstances, merger will act to combine separate interests that belong to one person. Merger does this by absorbing the smaller interest into the larger interest or by combining the two interests into a larger interest or at least into a single interest. For our purposes, we apply the merger doctrine to combine a present interest and a future interest. Consider the following:

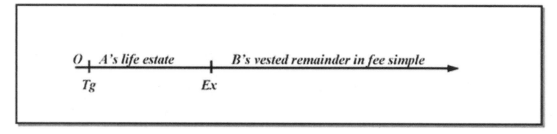

Our illustration is:

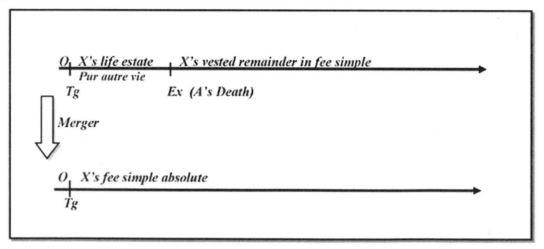

Suppose, further, that both A and B sell their interests to X. X holds a life estate for the life of A and a vested remainder in fee simple. The common law employed the concept known as merger to explain that X has a fee simple. The doctrine of merger was used to reclassify the two lesser interests X purchased into the greater interest of a fee simple absolute. If you study merger in more depth in your property class, then you will learn that when courts decide whether to apply or not apply merger, they carefully consider whether the owner of the interests under consideration for merger would reasonably intend or want merger to occur. In our example, A would have been liable to B for waste, but when both the life estate and vested remainder are conveyed to X, X holds both the potential liability for waste and the potential cause of action for waste. Thus, merging the two interests seems reasonable.

As another example, suppose:

Example 68

O → the Church, its successors and assigns* as long as the land is used as a church.

*The phrase "successors and assigns" is used in place of "and his heirs" when the grantee cannot have "heirs."

Our illustration is:

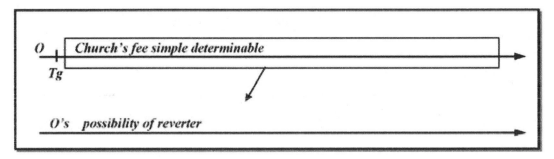

If the Church conveys its interest back to O, then the common law, via the merger doctrine, would recognize a fee simple in O.

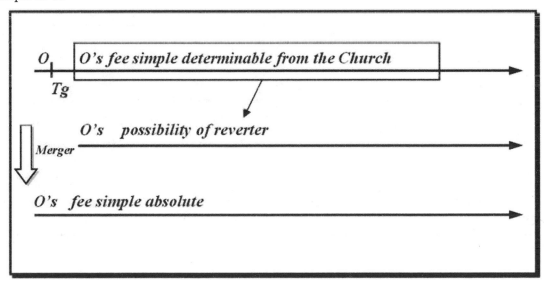

Now, suppose:

Example 61 (yet again)

O → A for life, then to B and his heirs if B marries C.

Our illustration, which is probably familiar since this is the third time you have encountered this example in this guide:

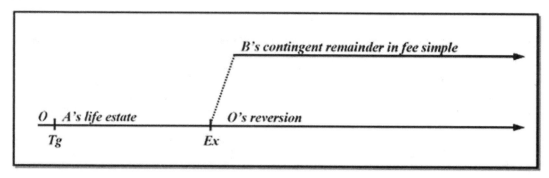

Suppose O conveys the reversion to A before B marries.

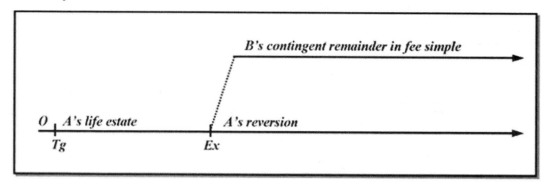

Here, too, the common law courts "saw" or "felt" or "decreed," as you prefer, that the life estate and reversion would combine into a fee simple. Once that happened, B's contingent remainder, not having a life estate to support it, would be destroyed. Poof! A has a fee simple absolute, and B has nothing.

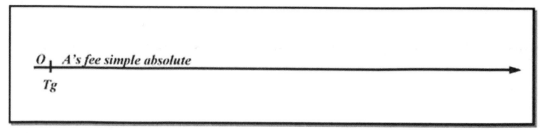

B's interest disappears forever. A similar result would occur if A had conveyed her life estate to O before B marries. The life estate would then merge into O's reversion. Not having met the deadline imposed for vesting of the contingent remainder, B's interest is destroyed.

You may be troubled that a life estate and a reversion are substantial enough or sufficient components of a fee simple to add up to a fee. You may also be troubled that a contingent remainder is being defeated somewhat mystically. Both of these ideas seem fair criticism in the rational light of the third millennium. However, apparently the contingent remainder, as it eventually emerged in the catalogue of estates in land and future interests, was closer to what we might call an expectancy. True, a contingent remainder could be devised and it was inheritable — provided, as suggested earlier, that the condition that made the interest contingent did not require survival. But a contingent remainder could not be alienated inter vivos, which does seem consistent with its destructibility.

Furthermore, destructibility was a functional doctrine that "cleansed" or simplified the state of the title, often leaving an unfettered fee simple. This fact may help dissipate the feeling that the doctrine of destructibility is a trap for an unwary grantor. Others, of course, find the magic of the doctrine one more jewel in the treasure box of property law.

By now, you might appreciate a definition of merger. The doctrine of merger provides that if successive vested estates come into the same hands, then the two estates are combined into the largest possible interest.

In the above examples, since the requisites for merger exist, A has a fee simple absolute. Merger ended the life estate at a time when the contingent remainder in B was not ready to vest. Thus, at common law, the contingent remainder in B was destroyed. After O's conveyance of his reversion to A, before B married C, the state of title is that A has a fee simple absolute. Our illustration is:

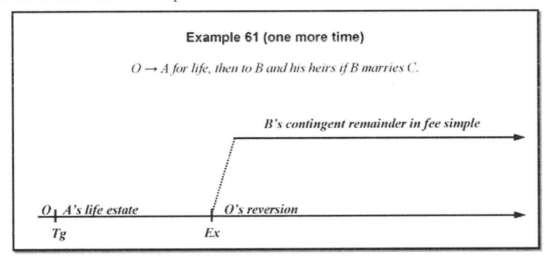

Example 61 (one more time)

O → A for life, then to B and his heirs if B marries C.

B's contingent remainder in fee simple

O *A's life estate*   *O's reversion*

Tg   *Ex*

Suppose O conveys his reversion to A:

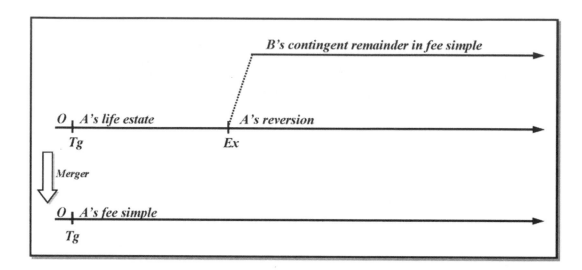

Instead, assume that A conveyed his life estate to O. O would get a fee simple absolute. Do you understand why?

On the other hand, assume B marries C before A dies. B's remainder vests and may not be destroyed by any action of A or O. The state of the title is now life estate in A and a vested remainder in B. O's reversion disappears because no facts exist that would allow the reversion to become possessory. Our illustration is:

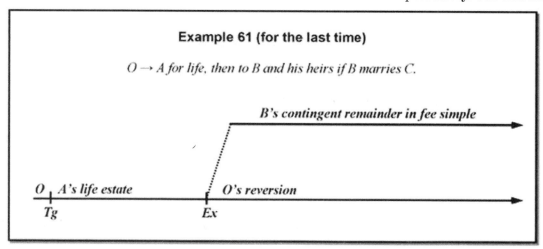

Suppose B marries C:

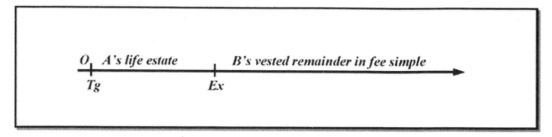

If you are not yet sick and tired of this example, then you might rework it through its various iterations. Okay! So you are sick and tired of this example. Let's move on to the fun exercise of destroying contingent remainders through forfeiture. This won't take too long.

3. Destruction of a Contingent Remainder by the Termination of the Prior Estate by Forfeiture

Suppose:

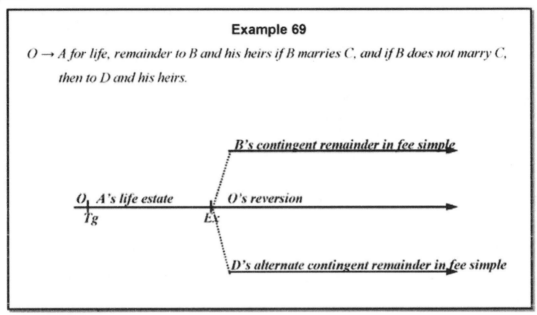

Example 69

$O \rightarrow A$ for life, remainder to B and his heirs if B marries C, and if B does not marry C, then to D and his heirs.

B's contingent remainder in fee simple

O, A's life estate   O's reversion

Tg   E

D's alternate contingent remainder in fee simple

At common law, some offenses, called felonies, carried a penalty of forfeiture of property. Assume A commits a felony, thereby forfeiting her life estate before B marries C. In that case, A's life estate has ended prematurely and the contingent remainders are destroyed. The state of the title after A's forfeiture: O has a fee simple absolute.

Instead, if one assumes that B marries C before A commits a felony, then a different result obtains. The state of the title after B's marriage: A has a life estate, B has a vested remainder in fee simple, O has nothing, and D has nothing. O's reversion disappears and D's alternative contingent remainder is destroyed. Thereafter, if A commits a felony, then the state of the title is: B has a fee simple absolute.

Of course, forfeiture is not a concept that survived in the course of the American reception of English common law, at least not on a long-term basis. However, as we have noted earlier, a valid gift requires the beneficiary's acceptance, and any beneficiary of a gift may "renounce" or refuse to accept the interest in that gift. A voluntary renunciation may result in the destruction of a contingent remainder as did involuntary common law forfeiture. For example:

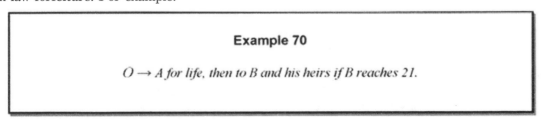

Example 70

$O \rightarrow A$ for life, then to B and his heirs if B reaches 21.

Our illustration is:

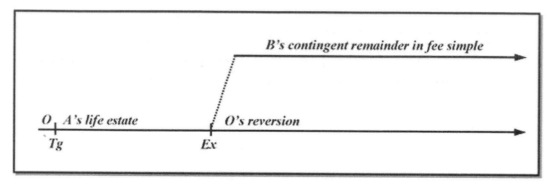

Suppose A decides to decline, or renounce, her life interest. Perhaps A believes the property is more of a liability than an asset. At common law, such a decision jeopardizes B's interest if B is not yet age 21. If A's interest ends prematurely by renunciation, then B's contingent remainder will be destroyed by failing to vest in time. O's interest will become possessory in fee simple. Perhaps in declining the gift, A may have ulterior motives — to defeat B.

4. Summary of Destructibility of Contingent Remainders

To summarize, depending on the development of facts extraneous to the grant, any contingent remainder in the grant might be destroyed before it has a chance to become vested. As you just learned, a contingent remainder may be destroyed (1) by failing to vest in time; (2) by merger; or (3) by forfeiture or renunciation. If the contingent remainder is destroyed by extraneous facts, then eliminate the contingent remainder when determining the state of the title.

On the other hand, if a contingent remainder becomes vested by reason of facts extraneous to the grant, then the reversion may disappear. To be a bit more definite, if a contingent remainder in fee simple absolute vests, then the reversion that had to follow that remainder does disappear. We remind you that we say "disappear" because a reversion is an alienable, inheritable, and devisable interest. A reversion is considered vested and thus not "destructible," but extraneous facts may make the reversion unnecessary to the state of the title. Remember, your ultimate task throughout this guide is to properly account for the full fee simple absolute. Thus, you may oftentimes need to find a reversion to account for the full fee simple absolute. When you don't need a reversion to account for the full fee simple absolute, then you don't have one — you don't have what you don't need. So, extraneous facts are important. Always consider them! Now, onward to a sub-category of the vested remainder, the vested remainder subject to open.

B. GIFTS TO A CLASS AND VESTED REMAINDERS SUBJECT TO OPEN

The family of remainders includes one subspecies of vested remainder that requires special attention. Suppose O makes the following bequest in a will:

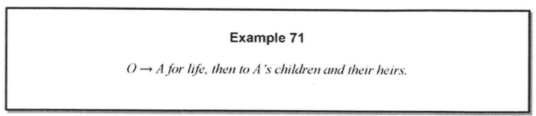

Example 71

O → A for life, then to A's children and their heirs.

Suppose, further, that A has no children. We illustrate this conveyance and this state of facts as follows:

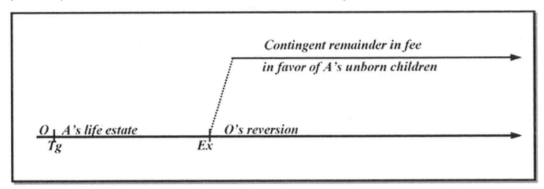

The bequest to "A's children and their heirs" is commonly called a class gift because it is made to a group of people. Rather than a bequest, this could have been made by deed and it could even involve a sale to A; however, the portion of the grant to the children of A is still commonly called a class gift. This gift of a future interest in Blackacre to the class of children of A is a contingent remainder because there is no person who meets the description of the beneficiary to whom the remainder belongs. As yet, the children of A are unborn, signaling a contingent remainder. Thus, no member of the class of children exists.

A contingent remainder to a class, like a contingent remainder to an individual, is destructible and inalienable inter vivos. Because this remainder is contingent and because no vested interest in the fee simple follows the contingent remainder, O keeps a reversion. Consider one further example:

Example 72

O → A for life, then to the children of A who reach 21 and their heirs.

Suppose A has two children, X, age 10, and Y, age 6. Our illustration is:

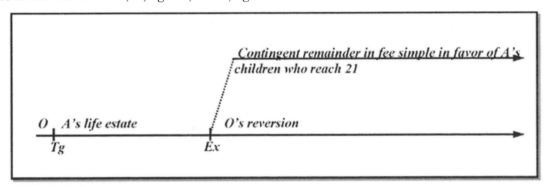

The class gift to A's children who reach age 21 is still a contingent remainder because it is given to a group of unascertained persons and perhaps even unborn children. No one yet fits the description so as to become an identifiable member of the class.

But what happens if one of the two children in this example reaches age 21, say, for example, Y? Perhaps X died at age 19. For purpose of stating the title, remainder is reclassified as vested. Thus, upon a child of A reaching age 21, the illustration becomes:

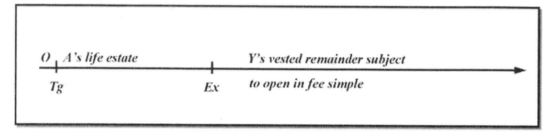

The phrase, "subject to open" in the diagram identifies a subspecies of vested remainder. Some authorities call this a vested remainder subject to partial divestment. A vested remainder subject to open results from a conveyance to a class where at least one class member is born and ascertainable and has met any condition precedent imposed on the class. Like other vested remainders, a vested remainder subject to open is indestructible, alienable inter vivos, devisable, and inheritable. But it is "subject to open" because for some period of time, the class is open. That is, the class can increase in number and thereby reduce X's share. For particular class gifts, such as a class gift "for life," circumstances could also cause the class to be reduced in size.

Suppose, instead, that both X and Y reach age 21. X and Y share a vested remainder subject to open in fee. X and Y hold a concurrent interest. At modern law, the type of concurrent interest would be a tenancy in common unless O's will specified that they would hold in joint tenancy with right of survivorship.

> Note that we said that X and Y share a vested remainder subject to open "in fee," not in "fee simple absolute." When we say "fee," we mean fee simple absolute. If we mean something less than a fee simple absolute, we will use all the necessary words, such as fee simple determinable and fee simple upon condition subsequent. When we say "fee simple interest" or "fee simple estate," we are generically referring to any kind of fee simple. Your teacher may or may not take these short cuts. Follow your teacher's lead on these short cuts, not ours.

Assuming that X and Y are tenants in common, suppose X dies, leaving a will in favor of his wife, W. W and Y will share the vested remainder subject to open in fee. If X died without a will, then X's property would pass to his heir, including X's share in the vested remainder subject to open.

If X and Y hold as joint tenants, which was the old common law presumption, but which could be expressly established today by the terms of O's grant, then when X died, Y would get X's share, whether X died intestate or whether X left a will devising all of his property to W. However, because the vested remainder subject to open is alienable inter vivos, X could have conveyed his interest in the vested remainder subject to open to B. If X had conveyed his interest, then the joint tenancy would have been severed into a tenancy in common, in which case B and Y would then hold the vested remainder subject to open as tenants in common.

Since a full discussion of the differences between concurrent interests (tenancy in common, joint tenancy, and tenancy by the entireties) is beyond the scope of this guide, we ask that you assume that all co-owners are tenants in common unless we expressly say otherwise and even though the preferred or default concurrent interest at common law was not the tenancy in common. We will briefly revisit the different kinds of concurrent interests in chapter six, but only for the limited purpose of teaching estates in land and future interests.

Some additional examples of gifts to a class may be useful for review and clarification. Suppose:

Example 73

O → A for life, then to the children of A and their heirs.

If A has no children, then the state of the title is: A has a life estate, the (unborn) children of A have a contingent remainder, and O has a reversion. The children of A do not have a contingent remainder subject to open. Legally speaking, there is no such interest.

If, in the above example, O conveys his reversion to A, then A will have, by the miracle of merger, a fee simple absolute. Merger destroys the contingent remainder in the children of A, because the remainder failed to vest before the termination of the prior estate.

If, on the other hand, a child, X, is born to A before O conveys his reversion, then the state of the title becomes: A has a life estate, and X, now in being, has a vested remainder subject to open in fee. O's reversion disappears because it is no longer needed to account for the full fee simple absolute. The remainder subject to open is not destructible. If X dies leaving the remainder to her spouse, H, then the state of the title will be: A has a life estate, and H has the vested remainder subject to open. (Remember, we asked you to assume tenancy in common.)

Other important aspects of gifts to a class include determining when a class gift closes. A class closes when no additional members can be added to the class, *e.g.*, when A dies in Example 73. For example, suppose O conveys "*to A for life, remainder to B's children and their heirs*," and on the date of the conveyance O, A, and B are living, and B has one child, X. The state of the title is: A has a life estate, and X has a vested remainder subject to open.

Now suppose B dies, survived by his child, X, and by A. The state of the title is: A has a life estate, and X has a vested remainder. Since the class has closed, X's remainder is no longer "subject to open."

You may rightly think that we are forgetting about "the birds and the bees." Suppose that B is a male and that his wife was pregnant when B died and that she thereafter gave birth to Y. As the common law evolved, if Y is born alive, Y would share with X. Our discussion from now on implicitly takes into account this period of gestation. So, for convenience, we will continue to say, in these circumstances, that the class closes at B's death, even though that is not strictly true if B is a male who dies leaving a pregnant wife who later delivers a live birth.

You may ponder the possibility that B and his wife created a frozen embryo before B died and that his wife several years later had that embryo implanted in her womb, resulting in the birth of Y. Suffice to say, the common law never imagined this set of facts. Some state legislatures have, so we will briefly return to this in chapter seven.

For a further example, suppose O conveys "*to A for life, remainder to B's children and their heirs.*" First assume that A dies when B is still alive but has no children. The state of the title would then be that O has a fee simple absolute. Do you understand why the contingent remainder was destroyed?

Instead, assume that when A died, B had a child, X, and that B is still alive. You might wonder now whether the gift remains open beyond A's death, if B survives A, to include children born to B thereafter. The common law slowly evolved to establish a complex but simply stated rule called "the rule of convenience." In this circumstance, absent a showing of intent to the contrary, this rule of construction would close the class at the end of A's life estate. Subject to the implicit gestation rule, above, no children born to B after A's death would share.

The rule of convenience closes a class as soon as a member of that class is entitled to demand distribution of his share. In this example, if a child of B had been born before A died, then that child will be entitled to possession when A dies. This fact will close the class at A's death unless O has expressed a different intent in the instrument that created the interests. Thus, in this example, X would have a fee simple absolute.

Class gifts involve other legal issues. You will encounter some of them in your course work in property, others in your wills and trusts course, and still others in the course on estate and gift tax. This chapter was intended only to provide an introduction to the family of remainders. The following summary and the problems in the review set will give you a chance to practice these new insights.

C. SUMMARY OF REMAINDERS

1. Vested Remainders (pre-1536)

a. Vested

Definition: A vested remainder is a remainder created in an identifiable grantee or identifiable group that is not subject to any condition and that is not subject to decrease or increase.

Here, and with all remainders, remember to first determine that the future interest *is* a remainder — *i.e.*, follows an expirable estate, is ready to take effect on expiration of the preceding estate, and does not take effect before expiration of the preceding estate, the three rules you learned in Chapter 2, Section B.

Examples 74, 75, and 76

O → A for life, then to B and his heirs.

O → A for life, remainder to B for life.

O → A for life, then to B and his heirs as long as the land is farmed.

In all of the above examples, in the classic common law language of estates in land, B is deemed to have a vested remainder. Notice in example 75 that if B dies before A, then B's interest disappears. That, however, is a function of the kind of present estate B will have. Further, in Example 76, B has an interest that, once it becomes possessory, might be lost on breach of condition. Again, this is a function of the kind of present estate the future interest will become, not a function of the kind of remainder B has.

Attributes of vested remainder: Alienable, devisable, inheritable.

b. Vested Subject to Open

Definition: A vested remainder subject to open is a remainder belonging to a class of people that may increase in number.

Examples 77, 78, and 79

O → A for life, then to the children of A and their heirs.

    [Assume A has one child, B.]

O → A for life, then to the children of C and their heirs.

    [Assume C has one child, B.]

O → A for life, then to B and his children.

In all three examples, B has a vested remainder subject to open.

Attributes of a vested remainder subject to open: Alienable, devisable, inheritable.

2. Contingent Remainders

Definition: A contingent remainder is a remainder that is subject to a condition precedent or created in an unborn or unascertainable person.

Examples 80, 81, 82, and 83

O → A for life, then to B and his heirs if B marries C. [Assume that B has not married C.]

O → A for life, remainder to the firstborn son of A and his heirs. [Assume A has no sons.]

O → A for life, then to B's heir. [Assume B is living.]

O → A for life, then to B and his heirs, if B marries C, otherwise to D and her heirs.

    [Assume B is living and unmarried.]

In all four examples, the remainders are contingent, and O has a reversion. In the first example, B has a contingent remainder in fee. In the second example, A's firstborn son has a contingent remainder in fee. In the third example, the person who on B's death is the heir to B's estate has a contingent remainder in fee. In the fourth example, B and D have alternate contingent remainders.

Attributes of a contingent remainder: A contingent remainder is destroyed if it fails to vest before expiration of the preceding estate. Failure to vest may occur if the condition precedent becomes impossible to perform or if the contingent remainder is destroyed by merger or by termination of the prior estate before expiration. A contingent remainder is not alienable inter vivos, but it is devisable and inheritable unless the condition that makes the interest a contingent remainder requires survivorship, in which case the interest would not be devisable or inheritable until the condition requiring survivorship has been met.

D. OUR ANALYTICAL APPROACH (MODIFIED)

We now modify our analytical approach by adding some additional matters covered in this chapter, which we **bold** so you may easily identify the additions.

First Determinations:

1. What did O have before making the grant?

    Assume O begins with a fee simple absolute unless otherwise stated.

2. What does A have?

    Fee simple absolute?

    Fee tail?

    Life estate?

    Fee simple determinable?

    Fee simple on condition subsequent?

3. If there are no further grants, what has O retained, if anything?

    Nothing if A has a fee simple absolute.

    Reversion if A has a life estate or a fee tail.

    Possibility of reverter if A has a fee simple determinable.

    Right of entry if A has a fee simple on condition subsequent.

Second Determinations:

If there are further grants, then ask, as to each one:

4. Is the interest a remainder?

    a. [Rule 1] Does the interest follow an expirable estate?

        i.   If no, then the interest is not a remainder. Strike the interest (it is void prior to 1536) and determine what is left in O, if anything, under First Determinations, question 3, above.

        ii. If yes, then the interest may be a remainder. Proceed to b, immediately below.

    b. [Rule 2] Will the interest take effect immediately upon the expiration of the preceding estate?

        i.   If no, then the interest is not a remainder. Strike the interest (it is void prior to 1536) and determine what is left in O, if anything, under First Determinations, question 3, above.

        ii. If yes, then the interest may be a remainder. Proceed to c, immediately below.

    c. [Rule 3] Can the interest take effect before the expiration of the preceding estate?

        i.   If yes, then the interest is not a remainder. Strike the interest (it is void prior to 1536) and determine what is left in O, if anything, under First Determinations, question 3, above.

        ii. If no, then the interest is a remainder. Proceed to 5, immediately below.

5. Since the interest is a remainder, what will the remainder be when it becomes possessory?

    Fee simple absolute?

    Fee tail?

Life estate?

Fee simple determinable?

Fee simple on condition subsequent?

6.   Is the remainder vested or contingent?

   a.   Is the holder of the remainder born and ascertainable?

      i.   If yes, then the remainder may be vested.

      ii.   If no, then the remainder is contingent, unless some extraneous facts show that the remainder has become vested.

      iii.   In either case, proceed to b. immediately below.

   b.   Is there a condition precedent to possession other than the expiration of the preceding interest?

      i.   If no (and if the holder of the remainder is born and ascertainable — answered under 6.a., above), then the remainder is vested.

      ii.   If yes (or if the holder of the remainder is unborn or unascertainable — answered under 6.a., above,) then the remainder is contingent.

   c.   Note: If a contingent remainder in one party (e.g., B) is immediately followed by another remainder in another party (e.g., C) that can become possessory only in exactly those circumstances in which the first party's (B's) remainder cannot, then both parties (B and C) have alternative contingent remainders.

7.   **If the remainder is vested, is the remainder a "class gift"?**

   a.   **If no, then the remainder is a vested remainder.**

   b.   **If yes, then the remainder is a vested remainder subject to open unless the class has closed by facts extraneous to the grant. Is the class closed?**

      i.   **If yes, then the class has closed and the remainder is a vested remainder.**

      ii.   **If no, then the remainder is a vested remainder subject to open unless extraneous facts have made the remainder a present possessory interest.**

8.   **If the remainder is contingent, has it been destroyed?**

   a.   **Has the contingent remainder been destroyed because it failed to vest in time — at or before the expiration of the preceding estate that supported the remainder?**

      i.   **If yes, then the remainder should be deleted from the grant and the state of the title should then be determined from what is left of the grant.**

      ii.   **If no, then proceed immediately to b., below.**

   b.   **Has the contingent remainder been destroyed by merger — by merging the preceding estate that supported the remainder with the next vested interest?**

      i.   **If yes, then the remainder should be deleted from the grant and the state of the title should then be determined from what is left of the grant.**

      ii.   **If no, then proceed immediately to c., below.**

   c.   **Has the contingent remainder been destroyed by termination (forfeiture or renunciation) of the preceding estate before its expiration?**

    i.   **If yes, then the remainder should be deleted from the grant and the state of the title should then be determined from what is left of the grant.**

    ii.   **If no, then proceed to 9., below**

9.   If the remainder is contingent, does O retain a reversion?

    Yes, unless O has otherwise accounted for the full fee simple absolute.

E.   REVIEW PROBLEMS (CIRCA 1500)

Please give the state of the title for each of the following. Assume that O has a fee simple absolute prior to the conveyance. You must give the state of the title for each of the separate fact situations. Assume each set of facts supplements the prior facts.

1.   O →   *W for life, then to A and his heirs if A survives W, and if A fails to survive W, then to B and his heirs.*

   a.   O, W, A, and B are all living.

   b.   B dies leaving a sole heir, D.

   c.   W dies.

   d.   A dies leaving a sole heir, E.

2.   O →   *A and the heirs of his body, then to the firstborn son of B and that son's heirs.*

   a.   O, A, and B are all living; neither A nor B has children. A and B are both married, but not to each other.

   b.   A has a son, C. A's wife dies in childbirth.

   c.   B has a son, D.

   d.   B dies.

   e.   A dies never having married again and with a will leaving all his property to E and his heirs.

3.   O →   *A for life, remainder to the children of A who survive A and their heirs.*

   a.   A is living but has no children. A is married.

   b.   A has a child, X.

   c.   A has a child, Y.

   d.   X dies, leaving H as an heir.

   e.   A dies.

4.   O →   *A for life, then to B and his heirs so long as liquor is not sold on the premises.*

   a.   O, A, and B are living.

   b.   A dies.

   c.   O dies leaving as his heir D.

   d.   B opens a liquor store on Blackacre.

Answers to Review Problems

Please give the state of the title for each of the following. Assume that O has a fee simple absolute prior to the conveyance. You must give the state of the title for each of the separate fact situations. Assume each set of facts supplements the prior facts.

1.   O →   *W for life, then to A and his heirs if A survives W, and if A fails to survive W, then to B and his heirs.*

   a.   O, W, A, and B are all living.
         W has a life estate.
         A has a contingent remainder in fee simple.
         B has an alternative contingent remainder in fee simple.
         O has a reversion.

   b.   B dies leaving a sole heir, D.
         No change except D has B's alternative contingent remainder in fee.

> Note the difference if the problem had said "A dies leaving a sole heir, D." While in theory A's contingent remainder is as inheritable as B's, the condition here requires A to survive W. Hence, if A predeceases W, the contingent remainder is destroyed and B's vested remainder follows W's life estate. O's reversion would disappear.

   c.   W dies.
         A has a fee simple absolute.

   d.   A dies leaving a sole heir, E.
         E has a fee simple absolute.

2.   O →   *A and the heirs of his body, then to the firstborn son of B and that son's heirs.*

   a.   O, A, and B are all living; neither A nor B have children. A and B are both married, but not to each other.
         A has a fee tail.
         The firstborn son of B has a contingent remainder in fee simple.
         O has a reversion.

   b.   A has a son, C. A's wife dies in childbirth.
         No change.

   c.   B has a son, D.
         A has a fee tail.
         D has a vested remainder in fee simple.

   d.   B dies.
         No change.

   e.   A dies never having married again, and with a will leaving all his property to E and his heirs.
         C has a fee tail.
         D has a vested remainder in fee simple.
         E has nothing.

3.   O →   *A for life, remainder to the children of A who survive A and their heirs.*

   a.   A is living but has no children. A is married.

A has a fee tail.

The children of A who survive A have a contingent remainder.

O has a reversion.

b. A has a child, X.

No change.

c. A has a child, Y.

No change.

d. X dies, leaving H as an heir.

No change. H inherits nothing. X must survive A to take.

e. A dies.

Y has a fee simple absolute.

4. $O \rightarrow$ *A for life, then to B and his heirs so long as liquor is not sold on the premises.*

a. O, A, and B are living.

O has a possibility of reverter.

A has a life estate.

B has a vested remainder in fee simple determinable.

b. A dies.

O has a possibility of reverter.

B has a fee simple determinable.

c. O dies leaving as his heir D.

No change except D has O's possibility of reverter.

d. B opens a liquor store on Blackacre.

D has a fee simple absolute.

Chapter 4

PRESENT AND FUTURE INTERESTS AFTER 1536

A. EXECUTORY INTERESTS AND THE FEE SIMPLE ON EXECUTORY LIMITATION

Look again at problem 3(c) in the review problems at the end of chapter two. O wants A to have a fee simple — "almost"; *i.e.*, she wants B to get the fee simple, if B returns from Rome. You should have decided that O could not accomplish that desire before 1536. That was true in the common law courts. We will continue to be concerned only with legal estates in land — as opposed not to "illegal estates" but to "equitable interests," which distinction shortly shall become clearer. However, to explain how O might accomplish her wish, we must turn our attention for a moment to the Court of Equity and to a legislative change in 1536.

In the period between 1066 and 1536, the world of the common law and the profession practiced by the common law lawyers expanded greatly. During this period of about five hundred years, the important common law courts had emerged, Parliament had become an important representative body that initiated significant legislation, and the body of common law principles had increased and become more detailed. From relatively simple beginnings, the forms of action had evolved to enable the common law courts to entertain more kinds of complaints and thus to award damages for more types of injuries.

At the same time, the procedural aspects of the forms of action, particularly the pleading stage, had become increasingly technical and slow. Further, the forms of action, even as multiple and flexible as they were, did not afford universal justice because if a particular claim did not fit precisely into the process and substance of at least one form of action and if it were not "perfectly" pleaded (presented) to the common law courts, then the claim failed. In a perfect world, some of these claims should have been allowed and a remedy provided, but the common law courts were more concerned about a perfectly pleaded world — that the claim perfectly fit into a recognized form of action. Thus, the common law courts refused to consider seemingly meritorious claims because the pleadings did not perfectly fit a recognized form (cause) of action.

During the same five-hundred-year period that produced the common law courts, Parliament, common law pleading, and an enlarged number of common law forms of action, an alternative channel of justice widened, in part, to respond to the disadvantages of the common law legal process. This alternative channel arose in an officer of the King's household called the Chancellor. As this office evolved, it increasingly became a source of relief for claims that were not recognized by the common law courts. Acting on behalf of the King, this household officer exercised a delegated authority to order compensation, decree specific performance, and otherwise compel activity that to him seemed just or "equitable." These alternative forms of relief came to be called "equity," and the alternative channel came to be called the court of equity (but officially, the Court of Chancery). As equity jurisdiction and relief expanded, clever lawyers filed claims in the courts of equity when they believed that equity would grant relief in circumstances where the common law courts would not — an early form of "forum shopping."

Initially, the petitions directed to the Chancellor probably represented unique problems. Later, many petitions fell into a few categories as the Chancellor's expertise became more specialized. One of the most important categories seems to have been petitions respecting conveyances of real property. These petitions asked that the Chancellor intervene to mitigate the hardship of results obtained at common law.

Take, for example, review problem 3(c) at the end of chapter two:

> *O → A and his heirs,* **but if B returns from Rome, then to B and his heirs.**

As you know, O's interest could not be carried out at common law. B's interest does not satisfy the definition of a remainder and no other future interest could be created in a third party. In the common law courts, the emphasized words were apparently void or at least were ignored, and A was treated as having a fee simple absolute.

Yet, to accomplish his desire, O could have constructed a conveyance that the Chancellor would have enforced. O could have created a **use**.

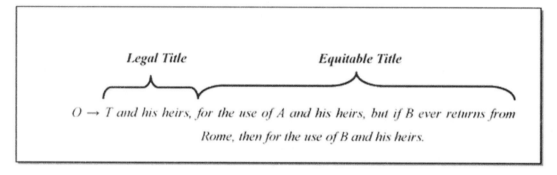

> Not everyone sees the recognition of the use as an historical event worthy of celebration. *See, e.g.,* G. Thompson, *Commentaries on the Modern Law of Real Property* § 4290, at 223 (J. Grimes ed., 1963):
>
>> But about the middle of the thirteenth century the "use" slithered into this Garden of Eden. Thus there developed a party whose rights in the land were not always visible since he might not be in open possession but which rights were protected by the equity courts. Uses apparently were not usually shown even on the manorial roles. Indeed secrecy was one of the major areas of usefulness.

This grant contains only one conveyance that the common law courts recognized: O has conveyed to T a fee simple absolute — the **legal** (common law) title to Blackacre. But the Chancellor would require T to manage the estate for the benefit of A and, if B returned from Rome, then for the benefit of B. Thus, A was regarded as having "equitable title," and B was regarded as having conditional future equitable title. Process in the Court of Chancery began with a petition. Discovery mechanisms, such as depositions and interrogatories, were available. A nonjury trial before the Chancellor followed. Eventually, if the Chancellor decided affirmatively for A and B, then a decree would issue, perhaps in the form of injunctive relief.

The process, the principles, and the remedies were all sufficiently different from those available in the common law courts so that the words "equitable rights" and "equitable relief" began to be used to describe them. For example, A and B have equitable rights resulting from the conveyance to T. T had the legal interest, and A and B had equitable interests. For reasons that are not altogether clear, the Chancellor was willing to enforce equitable future interests in a grantee that did not satisfy the common law conveyancing rules. His willingness to recognize future interests in grantees that did not satisfy the strict common law for remainders greatly added to the Chancellor's jurisdiction and power. The use provided other advantages as well. The use became a popular tax-avoidance device and also permitted owners of interests in land to devise such interests long before the Statute of Wills was enacted in 1540.

In 1536, Parliament passed the Statute of Uses, 27 Hen. VIII, Ch. 10. This Statute gave legal (common law) status to interests had been only enforceable in equity through the use. As a result of the Statute of Uses, some interests that had been previously recognized only in the court of equity gained protection in the common law courts. This allowed the common law courts to recapture lost judicial business at the jurisdictional expense of the court of equity. Thus, the Statute of Uses, you will be glad to know, did not make illegal or change the treatment of any of the present or future interests you have already mastered, so don't discard what you have already learned. The key difference is that some interests that were void at common law prior to 1536 became valid as new legal interests.

As a result of the Statute of Uses, the list of common law estates in land was expanded to include one new present interest and one new future interest. The new present interest is the "fee simple on executory limitation." The new future interest is an "executory interest." The relationship between these new estates is similar to the relationship between the old fee simple determinable and the possibility of reverter — the difference being that the executory interest is a future interest in a **grantee** while, as you know, a possibility of reverter was always in the **grantor**. This similarity leads us to diagram these two conveyances very much alike:

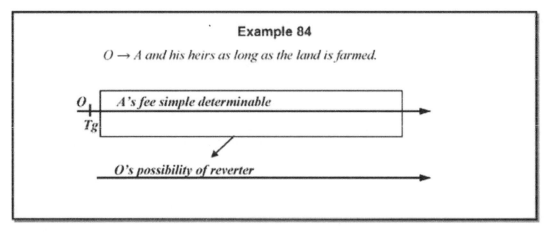

Example 84

$O \rightarrow A$ and his heirs as long as the land is farmed.

O
Tg
A's fee simple determinable

O's possibility of reverter

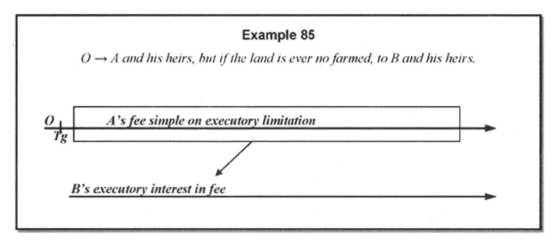

Example 85

$O \rightarrow A$ and his heirs, but if the land is ever no farmed, to B and his heirs.

O
Tg
A's fee simple on executory limitation

B's executory interest in fee

The fee simple on executory limitation was alienable, inheritable, and devisable (after the Statute of Wills in 1540). The executory interest was inheritable and devisable (after 1540) but was originally inalienable inter vivos (by either gift or sale).

Here are some more examples of these "new" estates:

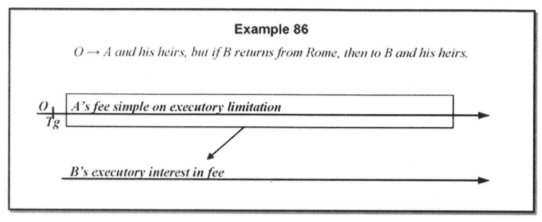

Hence, the grantor's wish in chapter two, problem 3(c) can now be met. The following example presents a bit of a problem:

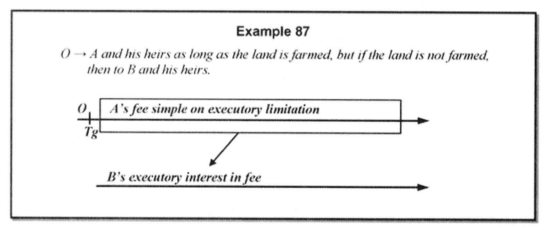

You should know, now, to call the future interest an executory interest in fee simple. But has A's present estate changed? It used to be called a "fee simple determinable" because all the words after "farmed" would have been disregarded before 1536 for violating the common law conveyancing rules.

Should we continue to call it a fee simple determinable now that the Statute of Uses allows the gift over to B? Or should we call it a fee simple on executory limitation, the new present estate, because it is now followed by an executory interest? Not all experts in this field would agree with that because some cases describe A's interest in Example 87 as a "fee simple determinable." Your property teacher, in fact, may think it is an important distinction, and we urge you to pay attention to your teacher in such matters. But we're going to call A's interest a fee simple on executory limitation, followed by B's executory interest in fee. This result has the attraction of keeping the two new estates related and furthermore leaves intact what you learned above — that a fee simple determinable is always followed by a possibility of reverter.

> For this initial presentation, what you choose to call A's interest in Example 87 doesn't matter very much. Why? Because, as you will learn in the next chapter, B's executory interest, though made lawful by the Statute of Uses, is nevertheless invalid by reason of the common law Rule Against Perpetuities. Thus, because of this Rule, A has a fee simple determinable, and O has a possibility of reverter. Stay tuned!

Let's consider another future interest in a grantee that was not permitted by the common law courts before 1536:

Example 88

O → A for life, then one year after A's death, to B and his heirs.

The future interest in B was too remote from A's life estate for the common law courts to tolerate. Recall that prior to 1536, a future interest in a grantee must be ready to become present possessory *immediately* upon the expiration of the preceding life estate. Thus, at common law, Example 88 would have resulted in a life estate in A and a reversion in O.

After 1536, a conveyance like Example 88 became legal:

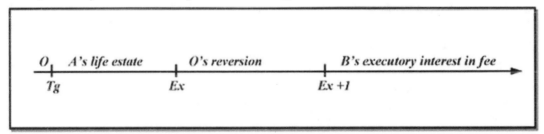

A has a life estate and B has an executory interest in fee. O takes a reversion in the property during the one-year hiatus. You will notice that O's reversion is subject to an executory interest, but this is typically left implicit rather than expressly stated. When the reversion becomes possessory, O's present estate will be a fee simple on executory limitation.

Note, too, that we can now have a conveyance that creates no new present estate in a grantee:

Example 89

O → B and his heirs upon his marriage.

B's interest is entirely future and would have been prohibited at common law prior to 1536. After the Statute of Uses, B has an executory interest in fee. O retains the present estate called a fee simple on executory limitation.

Look back over the six examples given above. Note that in some of them — Examples 85, 86, and 87 — the possession of the property, if it changes at all, will go from A to B. In some of them — Nos. 88 and 89 — the possession will go from O to B. The first kind of executory interest is called "shifting," and the second kind is called "springing." This is not a very important distinction, and little if anything — other than perhaps your exam score — turns on this classification. But the terms are still used and you should use them properly. In case you'd like more formal definitions, here they are:

(a) **_Shifting_** executory interests are those that, before 1536, would have failed because they attempted to cut short the prior estate and thus take effect before the expiration of the preceding life estate or fee tail.

(b) **_Springing_** executory interests are those that, prior to 1536, would have failed because they took effect at a time subsequent to the expiration of the preceding estate.

The Statute of Uses added new interests to an existing system. As we have learned, the inventory of estates in land and future interests increased by the addition of fees on executory limitation and executory interests. The ultimate impact of this result may not have been fully anticipated by those early legislators. If so, then they are not without counterparts today.

But the Statute of Uses left intact all the estates that had been valid before 1536, so all that you learned about the five present and five future interests in the first three chapters remains true for a few hundred more years — that is, for two more chapters. The Statute recognized a new present estate and a new future interest, but it truly only puts an "overlay" of an executory regime onto the existing system.

This new regime includes the refinement of the reversion as illustrated above, as well as a refinement of the vested remainder, which we now explain. Consider the following example:

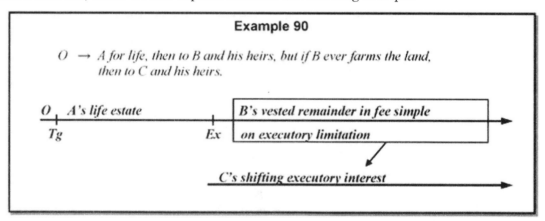

Example 90 is really not very new. Merely apply your old task of identifying what interest B will have when his interest becomes possessory. Here, B's present interest will be a fee simple on executory limitation. B's remainder is vested because there is no condition precedent, and B is born and ascertainable. B (or someone who succeeds to B's interest) is certain to come into possession of Blackacre; however, B may lose it to C after receiving possession if B does not possess it according to the condition (B must never farm). After the Statute of Uses recognized executory interests, O was able to create a future interest on executory limitation, _e.g._, B's vested remainder in fee simple on executory limitation, above.

Now, try another example.

Example 91

*O → A for life, then to B and his heirs, but if A ever farms the land,
then to C and his heirs.*

What is the state of the title? Well, A has a life estate. B's remainder appears to be vested by the usual tests: B is born and ascertainable, and no condition precedent exists. But, wait a minute. Consider the "but if" provision.

The "but if . . ." clause is a condition subsequent. The definition of a vested remainder evolved well before the Statute of Uses, and the language associated with a condition precedent ("if . . .") and a condition subsequent ("but if . . .") probably became standard language relatively early. The Statute of Uses, as you know, changed none of the remainder rules. Hence, the recognition of the legitimacy of a condition subsequent did not, in itself, make a remainder subject to a condition subsequent, contingent rather than vested.

So, you conclude, B has a vested remainder before 1536 and even after 1536. Remember that the Statute of Uses recognized only new interests and didn't change old interests. After the Statute of Uses, however, a remainder, although vested, may be "divested" before it ever becomes possessory. B, in our example, has such a remainder: a vested remainder subject to divestment — some texts and your teacher may call this a vested remainder subject to complete defeasance. If B's interest ever becomes possessory, that is, if B's interest avoids divestment while a remainder, then B will hold in fee simple. Thus, the complete name for B's future interest is a vested remainder subject to divestment in fee simple. C has a shifting executory interest in fee.

So far our classification scheme is rather tidy: B has a vested remainder subject to divestment in fee if B may lose his remainder while it is still a remainder, *e.g.*, Example 91. On the other hand, B has a vested remainder in fee simple on executory limitation if B may lose his interest after it becomes possessory, *e.g.*, Example 90.

But suppose B could lose the interest either while the interest is a remainder or after it becomes possessory? Consider:

Example 92

O → A for life, then to B and his heirs, but if B dies under age 21, then to C and his heirs.

Of course, B could die younger than age 21 either during A's life, thereby divesting the remainder, or after A's death, thereby removing B from possession. From what you have learned from the two previous examples, you might choose to call B's interest a vested remainder subject to divestment in fee simple on executory limitation. If your elocution is up to the task, then you may say that, but calling it a vested remainder subject to divestment in fee will do nicely. In other words, the standard classification labeling scheme is to describe B's interest as a vested remainder subject to divestment in fee.

Compare O's interest in Example 88. Note the limited description of O's future interest. In that example, we described O as having a reversion, not a reversion in fee simple on executory limitation.

> Look again at Example 92 and suppose that B dies at age 19. The remainder is destroyed for sure, but does A lose possession? If O wanted A to lose possession on B's untimely death, the present estate would be called **a life estate on executory limitation**. As you will learn in chapter six, this grant was permitted after 1536, but it had to be worded very clearly. The grant in Example 92 is not clear enough, so A has a life estate.

The above examples illustrate the fact that, after executory interests are recognized, a further subspecies of the vested remainder is recognized: vested subject to divestment. A vested remainder subject to divestment is a vested remainder subject to a particular type of executory interest.

Let's do a quick review of Examples 90, 91, and 92. Notice that in Example 90, B (or his successor) will get possession of the land, but possession might later be lost due to a condition. Thus, B has a vested remainder in fee simple on executory limitation in fee.

In example 91, B (or his successor) might not get possession due to a condition, but if he does get possession, then he will not later lose possession due to a condition. Here, B gets a vested remainder subject to divestment in fee.

In example 92, B might or might not get possession due to a condition, and if he does get possession, then he might or might not later lose possession due to a condition. Here B gets a vested remainder subject to divestment in fee.

Now you have it. This chapter has described certain changes made in 1536, and when you have mastered these changes you have mastered the basic common law system of estates in land and future interests. Good job! You have learned six basic present interests and six basic future interests.

Okay, we may be oversimplifying, because a vested remainder, one of the six future interests, comes in four flavors:

(1)   a vested remainder is vested indefeasibly, that is, in an identifiable person, without a condition precedent and without being subject to an executory interest or a condition subsequent;

(2)   a vested remainder may be subject to open;

(3)   after the Statute of Uses, a vested remainder can be vested subject to divestment; or

(4)   after the Statute of Uses, a vested remainder can be vested on executory limitation.

Flavors 3 and 4 are forms of a vested remainder that are subject to an executory interest. Problem 4 of the review problems at the end of this chapter explores these flavors in more detail. But recognize that as vested remainders, all four flavors are inheritable, devisable, and alienable inter vivos.

In later chapters we will introduce you to some complexities and show you some cases and statutes that changed the basic system, but for now, you have learned the basic concepts and vocabulary. Take a look at the review charts. Test your knowledge with the review problems.

B.   REVIEW MATERIALS

On the next two pages you will find two charts summarizing the information that you have learned to this point. Both charts may be used for review. You might also use the first chart to create the various interests described. For example, can you write a grant that creates a shifting executory interest in fee simple determinable? You can then use the second chart to determine whether such an interest is alienable inter vivos.

PRESENT AND FUTURE INTERESTES CREATED FROM A FEE SIMPLE ABSOLUTE IN LAND (1700)		
PRESENT INTEREST	POSSIBLE FUTURE INTERESTS	
Created in Transferee	In Transferor or His Estate	In Transferee(s)
Fee Simple Absolute	None	None
Fee Tail	Reversion	Vested Remainder • *e.g.*, in fee simple . . . no further interest • in fee simple on executory limitation . . . executory interest in subsequent transferee • in life estate . . . reversion Contingent Remainder • *e.g.*, in fee simple . . . reversion • in fee simple . . . alternative contingent remainder . . . reversion Executory Interest • *e.g.*, in fee simple . . . no further interest
Life Estate	Reversion	Same as for fee tail
Fee Simple Determinable	Possibility of Reverter	None
Fee Simple Subject to Condition Subsequent	Right of Entry (Power of Termination)	None
Fee Simple on Executory Limitation	Depends on type of executory interest created	*Executory Interest* • *e.g.*, in fee simple . . . no further interest • in life estate . . . reversion in grantor

SUMMARY OF TRANSFERABILITY (1700)			
Present Interests	**Alienable Inter Vivos**	**Devisable**	**Inheritable**
Fee Simple Absolute	Yes	Yes	Yes
Fee Tail	Limited	No	Modified
Life Estate	Yes	No	No
Fee Simple Determinable	Yes	Yes	Yes
Fee Simple on Condition Subsequent	Yes	Yes	Yes
Fee Simple on Executory Limitation	Yes	Yes	Yes
Future Interests			
Reversion	Yes	Yes	Yes
Possibility of Reverter	No	No*	Yes
Right of Entry	No	No	Yes
Remainder:			
Vested	Yes	Yes	Yes
Contingent	No	Yes	Yes
Executory Interest	No	Yes	Yes
* The answer here depends on an interpretation of the original English Statute of Wills (1540), as amended in 1542. The Statute provided for the devise of estates "in possession, reversion or remainder." Some authorities state that a possibility of reverter, like a right of entry, was not within the 1542 amendment. Other authorities disagree. *See* John A. Borron, Jr., *Simes & Smith, The Law of Future Interests* § 1901 (3d ed. 2011).			

C. OUR ANALYTICAL APPROACH (FURTHER MODIFIED AFTER 1536)

We now modify our analytical approach by adding some additional matters covered in this chapter, which we **bold** so you may easily identify the additions.

First Determinations:

1. What did O have before making the grant?

    Assume O begins with a fee simple absolute unless otherwise stated.

2. What does A have?

    Fee simple absolute?

    Fee tail?

    Life estate?

    Fee simple determinable?

    Fee simple on condition subsequent?

3. If there are no further grants, what has O retained, if anything?

    Nothing if A has a fee simple absolute.

    Reversion if A has a life estate or a fee tail.

    Possibility of reverter if A has a fee simple determinable.

    Right of entry if A has a fee simple on condition subsequent.

Second Determinations:

If there are further grants, then ask, as to each one:

4. Is the interest a remainder?

    a. [Rule 1] Does the interest follow an expirable estate?

        i. **If no, then the interest is not a remainder.** ~~Strike the interest (it is void prior to 1536) and determine what is left in O, if anything, under First Determinations, question 3, above.~~ **Proceed to Third Determinations, below.**

        ii. If yes, then the interest may be a remainder. Proceed to b, immediately below.

    b. [Rule 2] Will the interest take effect immediately upon the expiration of the preceding estate?

        i. **If no, then the interest is not a remainder.** ~~Strike the interest (it is void prior to 1536) and determine what is left in O, if anything, under First Determinations, question 3, above.~~ **Proceed to Third Determinations, below.**

        ii. If yes, then the interest may be a remainder. Proceed to c, immediately below.

    c. [Rule 3] Can the interest take effect before the expiration of the preceding estate?

        i. **If yes, then the interest is not a remainder.** ~~Strike the interest (it is void prior to 1536) and determine what is left in O, if anything, under First Determinations, question 3, above.~~ **Proceed to Third Determinations, below.**

        ii. If no, then the interest is a remainder. Proceed to 5, immediately below.

5. Since the interest is a remainder, what will the remainder be when it becomes possessory?

Fee simple absolute?

Fee tail?

Life estate?

Fee simple determinable?

Fee simple on condition subsequent?

6. Is the remainder vested or contingent?

   a. Is the holder of the remainder born and ascertainable?

      i.   If yes, then the remainder may be vested.

      ii. If no, then the remainder is contingent, unless some extraneous facts show that the remainder has become vested.

      iii. In either case, proceed to b, immediately below.

   b. Is there a condition precedent to possession other than the expiration of the preceding interest?

      i.   If no (and if the holder of the remainder is born and ascertainable — answered under 6.a, above), then the remainder is vested.

      ii. If yes (or if the holder of the remainder is unborn or unascertainable — answered under 6.a, above), then the remainder is contingent.

   c. Note: If a contingent remainder in one party (*e.g.*, B) is immediately followed by another remainder in another party (*e.g.*, C) that can become possessory only in exactly those circumstances in which the first party's (B's) remainder cannot, then both parties (B and C) have alternative contingent remainders.

7. If the remainder is vested, is the remainder a "class gift"?

   a. If no, then the remainder is a vested remainder.

   b. If yes, then the remainder is a vested remainder subject to open unless the class has closed by facts extraneous to the grant. Is the class closed?

      i.   If yes, then the class has closed and the remainder is a vested remainder.

      ii. If no, then the remainder is a vested remainder subject to open unless extraneous facts have made the remainder a present possessory interest.

8. If the remainder is contingent, has it been destroyed?

   a. Has the contingent remainder been destroyed because the remainder failed to vest in time — at or before the expiration of the preceding estate that supported the remainder?

      i.   If yes, then the remainder should be deleted from the grant and the state of the title should then be determined from what is left of the grant.

      ii. If no, then proceed immediately to b., below.

   b. Has the contingent remainder been destroyed by merger — by merging the preceding estate that supported the remainder with the next vested interest?

      i.   If yes, then the remainder should be deleted from the grant and the state of the title should then be determined from what is left of the grant.

      ii. If no, then proceed immediately to c., below.

    c.   Has the contingent remainder been destroyed by termination (forfeiture or renunciation) of the preceding estate before its expiration?

       i.   If yes, then the remainder should be deleted from the grant and the state of the title should then be determined from what is left of the grant.

      ii.   If no, then proceed to 9., below

9.   If the remainder is contingent, does O retain a reversion?

    Yes, unless O has otherwise accounted for the full fee simple absolute.

10.   **[Reserved for next chapter.]**

Third Determinations:

11.   **Since the interest is not a remainder, consider the new interests that are possible after the Statute of Uses (1536).**

    a.   **Reclassify the interest that was invalid prior to 1536 as an "executory interest" in fee or as one of the five possessory estates, as appropriate.**

       i.   **If this interest can become possessory immediately following the interest of a prior grantee, then the interest is a "shifting executory interest."**

      ii.   **If this interest can become possessory immediately from the grantor, then the interest is a "springing executory interest."**

    b.   **Next classify the present or future interest that immediately precedes the executory interest:**

       i.   **If the immediately preceding interest is only implicit, due to a gap in possession between the expiration of the preceding estate and the executory interest, then the grantor retains a "reversion" and the executory interest is then a "springing" one.**

    c.   **When the reversion becomes possessory, it will be a present estate "on executory limitation" — most likely a "fee simple on executory limitation."**

       i.   **If the immediately preceding future interest will become possessory, but might thereafter be lost due to a condition subsequent expressed in the grant, then the immediately preceding interest is "on executory limitation."**

      ii.   **If the executory interest does not fall under i, immediately above, then the interest is "subject to divestment."**

     iii.   **Caution: In making this analysis, be sure that the two future interests are not alternative contingent remainders. Remember the distinction between conditions precedent and conditions subsequent.**

D. REVIEW PROBLEMS

1. Give the "state of the title" for each of the grants below. That is, what present or future interest in Blackacre is conveyed to each of the parties at *Tg*, 1700?

    a. *O →* *A and his heirs, but if B should return from Rome, to B and his heirs.*

        [O, A, and B are living. B is in Rome.]

        O has _____

        A has _____

        B has _____

    b. *O →* *A and his heirs, but if A should marry B, to C and his heirs.*

        [O, A, B, and C are living. A is unmarried.]

        O has _____

        A has _____

        B has _____

        C has _____

    c. *O →* *A for life, and one year after A's death, to B and his heirs.*

        [O, A, and B are living.]

        O has _____

        A has _____

        B has _____

    d. *O → A and his heirs upon A's marriage.*

        [*O* and A are living. A is unmarried.]

        O has _____

        A has _____

    e. *O →* *A for life, then to B and his heirs, but if B dies before age 21, then to C and his heirs.*

        [O, A, B, and C are living. B is 19.]

O has _____

A has _____

B has _____

C has _____

2. In each case, what is B's interest? [Tg = 1591.]

    a.   *O →* *A and his heirs, but if the land is not farmed, to B and his heirs.*

        [B is living. The land is being farmed.]

    b.   *O →* *A for life, then to W for life, then if Z is still alive, to C for life, otherwise to B and his heirs.*

        [A, W, Z, C, and B are living.]

    d.   *O →* *A for life, then to B and his heirs.*

        [A and B are living.]

3. In each case, O is your client in 1591. If possible, construct a grant that will dispose of her property in the way she desires. If this can't be done, explain why.

    a.   O wants A to have a fee simple — "almost"; *i.e.,* she never wants the land to be used for commercial purposes, with the additional condition that if the land *is* ever used for commercial purposes, she wants it to go to another friend, C, for that friend's life.

    b.   O wants her friend A to have the land for A's lifetime and then she wants it to go to her friend B's youngest son, but only if B marries C. If B doesn't marry C, then O wants the land to go to the Church, but only for as long as it is used for Church purposes.

4. Give the state of the title. Assume the grant is in 1591:

    a.   *O →* *A for life, then if A has joined the Church, to B and his heirs, but if A has not joined the Church, then to Church and its successors and assigns.*

        [O, A, and B are living. A is not a member of the Church.]

    O has _____

    A has _____

    B has _____

    Church has_____

b. *O →*   *A for life, then to B and his heirs, but if A joins the Church, then upon A's death, to the Church and its successors and assigns.*

   [O, A, and B are living. A is not a member of the Church.]

   A has _____

   B has _____

   C has _____

c. *O →*   *A for life, then to B and his heirs, but if B joins the Church after taking possession, then to the Church and its successors and assigns.*

   [O, A, and B are living.]

   A has _____

   B has _____

   Church has _____

d. *O →*   *A for life, then to B and his heirs, but if B joins the Church, then upon A's death, to the Church and its successors and assigns.*

   [O, A, and B are living. B is not a member of the Church.]

   A has _____

   B has _____

   C has _____

e. *O →*   *A for life, then to B and his heirs, but if B does not survive A, then to C and his heirs.*

   [O, A, B, and C are living.]

   O has _____

   A has _____

   B has _____

   C has _____

f. *O →*   *A for life, then, if B survives A, to B and his heirs, but if B does not survive A, then to C and his heirs.*

[O, A, B, and C are living]

O has _____

A has _____

B has _____

C has _____

5.   Give the state of the title; assume in both cases that A and B are living and that A is farming the land:

a. $O \rightarrow$ *A and her heirs, but if the land ceases to be farmed by A, then to B and his heirs.*

O has _____

A has _____

B has _____

b. $O \rightarrow$ *A and her heirs as long as the land is farmed by A, then to B and his heirs.*

O has _____

A has _____

B has _____

Answers to Review Problems

1.   Give the "state of the title" for each of the grants below. That is, what present or future interest in Blackacre is conveyed to each of the parties at **Tg**, 1700?

    a.   *O →*   *A and his heirs, but if B should return from Rome, to B and his heirs.*

                  [O, A, and B are living. B is in Rome.]

        O has nothing.

        A has a fee simple on executory limitation.

        B has a shifting executory interest in fee simple.

    b.   *O →*   *A and his heirs, but if A should marry B, to C and his heirs.*

                  [O, A, B, and C are living. A is unmarried.]

        O has nothing.

        A has a fee simple on executory limitation.

        B has nothing. (Don't worry about what entitlements B might have as A's spouse.)

        C has a shifting executory interest in fee simple.

    c.   *O →*   *A for life, and one year after A's death, to B and his heirs.*

                  [O, A, and B are living.]

        O has a reversion.

        A has a life estate.

        B has a springing executory interest in fee simple.

> Your teacher may want you to call O's interest a reversion in fee simple on executory limitation.

    d.   *O →*   *A and his heirs upon A's marriage.*

                  [O and A are living. A is unmarried.]

        O has a fee simple on executory limitation.

        A has a springing executory interest in fee simple.

    e.   *O →*   *A for life, then to B and his heirs, but if B dies before age 21, then to C and his heirs.*

                  [O, A, B, and C are living. B is 19.]

        O has nothing.

        A has a life estate.

        B has a vested remainder subject to divestment in fee.

        C has a shifting executory interest in fee simple.

2.   In each case, what is B's interest? [**Tg** = 1591.]

    a.   *O →*   *A and his heirs, but if the land is not farmed, to B and his heirs.*

                  [B is living. The land is being farmed.]

        B has a shifting executory interest in fee simple.

    b.   *O →*   *A for life, then to W for life, then if Z is still alive, to C for life, otherwise to B and his heirs.*

                  [A, W, Z, C, and B are living.]

        B has an alternative contingent remainder in fee simple.

    c.   *O →*   *A for life, then to B and his heirs.* [A and B are living.]

        B has a vested remainder in fee simple.

3.   In each case, O is your client in 1591. If possible, construct a grant that will dispose of her property in the way she desires. If this can't be done, explain why.

    a.   O wants A to have a fee simple — "almost"; *i.e.*, she never wants the land to be used for commercial purposes, with the additional condition that if the land *is* ever used for commercial purposes, she wants it to go to another friend, C, for that friend's life.

        O → *A and his heirs, but if the land is ever used for commercial purposes, then to C for life.*

    b.   O wants her friend A to have the land for A's lifetime and then she wants it to go to her friend B's youngest son, but only if B marries C. If B doesn't marry C, then O wants the land to go to the Church, but only for as long as it is used for Church purposes.

        O → *A for life, then if B marries C, to B's youngest son and his heirs, otherwise to the Church as long as it is used for Church purposes.*

4.   Give the state of the title. Assume the time of the grant is 1591.

    a.   *O →* A for life, then if A has joined the Church, to B and his heirs, but if A has not joined the Church, then to the Church and its sucessors and assigns.

        [O, A, and B are living. A is not a member of the Church.]

A has a life estate.

B and the Church have alternative contingent remainders.

O has a reversion.

    b.   *O →* A for life, then to B and his heirs, but if A joins the Church, then upon A's death, to the Church and its successors and assign.

        [O, A, and B are living. A is not a member of the Church.]

A has a life estate.

B has a vested remainder subject to divestment in fee.

The Church has a shifting executory interest in fee.

O has nothing.

Note that B and the Church do not have alternative contingent remainders because there is no condition precedent language, only condition subsequent language. B may not get the land, but if he does get it, he will keep it.

    c.   *O →* A for life, then to B and his heirs, but if B joins the Church after taking possession, then to the Church and its successors and assigns.

        [O, A, and B are living.]

A has a life estate.

B has a vested remainder in fee simple on executory limitation.

The Church has a shifting executory interest in fee.

O has nothing.

Note that by the express terms of this grant, if B joined the Church while A was alive, he would still get the land. This may not have been what O subjectively intended, but it is what O objectively intended (*i.e.*, stated in the grant).

    d.   *O →* A for life, then to B and his heirs, but if B joins the Church, then upon A's death, to the Church and its successors and assigns.

        [O, A, and B are living. B is not a member of the Church.]

A has a life estate.

B has a vested remainder subject to divestment in fee.

The Church has a shifting executory interest in fee.

O has nothing.

    e.   *O →* A for life, then B and his heirs, but if B does not survive A, then to C and his heirs.

        [O, A, B, and C are living.]

A has a life estate.

B has a vested remainder subject to divestment in fee.

C has a shifting executory interest in fee.

O has nothing.

Note that B and C do not have alternative contingent remainders because there is no condition precedent language, only condition subsequent language. B may not get the land, but if he does get it, he will keep it.

f.   O →   A for life, then, if B survives A, to B and his heirs, but if B does not survive A, then to C and his heirs.

[O, A, B, and C are living.]

A has a life estate.

B and C have alternative contingent remainders.

O has a reversion.

In (f), B's survivorship is a condition precedent to B taking possession at all. But if B does survive A, then B will have a fee simple absolute. If B does not survive A, then C will have fee simple absolute when A dies. But why is the answer to (f) not exactly the same as the answer to (e)? A short but somewhat unsatisfactory answer is because the phrase "if B survives A" is present in (f) but missing from (e). The other grants may help explain the difference, but the difference is a subtle one. We've put the explanation here in the review problems instead of in the main text of the chapter to indicate that we consider it "advanced learning."

Reread the "but if" clause in (b), (c) and (d). In (b), the condition will be broken, if ever, during A's lifetime — A cannot join the Church after he is dead. The condition in (c) will be broken, if ever, only after A's death, when B comes into possession and begins to use the land. Finally, in (d), the condition may be broken either during A's life, or after A's death.

In each of (b), (c) and (d), B has a vested remainder because he is ready to take the property on A's death and there is no condition precedent to his taking. You might contend that (b) contains a condition precedent — that A not join the Church, but the common law considered a condition contained in a "but if" clause a condition subsequent. Thus, we call B's interest in (b) a vested remainder subject to divestment in fee because the remainder may be lost through breach of condition only during the period of time it is a future interest. B's interest in (c) is a vested remainder in fee simple on executory limitation, not a vested remainder subject to divestment, because B can lose his fee simple only after he comes into possession. B's interest in (d), which might be lost either before or after B takes possession, may be described by the following mouthful: a vested remainder subject to divestment in fee simple on executory limitation. However, as noted earlier, it is typical to describe B's interest as a vested remainder subject to divestment in fee.

Finally, what about (e)? The "but if" condition in this example will be broken, if ever, during A's life (by B's death). Hence, (e) resembles example (b), and B has a vested remainder subject to divestment in fee. The difference between (a) and (e) and between (e) and (f) lies in the legal consequence that the "but if" clause in (e) acts as a condition subsequent to divest a vested remainder. In (a) and (f), however, the language of the conveyance establishes the first remainder as contingent (subject to a condition precedent); the second remainder is deemed also to be subject to a condition precedent by virtue of following a contingent remainder. Because the remainders in (a) and (f) are contingent, O keeps a reversion.

One final complexity: look again at (b) and (e), the two instances in which B's interest is classified as a vested remainder subject to divestment in fee. Suppose A renounces his life estate. B's remainder is vested, so B comes into possession immediately. However, the condition, which before renunciation looked like it would be broken, if ever, *before* B took possession, may now be broken *after* B takes possession because A is still alive. The condition is still viable and may remove B from possession. That is what we usually call a fee simple on executory limitation. Thus, B's interest following renunciation by A is a fee simple on executory limitation. The lesson: remember to consider the possible relevancy of extraneous facts.

This box has generated many student concerns over the years. In our view, if you have the rest figured out, then you are in good shape.

5.   Give the state of the title; assume in both cases that A and B are living and that A is farming the land:

   a. $O \rightarrow$ A and her heirs, but if the land ceases to be farmed by A, then to B and his heirs.

         A has a fee simple on executory limitation.

         B has a shifting executory interest in fee.

         O has nothing.

   b. $O \rightarrow$ *A and her heirs as long as the land is farmed by A, then to B and his heirs.*

         A has a fee simple on executory limitation.

         B has a shifting executory interest in fee.

         O has nothing.

> Here's a point we made above in the text. We will call A's interest in both 5(a) and 5(b) a fee simple on executory limitation for what we think are proper pedagogic reasons. We understand, though, that from the perspective of the cases, 5(b) might more properly give A a fee simple determinable. Take your lead from your property teacher on this one. We all agree that B's interest in both cases is a shifting executory interest in fee.

Chapter 5

LATER MODIFICATION OF THE BASIC COMMON LAW

Common Law Responses to the Statute of Uses

You have learned so far the vocabulary and many of the concepts necessary for you to maneuver in the area of estates in land and future interests. You have learned six basic present estates and six basic future interests. You have also learned that the concept of remainders has several subconcepts: vested, vested subject to open, vested subject to divestment, vested on executory limitation, and contingent. You also know that the Statute of Uses led to the executory interest, that the recognition of the executory interest produced a new kind of fee — the fee simple on executory limitation — and that the existence of executory interests also resulted in the concept of a vested remainder subject to divestment.

All the ramifications of the Statute of Uses were not foreseen nor were they necessarily foreseeable. One of the features of the evolution of the common law, at least the common law of property, has been the elaboration of ideas in unforeseen yet functional directions. As Professor Rabin notes, "Most changes in the law create important unanticipated side effects. These side effects are sometimes beneficial and sometimes harmful." E. Rabin, *Fundamentals of Modern Real Property* 22 (1974). Who would have thought, for example, that the only lasting consequence of the Eighteenth Amendment to the United States Constitution would be the proliferation of organized crime? Perhaps because the law of property is so old, perhaps because the common law of property is remarkably durable, and perhaps because the law of property is so uniquely of common law origin, property law especially illustrates the pragmatic, yet haphazard, course of common law evolution. This chapter is designed to describe one part of that haphazard evolution: the response of the common law of real property to the Statute of Uses. First, however, you will need to recall that special attribute of a contingent remainder, destructibility.

A. THE DESTRUCTIBILITY OF CONTINGENT REMAINDERS: A REVIEW

Contingent remainders were destructible in several ways. Three primary situations could cause a contingent remainder to be destroyed: merger, forfeiture, and natural expiration.

1. Merger

Merger applies when one person owns a possessory estate or a vested future interest — a reversion or a vested remainder — and the *next* vested future interest. Under some circumstances, the lesser of the two interests will be absorbed by the greater. Example 93 illustrates merger. Compare Examples 93 and 94.

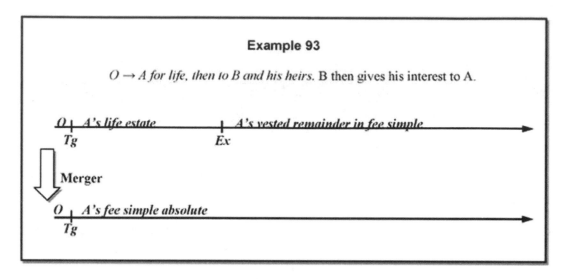

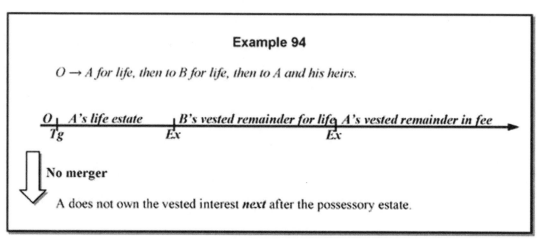

Merger can result in the destruction of contingent remainders. For example, if the prior estate that supports the contingent remainder ceases to exist as a result of merging into a larger estate, then the dependent contingent remainder is destroyed.

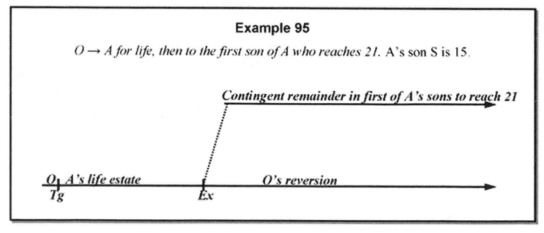

No merger occurs in Example 95 because A has only the possessory estate. Suppose, however, that O conveys her reversion to A (recall that reversions are alienable). Now, A owns the possessory estate and the next vested interest, and they merge:

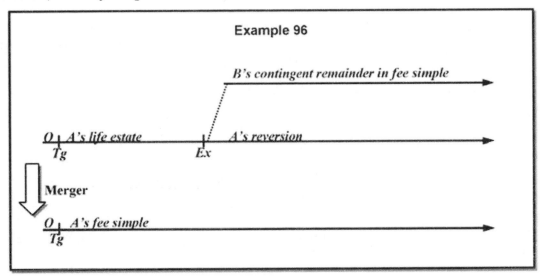

B's contingent remainder is destroyed, thus illustrating one example of the destructibility of contingent remainders — destruction as a consequence of merger.

Merger does not occur and thus does not destroy contingent remainders when all the interests involved were created by one grant. Note that in Example 95, the contingent remainder was destroyed by O's second conveyance of her reversion to A.

Consider the following example:

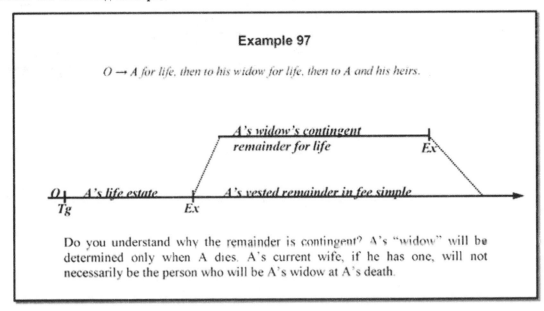

A owns the possessory estate and the next vested interest, but the estates do not merge to destroy the contingent remainder in A's surviving wife because all the estates were created with one grant. Note, however, that A may convey a fee simple absolute to B by selling both his life estate and his vested remainder to B. The requisites of merger are met because the appropriate estates are held by a single person and the situation was not created by a single conveyance.

2. Forfeiture

Forfeiture of the present estate destroys a dependent contingent remainder.

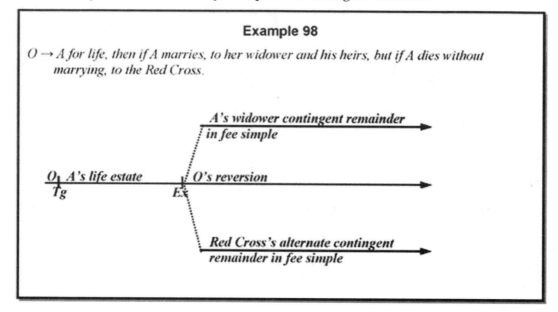

Example 98

O → A for life, then if A marries, to her widower and his heirs, but if A dies without marrying, to the Red Cross.

A's widower contingent remainder in fee simple

O A's life estate
Tg   *E.x O's reversion*

Red Cross's alternate contingent remainder in fee simple

Now, suppose A renounces her life estate or, at early common law, commits a felony. The contingencies are not ready to be tested, and hence we cannot choose between the alternative contingent remainders. O's reversion, on the other hand, is vested and O stands ready to take at any time. What if O is dead? Remember, a reversion is inheritable, so O's heir stands ready to take at any time. Thus, if A renounces, the contingent remainders are destroyed, and O or O's successors take possession in fee simple. O takes in fee simple because, under the terms of the grant, after the destruction of the contingent remainders, no one else has any interest.

3. Natural Expiration

A contingent remainder also is destroyed if the estate preceding it expires before the remainder becomes vested. This possibility provides frequent opportunities for destruction of contingent remainders.

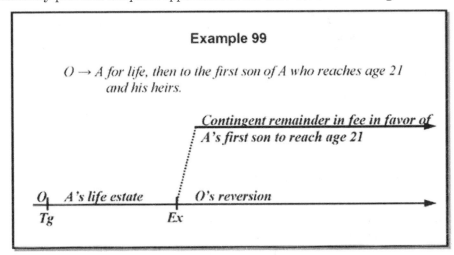

Example 99

O → A for life, then to the first son of A who reaches age 21 and his heirs.

Contingent remainder in fee in favor of
A's first son to reach age 21

O   *A's life estate*   *O's reversion*
Tg   Ex

The remainder will be contingent until one of A's sons reaches age 21. If A dies when his oldest son is 19, the contingent remainder is destroyed, and O takes his reversion. What happens two years later when the son reaches age 21? Nothing. The contingent remainder was destroyed by failing to vest in time.

4. Summary

Three primary instances illustrate the doctrine of the destructibility of contingent remainders: merger, forfeiture, and natural expiration. True, in many states today, contingent remainders are not destructible due to judicial abolition or statutory removal of the doctrine. Here, as always, we are talking about the state of the early common law. We postpone "modern" inquiries until chapter seven.

Remember, vested remainders are not destructible. We are dealing here with the destructibility of **contingent** remainders. Remember, too, that we are dealing here with the destructibility of contingent **remainders.** The same rules do not apply to executory interests or other future interests, as will be further considered in the next section.

B. THE INDESTRUCTIBILITY OF EXECUTORY INTERESTS AND *PELLS* AND *PUREFOY*

Contingent remainders and executory interests are very much alike. For example, both were devisable and inheritable, and both were inalienable inter vivos at common law. Further, both can operate similarly. Compare:

Examples 100 and 101

O → A for life, remainder to B and his heirs if B marries C.

    B has a contingent remainder in fee.

O → B and his heirs if B marries C.

    B has a springing executory interest in fee.

B's interest in both parts of Examples 100 and 101 is dependent on an event that may or may not occur. The "contingency" of each probably made both interests inalienable at common law.

For reasons that are obscure, the common law courts were initially uncertain whether executory interests were destructible or indestructible. In *Pells v. Brown*, Cro. Jac. 490, 79 Eng. Rep. 504 (1620), however, the common law judges finally decided that executory interests were indestructible.

As a result of the decision in *Pells v. Brown*, classification as a contingent remainder rather than an executory interest had important consequences. Contingent remainders would continue to be destructible. Executory interests, on the other hand, would be indestructible. Both rules — that a contingent remainder is destructible and that an executory interest is indestructible — are rules of law. Subsequently, in *Purefoy v. Rogers*, 2 Wm. Saund. 380, 85 Eng. Rep. 1181 (1670), the court laid down a rule of construction that a future interest would be construed as a contingent remainder rather than as an executory interest if the future interest was capable of taking effect as a contingent remainder. A rule of construction is used as an aid to assist the court in determining the likely intent of the parties. *See* text at Example 27, chapter two. In contrast, the parties' intent is irrelevant when applying a rule of law. Compare:

Example 102

O → A for life, remainder to B and his heirs if B has reached age 21.
    B is age 19; A is living.

    B has a contingent remainder because it is possible that B will reach 21 before A dies.

Example 103

O → A for life, and one day later to B and his heirs if B has reached age 21.
   A is living; B is 19.

B has an executory interest because, as the grant is written, the one-day hiatus between the expiration of A's life estate and B's right to take possession, assuming B has reached 21, prevents this interest from being classified as a remainder.

Note that the rules of *Pells v. Brown* and *Purefoy v. Rogers* added a good deal of flexibility to the common law of property. Through a careful (or careless) choice of words, a grantor could create either a destructible or an indestructible interest. In a choice between the two, when the grant was susceptible of being interpreted or construed as creating either a contingent remainder or an executory interest, the law preferred the destructible contingent remainder interest.

C. THE RULE AGAINST PERPETUITIES

The course of property law, however, is not smooth. In *The Duke of Norfolk's Case*, 3 Ch. Cas. 1 (1681), a principle surfaced that acted as a curb on the executory interest. Over the next 150 years, this principle, a true child of the common law, was refined into what would be called the Rule Against Perpetuities (RAP). Although *The Duke of Norfolk's Case* was an equity case, this fact does not diminish the charm of the metaphor.

We have chosen the year 1700 as the reference date for your learning of the common law. We regard changes in law after 1700 (discussed in chapter seven) as modern variations. We choose the year 1700, in part, because by that time the Rule Against Perpetuities had been conceived, if not christened.

In *The Duke of Norfolk's Case*, the court decided that executory interests, to be valid and enforceable as written, had to be **sure** to become possessory within a certain period. The beginning of the period was the time of the grant — the date we've been calling **Tg**. Note that for wills, the time of the grant would be the date of the testator's death. The endpoint of the period, however, was not set at a fixed number of years. Those early judges would have saved many generations of law students and lawyers considerable trouble by saying that all executory interests must become possessory within a fixed period from the time of the grant, *e.g.*, fifty years, but these judges did not so decree.

The impetus of the RAP was to keep the original grantor, O, from controlling the disposition of the property through the use of this new, flexible, and indestructible executory interest for too long a period after O's conveyance. Instead of allowing O a fixed period to control the destiny of the land, which certainly would have been easier to apply, the endpoint of the RAP's period is set according to the lives of certain persons living at **Tg**, the so-called "lives in being" or "measuring lives." As it eventually evolved, the RAP usually is stated: "No interest is good unless it must vest, if at all, within 21 years following a life or lives in being at the creation of the interest."

You should recognize that the RAP "voids" future interests that do not become vested "soon enough." In describing the effect of violating RAP, we use "voids" rather than "destroys" to distinguish the RAP from the doctrine of destructibility of contingent remainders. The RAP limits the impact of future interests by restricting their enforceability. The RAP represents a belief that, in the long run, property is best utilized when the living, not the dead, control the disposition of property.

The RAP requires (1) that an interest "vest" and (2) that it vest "soon enough." The word "vest" is a term of art that varies in precise meaning from one interest to another. The phrase "soon enough" represents a formula. The RAP permits interests to be "unvested" for a limited period of time, *i.e.*, during the lives of certain individuals living on the date of the conveyance plus 21 years.

.All of the present estates in land satisfy the RAP because, for purposes of the RAP, possessory interests are deemed to be "vested" from the moment of their creation. The three kinds of future interests in a grantor — the possibility of reverter, the right of entry, and the reversion — also satisfy the RAP because they too are considered "vested" from the moment of creation. Future interests in a grantee, however, involve a more subtle analysis.

The primary purpose of this chapter is to introduce you to a key reason for the RAP: to curb the newly recognized, very flexible, and otherwise indestructible executory interest. Let's restate the RAP as it applies to executory interests:

> **No executory interest is good unless it must become possessory (or becomes a vested remainder), if at all, within 21 years following a life or lives in being at the creation of the interest.**

Note that, subject to the parenthetical, the word "vested" in the more general statement of the RAP becomes "possessory" here. The period of time allowed by the formula is grasped most clearly by examining selected conveyances.

Consider an executory interest that violates the RAP:

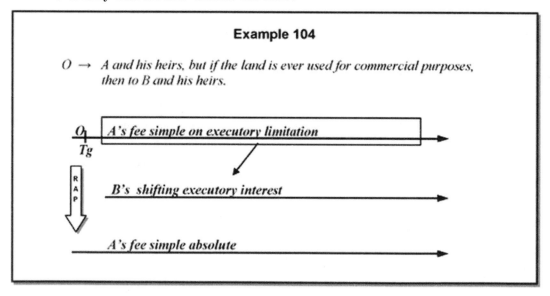

Example 104

$O \rightarrow$ *A and his heirs, but if the land is ever used for commercial purposes, then to B and his heirs.*

A's fee simple on executory limitation

B's shifting executory interest

A's fee simple absolute

Why? Because B's executory interest will not vest until B's interest becomes possessory — that is, if and when the land is used for commercial purposes. Note the uncertainty as to when B's executory interest will become possessory. In other words, there is no guarantee that the event will occur within 21 years of the death of any of the relevant persons alive at the time of the grant — O, if the conveyance was by deed, and A and B (the measuring lives). The RAP says "must" and requires just such a guarantee. Hence, B's interest is void. Because B's interest is void, you must remove B's interest from the grant and then determine what is left. A fee simple in A. Simple!

We have used variations of this example before. Note the evolution:

Example 32:   *O → A and his heirs as long as the land is farmed, then to B and his heirs.*

                         Before 1536, B's interest is void because it is not a remainder.

Example 87:   *O → A and his heirs as long as the land is farmed, but if the land is not farmed, then to B and his heirs.*

                         In 1536, the Statute of Use validates B's interest as a shifting executory interest.

Example 104:   *O → A and his heirs, but if the land is used for commercial purposes, then to B and his heirs.*

                         By 1700, the Rule Against Perpetuities has evolved to destroy B's interest as not certain to vest in time.

In the following example, the future interest does not violate the RAP.

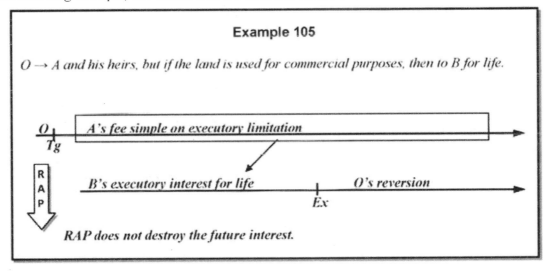

Example 105

O → A and his heirs, but if the land is used for commercial purposes, then to B for life.

A's fee simple on executory limitation

B's executory interest for life   O's reversion

RAP does not destroy the future interest.

Why not? Because B's interest will vest, *if ever*, during his life. B's executory interest is in a life estate. That is soon enough for the RAP: B is alive at the time of the grant, and B's interest will vest (become possessory), if it ever does, within his lifetime. Thus, B's interest is valid (*i.e.*, not voided by the RAP). The "measuring lives" are A and B, and if O has conveyed by deed, O. We must determine with certainty that at least one measuring life will validate the conveyance for purposes of the RAP. Since B will take, if he ever does, during his life, then the interest is valid.

Consider another executory interest that does not violate the RAP.

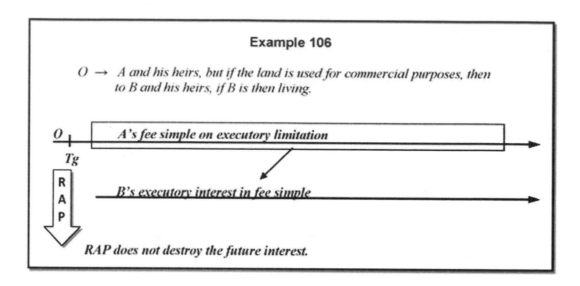

Example 106

O → A and his heirs, but if the land is used for commercial purposes, then to B and his heirs, if B is then living.

A's fee simple on executory limitation

B's executory interest in fee simple

RAP does not destroy the future interest.

Once again, B's interest will vest, **if at all**, during B's lifetime, due to the survivorship requirement. B's interest is good.

But now consider an executory interest that violates the RAP.

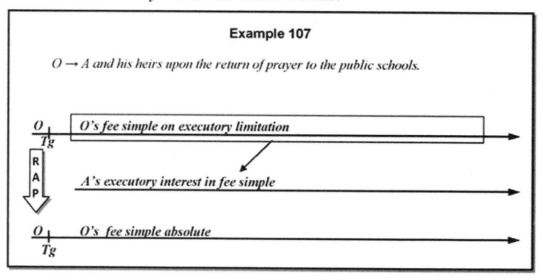

Example 107

O → A and his heirs upon the return of prayer to the public schools.

O's fee simple on executory limitation

A's executory interest in fee simple

O's fee simple absolute

Here, the measuring lives, O and A, might die **and** more than 21 years may pass before prayer returns to the public schools. Hence, A's executory interest is void because it violates the RAP. Thus, O has a fee simple absolute.

Consider yet another executory interest that violates the RAP.

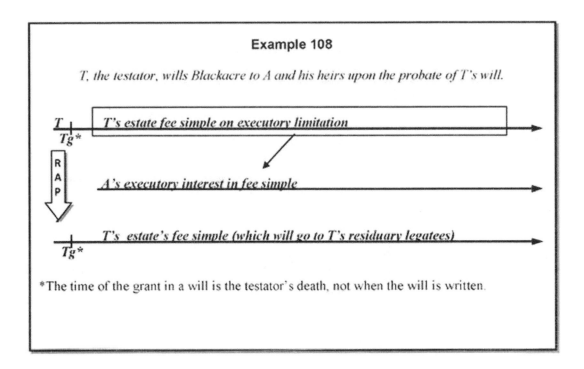

The result in this grant may be hard to believe. Because the RAP requires a *guarantee* that A's interest will vest within the relevant measuring lives plus 21 years from the *Tg*, the future interest in A fails. Justice sometimes works slowly. We cannot guarantee that T's estate will be probated in time, although we recognize that it is highly likely to be probated within 21 years of A's death. But because we cannot guarantee this, A's interest is void. This example illustrates the fact that the proper application of the RAP involves some quite fantastic possibilities; in this case, one must envision a very slothful probate court. In other cases, courts have hypothesized children born of very old people, or born of very young people, or widows who have not yet been born at the time of their husband-to-be's adulthood. All of this shows that when the RAP says "must vest" it means *must* vest. So, let your imagination run wild, but keep it grounded in remote possibilities, not in science fiction.

Consider additional examples of future interests that violate the RAP:

Examples 109 and 110

T wills Blackacre to A and B and their heirs upon the distribution of his estate.

T wills Blackacre to A and B and their heirs upon the end of the war.

How can T get Blackacre to A and B? Consider two valid grants that guarantee that the future interests will vest, if they ever do, within the lives of the grantees:

Examples 111 and 112

T wills Blackacre to A and B and their heirs upon the probate of T's will, if either is then living.

T wills Blackacre to A and B for their joint lives and for the life of the survivor, upon the probate of T's will.

Now consider this grant:

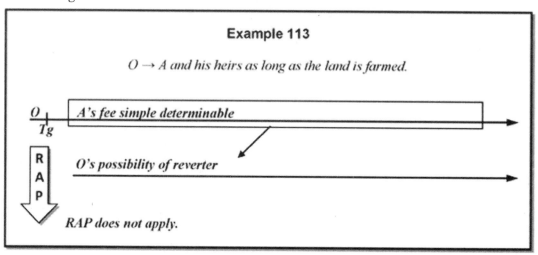

Example 113

O → A and his heirs as long as the land is farmed.

A's fee simple determinable

O's possibility of reverter

R A P

RAP does not apply.

"Wait a minute," you say. "Why doesn't the RAP void O's possibility of reverter? The possibility of revereter won't become possessory until the land is not farmed, which is not certain to be soon enough for the RAP." That is observant, clever, and logical, but irrelevant. The RAP doesn't apply to possibilities of reverter. Note that, while earlier diagrams said "RAP does not void the future interest," here we've said "RAP does not apply." This distinction is pretty fine and mostly historical but important. Recall that the possibility of reverter was in place as a recognized legal future interest well before the Statute of Uses, the *Duke of Norfolk's Case*, or the RAP. The possibility of reverter, like the right of entry, the reversion, and the vested remainder, was deemed "vested" for purposes of the RAP from the moment of its creation.

Now consider:

Example 114

O → A and his heirs as long as the land is farmed, then to B and his heirs.

Similar examples were considered in chapter four, and you may recall that there is a debate about what to call the present estate. We decided to call it A's fee simple on executory limitation, followed by B's executory interest. Some others would call it A's fee simple determinable, followed by B's executory interest.

Regardless of what we or others name it to start with, we all end up in agreement. Why? Because, after applying the RAP, we all agree that B's executory interest violates the RAP. Why is that? Because B's interest might fail to vest in time — within the lives in being of O, if O conveyed by deed, and A and B, plus 21 years. Once you strike B's executory interest for violating the RAP, A is left with a fee simple determinable, and O has a possibility of reverter.

To be a bit more specific, we reach this by voiding B's future interest — by crossing out words until we are at a point where the grant makes sense, back to the word "farmed." What is left is clearly a fee simple determinable, followed, as always, by a possibility of reverter.

So, are you with us? Recall that we renamed A's interest after 1536 in fee simple on executory limitation so that you could stick with the rule that a possibility of reverter *always* follows a fee simple determinable. Remember, when you apply the RAP, you have to remember to cross out words only back to the point where the grant makes sense.

Now consider:

Example 115

O → A and his heirs, but if the land is not farmed, then to B and his heirs.

B's executory interest violates the RAP. But here, we cross out words back to "heirs." You can't stop crossing out at "farmed." If you stop there, what's left makes no sense. So, A has a fee simple and O has nothing.

Note the difference with this example:

Example 116

O → A and his heirs as long as the land is farmed, then to B and his heirs.

B's executory interest violates the RAP. Here, we need only cross out words back to "farmed." Thus, A has a fee simple determinable, and O has a possibility of reverter.

The Duke of Norfolk's Case resulted in a curb on executory interests. The permutations of the Rule Against Perpetuities were not detailed in this case but rather worked out in subsequent cases over the next two hundred years. *See generally* J. Dukeminier & S. Johanson, *Family Wealth Transactions: Wills, Trusts and Estates* 970-77 (2d ed. 1978). For example, the traditional formula that describes the period of time allowed by the RAP was not settled until 1833. *Id.* at 976 (citing *Cadell v. Palmer*, 1 Cl. & Fin. 372, 6 Eng. Rep. 956 (H.L. 1832, 1833)). Further, the application of the RAP to class gifts was not stated clearly until 1817. *Id.* at 1006 (citing *Leake v. Robinson*, 2 Mer. 363, 35 Eng. Rep. 979 (Ch. 1817)). The classic formulation of the RAP is found in a treatise written by an American in 1886, John Chipman Gray, *Rule Against Perpetuities* 970 (1st ed. 1886). But to simplify RAP, we round off these dates to about 1700 — a bit early, but close enough for our purposes.

The Rule Against Perpetuities was an important and far-reaching reaction to the Statute of Uses, but not the only one.

The Statute of Wills was passed in 1540 in response to complaints by landowners that the Statute of Uses had eliminated indirect mechanisms for devising land. *See* T. Plucknett, *A Concise History of the Common Law* 587 (5th ed. 1956). Prior to 1536, landowners had devised land by making special conveyances to uses. The Statute of Wills permitted owners of present estates in land to devise them at common law. An amendment to the Statute of Wills in 1543 permitted those who held certain future interests to devise them. *See* John A. Borron, Jr., *Simes & Smith, The Law of Future Interests* § 1901 (3d ed. 2011).

Finally, despite the Statute of Uses, by 1700 real property lawyers had developed a permanent place for equitable property interests. Certain conveyances were recognized as primarily within the jurisdiction of the court of equity. From such exceptional conveyances "to use" evolved the modern trust. The system of estates in land and future interests in 1700 continues to include equitable as well as legal interests. *See* A. James Casner et. al, *Cases and Text on Property* 316-318 (5th ed. 2004).

For purposes of a basic introduction to the RAP, an understanding of its application to executory interests should suffice. Consider the review chart that follows, and then try the problems that follow the chart. Some of these problems illustrate the application of RAP to more future interests than executory interests, but the RAP most profoundly affected the executory interest.

D. REVIEW TABLE FOR THE RAP

Present Possessory Estates

>> All present possessory interests are *vested* and thus neither subject to nor voided by the RAP.

> › However, a possessory interest may be ***affected*** by the RAP. For instance, if an executory interest is voided by the RAP, the preceding estate might change, e.g., a fee simple on executory limitation might become a fee simple absolute.

Future Interests in the Grantor

>> All future interests in the grantor — the reversion, the possibility of reverter, and the right of entry — are *vested* and thus neither subject to nor voided by the RAP.

Future Interests in Grantees and Devisees

>> A springing executory interest is subject to and voided by the RAP if it is not certain to become possessory within the RAP period.

>> A shifting executory interest and contingent remainder are subject to and voided by the RAP if they are not certain to become a vested remainder or possessory within the RAP period.

>> As a class gift, a vested remainder subject to open is subject to the RAP. A vested remainder subject to open ***vests for RAP purposes*** when the class closes and when any conditions precedent are met for each and every class member. The class must be certain to close and any conditions precedent must be certain to be met or to fail within the RAP period or the ***entire*** class gift is void.

> › Remember that a class closes either (1) when there can be no more members added to the class or (2) by application of the "rule of convenience," discussed in chapter four, Section B, which closes a class when a member of that class is entitled to demand distribution of his or her share.

>> A vested remainder, other than a vested remainder subject to open, is not subject to nor voided by the RAP.

> › However, a vested remainder subject to divestment may be ***affected by*** the RAP. For instance, if an executory interest is voided by the RAP, a preceding estate might change, e.g., a vested remainder subject to divestment may become a vested remainder in fee simple absolute.

E. OUR ANALYTICAL APPROACH (FURTHER MODIFIED)

We now modify our analytical approach by adding some additional matters covered in this chapter, which we **bold** so you may easily identify the additions.

First Determinations:

1. What did O have before making the grant?

    Assume O begins with a fee simple absolute unless otherwise stated.

2. What does A have?

    Fee simple absolute?

    Fee tail?

    Life estate?

    Fee simple determinable?

    Fee simple on condition subsequent?

3. If there are no further grants, what has O retained, if anything?

    Nothing if A has a fee simple absolute.

    Reversion if A has a life estate or a fee tail.

    Possibility of reverter if A has a fee simple determinable.

    Right of entry if A has a fee simple on condition subsequent.

Second Determinations:

If there are further grants, then ask, as to each one:

4. Is the interest a remainder?

    a.   [Rule 1] Does the interest follow an expirable estate?

        i.   If no, then the interest is not a remainder. Proceed to Third Determinations, below.

        ii. If yes, then the interest may be a remainder. Proceed to b, immediately below.

    b.   [Rule 2] Will the interest take effect immediately upon the expiration of the preceding estate?

        i.   If no, then the interest is not a remainder. Proceed to Third Determinations, below.

        ii. If yes, then the interest may be a remainder. Proceed to c, immediately below.

    c.   [Rule 3] Can the interest take effect before the expiration of the preceding estate?

        i.   If yes, then the interest is not a remainder. Proceed to Third Determinations, below.

        ii. If no, then the interest is a remainder. Proceed to 5, immediately below.

5. Since the interest is a remainder, what will the remainder be when it becomes possessory?

    Fee simple absolute?

    Fee tail?

    Life estate?

    Fee simple determinable?

Fee simple on condition subsequent?

6.   Is the remainder vested or contingent?

    a.   Is the holder of the remainder born and ascertainable?

        i.   If yes, then the remainder may be vested.

        ii.   If no, then the remainder is contingent, unless some extraneous facts show that the remainder has become vested.

        iii.   In either case, proceed to b. immediately below.

    b.   Is there a condition precedent to possession other than the expiration of the preceding interest?

        i.   If no (and if the holder of the remainder is born and ascertainable — answered under 6.a, above), then the remainder is vested.

        ii.   If yes (or if the holder of the remainder is unborn or unascertainable — answered under 6.a, above), then the remainder is contingent.

    c.   Note: If a contingent remainder in one party (*e.g.*, B) is immediately followed by another remainder in another party (*e.g.*, C) that can become possessory only in exactly those circumstances in which the first party's (B's) remainder cannot, then both parties (B and C) have alternative contingent remainders.

7.   If the remainder is vested, is the remainder a "class gift"?

    a.   If no, then the remainder is a vested remainder.

    b.   If yes, then the remainder is a vested remainder subject to open unless the class has closed by facts extraneous to the grant. Is the class closed?

        i.   If yes, then the class has closed and the remainder is a vested remainder.

        ii.   If no, then the remainder is a vested remainder subject to open unless extraneous facts have made the remainder a present possessory interest.

        iii.   **Does the vested remainder subject to open violate the RAP? See Fourth Determinations, below.**

8.   If the remainder is contingent, has it been destroyed?

    a.   Has the contingent remainder been destroyed because the remainder failed to vest in time — at or before the expiration of the preceding estate that supported the remainder?

        i.   If yes, then the remainder should be deleted from the grant and the state of the title should then be determined from what is left of the grant.

        ii.   If no, then proceed immediately to b., below.

    b.   Has the contingent remainder been destroyed by merger — by merging the preceding estate that supported the remainder with the next vested interest — **arising from more than the original grant?**

        i.   If yes, then the remainder should be deleted from the grant and the state of the title should then be determined from what is left of the grant.

        ii.   If no, then proceed immediately to c., below.

    c.   Has the contingent remainder been destroyed by termination (forfeiture or renunciation) of the preceding estate before its expiration?

    i.   If yes, then the remainder should be deleted from the grant and the state of the title should then be determined from what is left of the grant.

    ii. If no, then proceed to 9., below.

9. If the remainder is contingent, does O retain a reversion?

    Yes, unless O has otherwise accounted for the full fee simple absolute.

10. **Is the contingent remainder void under RAP? See Fourth Determinations, below.**

Third Determinations:

11. Since the interest is not a remainder, consider the new interests that are possible after the Statute of Uses (1536).

    a. Reclassify the interest that was invalid prior to 1536 as an "executory interest" in fee or as one of the five possessory estates, as appropriate.

        i.   If this interest can become possessory immediately following the interest of a prior grantee, then the interest is a "shifting executory interest."

        ii. If this interest can become possessory immediately from the grantor, then the interest is a "springing executory interest."

    b. Next classify the present or future interest that immediately precedes the executory interest:

        i.   If the immediately preceding interest is only implicit, due to a gap in possession between the expiration of the preceding estate and the executory interest, then the grantor retains a "reversion" and the executory interest is then a "springing" one.

    c. When the reversion becomes possessory, it will be a present estate "on executory limitation" — most likely a "fee simple on executory limitation."

        i.   If the immediately preceding future interest will become possessory, but might thereafter be lost due to a condition subsequent expressed in the grant, then the immediately preceding interest is "on executory limitation."

        ii. If the executory interest does not fall under i, immediately above, then the interest is "subject to divestment."

        iii. Caution: In making this analysis, be sure that the two future interests are not alternative contingent remainders. Remember the distinction between conditions precedent and conditions subsequent.

12. **Is the executory interest void under RAP? See Fourth Determinations, below.**

Fourth Determinations (RAP)

Note: You should have already classified the interests without regard to the RAP.

13. **Identify the interests that are subject to the RAP: executory interests, contingent remainders, and vested remainders subject to open.**

14. **As to each interest that is subject to the RAP, will the interest vest soon enough, if the interest ever does vest, within the lives in being plus 21 years?**

    <u>Basic vesting inquiry:</u>

    If the interest is certain to vest in time, then the interest is valid (*i.e.* does not violate RAP). If there is any possibility that the interest may not vest in time, then the interest violates RAP. Note: the fact that an interest may never vest is irrelevant for purposes of RAP. The key is that,

if the interest ever does vest, the interest must vest in time.

The other keys to RAP are "Measuring Lives" and "Vesting Rules."

<u>Measuring lives:</u>

Measuring lives are the relevant lives in being at the time of the grant, that is, the lives to consider for purposes of applying the "lives in being plus 21-year" RAP period. Consider extraneous facts, such as whether a particular person is alive at the time of the grant, *e.g.*, a testator is not alive at the time of the grant because a will takes effect on the testator's death. Sometimes, measuring lives are implied from the language of the grant.

<u>RAP Vesting Rules:</u>

Contingent remainders vest when they become either vested remainders or present estates.

Executory interests vest when they become present estates, and in the case of shifting executory interests, also when they become vested remainders.

Vested remainders subject to open vest for RAP purposes when no more members of the class can be added, *i.e.*, when the class closes. If the class might not close within the RAP period, the entire class gift is void.

15. If the interest is void, then strike the offending interest by using the "cross-out rule." Strike the words of the offending interest back to where the remaining words, if any, can stand alone and still make sense.

16. Then reclassify the interests by reconsidering the first three Determinations, above.

F. REVIEW PROBLEMS (CIRCA 1700)

Please give the state of the title for each of the following problems:

1. *O →* *A and his heirs as long as the land is farmed, and then to B and his heirs.*

   Assume O, A, and B are living.

   A has _____

   B has _____

   O has _____

2. *O →* *B for life, then to B's eldest son for life, then to C and his heirs as long as the land is farmed, then to X and his heirs.*

   Assume O, B, C, and X are living and B has no sons.

   B has _____

   B's eldest son has _____

   C has _____

   X has _____

   O has _____

3. *O →* *B for life, then to B's eldest son for life, then to C and his heirs, but if liquor is ever sold on the premises during B's or C's lifetime, then to X and his heirs.*

   Assume O, B, C, and X are living, and that B has no sons.

   B has _____

   B's eldest son has a _____

   C has _____

   X has _____

   O has _____

4. *O →* *B for life, then to the Church, but if and when a male descendant of B changes his name to "O," then to such descendant and his heirs.*

   Assume O and B are living. All of B's living descendants are named "B." B has three living sons.

B has _____

The Church has _____

The male descendant of B who changes his name to O has _____

O has _____

5. $O \rightarrow$ *B for life, then to the Church, but if and when B or one of his now-living sons changes his name to "O," then to such person and his heirs.*

Assume O, B, and three living sons of B, none named O, are living.

B has _____

The Church has _____

B or one of his now-living sons has _____

O has _____

6.   Compare the following three problems:

$O \rightarrow$ *A and his heirs 25 years after all the people now living the world are dead.*

$O \rightarrow$ *A and his heirs 20 years after all the people now living in the world are dead.*

$O \rightarrow$ *A and his heirs 20 years after all the living descendants of Elizabeth II are dead.*

7. $O \rightarrow$ *A and his heirs of his body, then to the grandchildren of C and their heirs.*

a. Assume C has a living child, X.

b. Assume that C has a living child, X, and that X has a living child, X'.

A has _____

Grandchildren of C have _____

O has _____

8. $O \rightarrow$ *A and his heirs upon the passage of 25 years.*

A has _____

O has _____

9. $O \rightarrow$ *A and his heirs as long as the land is farmed, then to the children of B for life.*

Assume B has a child C.

A has _____

B's children have _____

O has _____

10. *O →*   *A for life, then to A's children for their lives, then to the next manager of the Chicago Cubs to win the World Series and that person's heirs.*

Assume A is an 80-year old widow and has living children X and Y. The Cubs are still "waiting 'til next year."

A has _____

A's chidren have _____

Manager has _____

O has _____

11. *O →*   (devises) *A for life, then to such of A's grandchildren living at O's death and any born within 5 years therefrom who are or thereafter attain age 21 and their heirs.*

Assume O dies when A is alive and when A has two children, X and Y, and a grandchild, X'.

A has _____

A's eligible grandchildren have _____

O has _____

12. *O →*   *A for life, then to A's widow for her life, then to the person serving as manager of the Chicago Cubs and that person's heirs.*

Assume O and A are living. A is unmarried.

A has _____

A's widow has _____

Manager has _____

O has _____

13. *O →*   *A and his heirs upon completion of the new law school.*

Assume the law school is under construction but not yet completed.

A has _____

O has _____

Answers to Review Problems (Circa 1700)

Please give the state of the title for each of the following problems:

1. $O \rightarrow$ *A and his heirs as long as the land is farmed, and then to B and his heirs.*
    Assume O, A, and B are living.

    Step One: ***Classify the interests without regard to the RAP.***
    A has a fee simple on executory limitation.
    B has a shifting executory interest in fee.
    O has nothing.

    Step Two: ***Identify the interests that are subject to the RAP.***
    B's executory interest.

    Step Three: ***Apply the RAP.***
    Because B's executory interest might not vest in time, it is void.

    Step Four: ***Apply the "cross-out rule," if applicable.***
    Use the "cross-out rule": starting backwards from the end, cross out until the grant makes sense; *i.e.*, back to the word "farmed."

    Step Five: ***What is the result?***
    A has a fee simple determinable.
    B has nothing.
    O has a possibility of reverter.

2. $O \rightarrow$ *B for life, then to B's eldest son for life, then to C and his heirs as long as the land is farmed, then to X and his heirs.*
    Assume O, B, C, and X are living and B has no sons.

    Step One: ***Classify the interests without regard to the RAP.***
    B has a life estate.
    B's eldest son has a contingent remainder in a life estate.
    C has a vested remainder in fee simple on executory limitation.
    X has a shifting executory interest in fee.
    O has nothing.

    Step Two: ***Identify the interests that are subject to the RAP.***
    B's oldest son's contingent remainder.
    X's executory interest.

    Step Three: ***Apply the RAP.***
    X's interest is void under the RAP. The contingent remainder is valid because it will vest or be voided at B's death.

    Step Four: ***Apply the "cross-out rule," if applicable.***
    Use the "cross-out rule": starting from the end, cross out until the grant makes sense; *i.e.*, back to the word "farmed."

    Step Five: ***What is the result?***
    B has a life estate.
    B's eldest son has a contingent remainder in a life estate.
    C has a vested remainder in fee simple determinable.
    X has nothing.
    O has a possibility of reverter.

3. $O \rightarrow$ *B for life, then to B's eldest son for life, then to C and his heirs, but if liquor is ever sold on the premises during B's or C's lifetime, then to X and his heirs.*
    Assume O, B, C, and X are living, and that B has no sons.

    Step One: ***Classify the interests without regard to the RAP.***
    B has a life estate.

B's eldest son has a contingent remainder for life.

C has a vested remainder subject to divestment in fee simple.

X has an executory interest in fee.

O has nothing.

Step Two: ***Identify the interests that are subject to the RAP.***

B's eldest son's contingent remainder.

Step Three: ***Apply the RAP.***

B's eldest son's contingent remainder is valid because if will vest, if ever, at B's death.

X's interest is valid because it will become possessory, if at all, within the lifetime of B and C.

Step Four: ***Apply the "cross-out rule," if applicable.***

Not applicable.

Step Five: ***What is the result?***

Unchanged.

You might want to call C's interest a vested remainder in fee simple on executory limitation in fee. This may be acceptable to your professor because the divesting condition can be broken either during B's lifetime, when the remainder is still a remainder, or in C's lifetime, after the remainder has become possessory. You might even want to call C's interest a vested remainder subject to divestment in fee simple on executory limitation. That's okay, too, though no court that we know of would require that much verbage.

---

4.   O → *B for life, then to the Church, but if and when a male descendant of B changes his name to "O," then to such descendant and his heirs.*

Assume O and B are living. All of B's living descendants are named "B." B has three living sons.

Step One: ***Classify the interests without regard to the RAP.***

B has a life estate.

The Church has a vested remainder subject to divestment in fee.

The first male descendant to change his name to O has a shifting executory interest in fee.

O has nothing.

Step Two: ***Identify the interests that are subject to the RAP.***

B's descendant's executory interest.

Step Three: ***Apply the RAP.***

The RAP voids the executory interest because there is no limit on how distant a descendant might be. A descendant of B could change his name to O, making the executory interest possessory (vested) more than 21 years after O, B and all three of B's sons are dead.

Step Four: ***Apply the "cross-out" rule, if applicable.***

Cross out back to "Church."

Step Five   ***What is the result?***

B has life estate.

The Church has a vested remainder in fee. Note that the Church's remainder subject to divestment is not subject to the RAP but the RAP affects it by changing it into a vested remainder in fee simple absolute.

Male descendant of B who changes his name to O has nothing.

O has nothing.

5. $O \rightarrow$ *B for life, then to the Church, but if and when B or one of his now-living sons changes his name to "O," then to such person and his heirs.*

Assume O, B, and three living sons of B, none named O, are living.

Because this is so similar to the prior problem, we will take a short cut, but you may still wish to take a step-by-step approach.

Here, the executory interest in the son who changes his name to O is valid because it will become possessory, if at all, in the lifetime of B and his three living sons, all of whom are lives in being at *Tg*. Therefore, the state of the title is:

B has a life estate.

The Church has a vested remainder subject to divestment in fee.

The first of B's now living sons to change his name to O has an executory interest.

O has nothing.

6.   Compare the following three problems:

$O \rightarrow$ *A and his heirs 25 years after all the people now living the world are dead.*

$O \rightarrow$ *A and his heirs 20 years after all the people now living in the world are dead.*

$O \rightarrow$ *A and his heirs 20 years after all the living descendants of Elizabeth II are dead.*

Regarding the first example, you may astutely note that A's springing executory interest is void because lives in being, plus 25 years, is too long. Thus, O retains a fee simple absolute, not fee simple on executory limitation.

Regarding the second example, RAP is not violated as lives in being plus 20 years is soon enough. However, the interest is void for indefiniteness, because there is no way to determine when the 20–year period will actually lapse. Thus, O has a fee simple absolute.

Regarding the third example, RAP is not violated and the interest is not void for indefiniteness because the descendants of Elizabeth II are easily determined and their dates of death will be a matter of public record. Indeed, the births and deaths of royal descendants are carefully recorded in England. So A has a springing executory interest. O has a fee simple on executory limitation.

7. $O \rightarrow$ *A and his heirs of his body, then to the grandchildren of C and their heirs.*

a.   Assume C has a living child, X.

b.   Assume that C has a living child, X, and that X has a living child, X'.

Step One: ***Classify the interests without regard to the RAP.***

a.   A has a fee tail.

C's grandchildren have a contingent remainder in fee.

O has a reversion.

b.   The same, except that X' has a vested remainder subject to open.

Step Two: ***Identify the interests that are subject to the RAP.***

a.   C's grandchildren's contingent remainder

b.   X' has a vested remainder subject to open

Step Three: ***Apply the RAP.***

a.   The RAP vesting rule for a contingent remainder is when it becomes a vested remainder.

The measuring lives are O, A, C and (implicitly) X, the living child of C.

We are asked to assume that C has a child X. Now we will apply RAP by considering possibilities.

Suppose that two years after the grant, C has a child Y, and A has child A'. Neither Y nor A' would be measuring lives because they were not born at the time of the grant. Then suppose that all the measuring lives (O, A, C, and X) die and the fee tail passes to A'. Thereafter, Y could have a child Y' (a grandchild of C) who would then share in what is now a vested remainder subject to open (now there is a member of the class, so the remainder is no longer contingent). And this class will not close until Y (who is now the only living child of C) dies. Y could live more than 21 years after the last measuring life died and the fee tail may still be possessory in A's lineal descendants. Because of this remote possibility, C's grandchildren's interest is void under RAP because it might fail to vest indefeasibly in time (the class may fail to close in time).

b. The analysis is the same, except that we begin with X' having a vested remainder subject to open. Because the exact same possibility could unfold, adding the untimely death of X', the vested remainder subject to open is void.

Step Four: ***Apply the cross-out rule, if applicable.***

Delete the contingent remainder.

Step Five ***What is the result?***

a.

A has a fee tail.

O has reversion.

When A's fee tail expires, O will have a fee simple absolute.

b.

A has fee tail.

O has a reversion.

When A's fee tail expires, O will have a fee simple absolute.

Compare: *O → A and the heirs of his body, then to the children of C and their heirs.*

A has a fee tail.

C's children have contingent remainders in fee.

O has a reversion.

Here C (a measuring life) could have children living at the time of the grant (*e.g.,* X) and more could be born thereafter (*e.g.,* Y). In this circumstance, Y would share the vested remainder subject to open with X. But the class will close when C dies, at which time any living children of C would have a vested remainder in fee (not a vested remainder subject to open in fee). Vested remainders are not subject to RAP.

Compare: *O → A for life, then to the <u>grandchildren</u> of C and their heirs.*

No RAP problem. Do you understand why?

C's grandchildren, if any, will take immediately upon A's death (A being a measuring life).

8. *O →   A and his heirs upon the passage of 25 years.*

O retains a fee simple on executory limitation.

A has an executory interest.

Applying RAP, A's executory interest is void. O and A could immediately die after the grant, and the executory interest would not become possessory within the measuring lives plus 21 years.

Thus, O has a fee simple absolute.

> Unfortunately, this question is tricky. Some courts *might* construe the passage of 25 years as a certainty, and *may* therefore hold that A's interest is immediately "vested" for purposes of RAP. Thus, in some states, this problem *may* be an exception to the rule that executory interests vest at possession.

9. $O \rightarrow$ *A and his heirs as long as the land is farmed, then to the children of B for life.*
                     Assume B has a child C.

Step One: ***Classify the interests without regard to the RAP.***

A has a fee simple on executory limitation.

The children of B have a shifting executory interest for life.

O has a reversion (the larger of O's possible interests).

Step Two: ***Identify the interests that are subject to the RAP.***

You must apply RAP to B's children's executory interest.

Step Three: ***Apply the RAP.***

The measuring lives are O, A, B and C.

B could have a child D, who could outlive all measuring lives by more than 21 years and, in the meantime, the land could continue to be farmed. Thus, the executory interest violates RAP.

Step Four: ***Apply the "cross-out" rule, if applicable.***

Cross out the interest back to "farmed."

Step Five   ***What is the result?***

A has a fee simple determinable.

O has a possibility of reverter.

Note that there is no such thing as an executory interest subject to open, and that all executory interests "vest" for RAP purposes at possession or in the case of shifting executory interests, also when they become vested remainders. On the other hand, vested remainders subject to open "vest" for purposes of the rule when the class closes (*i.e.*, when there can never be any more members of the class).

10. $O \rightarrow$ *A for life, then to A's children for their lives, then to the next manager of the Chicago Cubs to win the World Series and that person's heirs.*
                     Assume A is an 80-year old widow and has living children X and Y. The Cubs are still "waiting 'til next year."

Step One: ***Classify the interests without regard to the RAP.***

A has a life estate.

A's children, X and Y, have vested remainders subject to open.

Coach has a contingent remainder in fee.

O has a reversion.

Step Two: ***Identify the interests that are subject to the RAP.***

The vested remainder subject to open and the contingent remainder.

Step Three: ***Apply the RAP.***

The vested remainder subject to open is valid because the class will close instantaneously at A's death. At A's death, the remainder to A's children will then become a vested present estate or the remainder might not ever become possessory because A may die without any children living. But neither possibility violates RAP. The key is that there is no possibility of "remote vesting" beyond the period allowed by the RAP.

The contingent remainder violates the RAP. Ignoring the biological clock, as common law courts would do, A might have a child Z after the grant. Z may outlive all measuring lives (O, A, X and Y) by more than 21 years. The contingent remainder may not vest in time because the next manager of the Cubs to win the World Series could be far into the future — long after the deaths of O, A, X, and Y plus 21 years. Thus, the contingent remainder in the coach is void.

Step Four: ***Apply the "cross-out" rule, if applicable.***,

Cross out back to the word "lives."

Step Five ***What is the result?***

A has a life estate.

A's children, X and Y, have a vested remainder subject to open for life.

O has a reversion.

This problem, often called "The Fertile Octogenarian," is based on a real case.

11.   *O* →   (devises) *A for life, then to such of A's grandchildren living at O's death and any born within 5 years therefrom who are or thereafter attain age 21 and their heirs.*

Assume O dies at a time when A is alive and when A has 2 children, X and Y, and a grandchild X'.

Step One: ***Classify the interests without regard to the RAP.***

A has a life estate.

X' (and any other grandchildren that are born within 5 years of O's death) must reach age 21 (we assume X' has not reached age 21 because that fact is not given) and A is alive. Thus, X' and any other grandchildren born within 5 years of O's death have a contingent remainder in fee. You might possibly argue that they have a springing executory interest in fee, depending on how you interpret the devise.

O's estate has a reversion or possibly a reversion in fee simple on executory limitation.

Note: Within limits, reasonable minds may differ about A's grandchildren's interests. For example, you might argue that X' has a vested remainder subject to open if X is already age 21 at O's death or when X' reaches age 21 during A's life.

As you will learn, your initial answer does not really matter provided it is one of these interests.

Step Two: ***Identify the interests that are subject to the RAP.***

Regardless of how you classify the future interest in A's grandchildren, you must consider RAP, as RAP applies to contingent remainders, executory interests, and vested remainders subject to open.

Step Three: ***Apply the RAP.***

Is there a remote possibility that the grandchildren's future interest in fee will fail to vest in time? Yes.

A may conceive or bear a child Z. Then, A, X, Y (as A's children, X and Y are implied measuring lives because they were alive at the time of the grant) and X', might all die. Thereafter, Z might conceive or bear a grandchild of A, Z', within 5 years of A's death. Yes, once again, we are ignoring the biological clock.

Note that O's devise is to *A's* grandchildren. These events would leave Z' as the only grandchild of A. If Z' attains age 21, Z' will fail to do so within the measuring lives plus 21 years. Thus, the future interest in the grandchildren is void.

Step Four: ***Apply the "cross-out" rule, if applicable.***

Although you could selectively cross out words to give the grandchildren a contingent remainder in fee, you probably need to cross out the whole interest in A's grandchildren.

Step Five ***What is the result?***

If you cross out the whole future interest, A has a life estate.

O's estate has a reversion.

This problem, often called "The Precocious Toddler," is based on a real case.

12. $O \rightarrow$ *A for life, then to A's widow for her life, then to the person serving as manager of the Chicago Cubs and that person's heirs.*

Assume O and A are living and A is unmarried.

Step One: ***Classify the interests without regard to the RAP.***

A has a life estate.

A's widow has a contingent remainder for life.

The manager has a contingent remainder in fee.

Step Two: ***Identify the interests that are subject to the RAP.***

The contingent remainder in A's widow.

The contingent remainder in the manager of the Cubs.

Step Three: ***Apply the RAP.***

The widow's contingent remainder for life presents no RAP problem. If she exists at A's death, she will take immediately.

But the manager's contingent remainder violates RAP. The remote vesting possibility is that A may marry a person, presently unborn, who survives O and A (the only reliable measuring lives) by more than 21 years. Thus, the contingent remainder in the manager is void.

Note that it would not matter if A were married at the time of the grant, because A's wife, at that time, might not ever be his widow.

Step Four: ***Apply the "cross-out" rule, if applicable.***

Delete the manager's interest.

Step Five   ***What is the result?***

A has a life estate.

A's widow has a contingent remainder for life.

O has a reversion.

This problem, often called "The Unborn Widow," is based on a real case.

13. $O \rightarrow$ *A and his heirs upon completion of the new law school.*

Assume the law school is under construction but not yet completed.

Step One: ***Classify the interests without regard to the RAP.***

A has a springing executory interest.

O has a fee simple on executory limitation.

Step Two: ***Identify the interests that are subject to the RAP.***

A's executory interest.

Step Three: ***Apply the RAP.***

The executory interest is void because there is no guarantee that the law school will be completed within 21 years after the deaths of O and A.

Step Four: ***Apply the "cross-out" rule, if applicable.***

Cross out the entire grant.

Step Five   ***What is the result?***

O has a fee simple absolute.

This problem, often called "The Tortoise Construction Company," is based on real cases.

Chapter 6

A FEW INTERESTING COMPLEXITIES

You have now learned the basic common law of estates and future interests. In this chapter, we present some miscellaneous complexities. The system of estates in land and future interests that you have learned so far was supplemented at common law by conceptual accidents and common law pragmatism; in addition, some policy choices reflected various rules of law or rules of construction. We have selected some of the more famous examples to discuss and illustrate.

Our selection of the complexities to be offered here is pretty idiosyncratic, and we have made decisions based more on what has caught our interest and what we think makes a good teaching point rather than on what has much relevance for your later practice or even for your present property course. We hope you find some of what follows interesting, rather than aggravating, but we doubt that your property teacher will cover all this material. Nevertheless, we have included the material that follows in the hope that some of it will enable you to practice what you have learned, as well as inspire you to learn more about estates and future interests.

A. THE LIFE ESTATE DETERMINABLE

You have learned a great deal about the various interests presented so far. For example, you have learned that a remainder can be vested or contingent, and that a vested remainder can be vested subject to open, vested subject to divestment, or vested on executory limitation. The common law may have been quite strict *within* the various categories, but it also was creative, at least, in the number of categories that were allowed.

You will encounter this creativity again as we consider the life estate determinable. Study the following, a chart that you may have begun to formulate in your own mind.

Opportunities for the Grantor to Place Conditions on the Grantee's Possession

	Without Express Condition	*Determinable*	*On Condition Subsequent*	*On Executory Limitation*
Fee Simple	√	√	√	√
Fee Tail	√			
Life Estate	√	*	This may not have been permitted at common law	This is permissible only if clearly expressed

We have previously discussed the checked squares. Let's now consider the life estate determinable — the square marked with an asterisk (*):

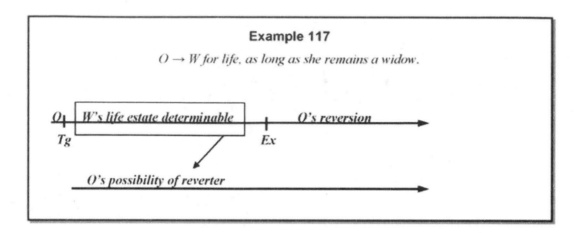

Example 117

O → W for life, as long as she remains a widow.

Here, in a life estate determinable, O appears to have retained two future interests: a reversion following W's life estate and a possibility of reverter if she remarries. The reversion is considered the "larger" or more certain estate and might be said to "gobble up" the possibility of reverter:

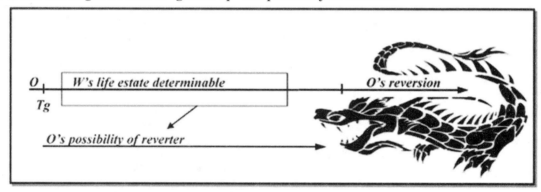

Hence, the term "reversion" refers to both parts of the grantor's retained future interest:

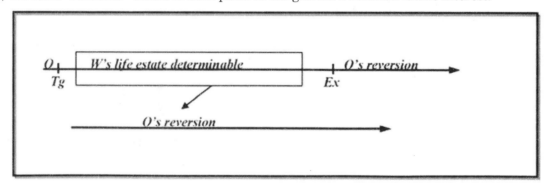

Hence, the "rule" is that when O creates a life estate determinable in A and keeps the future interest for himself, O retains a reversion. Why is this important? Consider that O may alienate a reversion inter vivos but not a possibility of reverter.

Well, then, what about:

Example 118

O → W for life, as long as she remains a widow, then to B and his heirs.

What does B have? In other words, what did O intend B to have? Did O intend that B take Blackacre on W's death regardless of whether W remarried, but did O want the property back if W remarried until her death, at which time it would pass to B? Or did O intend that B take the property only if W remarried, leaving O with a reversion if W died unmarried? Or, did O intend that B take immediately when W either died or remarried? Consider:

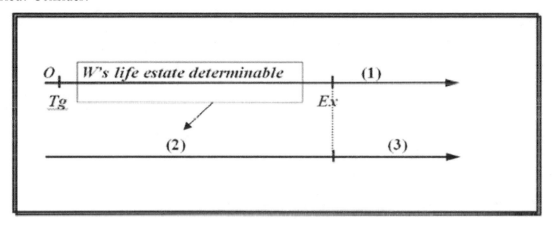

We have three possible chunks of future interest, and we are not sure how much O intended B to have. Remember, however, that the common law decided that when O created a life estate determinable and no future interest in a grantee, he kept a reversion for himself. What shall we presume when O creates a future interest in a grantee when he might have kept a reversion? Perhaps we should presume that O intended B to have all that O might have retained. This result can be reached by resorting to a rule of construction that construes the grant against O by presuming that O intended to part with the full fee simple absolute interest. Thus, we presume that O intended to retain no interest. We then recognize that B apparently gets two future interests: a remainder, which become possessory if W dies unmarried, and an executory interest, which becomes possessory if W remarries; however, just as in the previous example, the interest that was considered the "larger" one — B's remainder — gobbles up the smaller interest — B's executory interest.

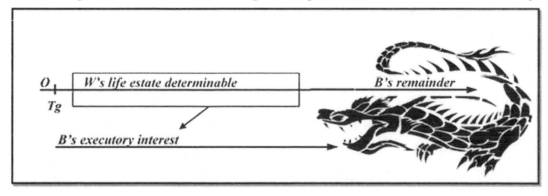

But this result seems a little anomalous in light of the fact that a remainder could **not** follow a **fee simple** determinable. Perhaps this is a conceptual accident. However, consider the practical consequences. A vested remainder is alienable inter vivos. An executory interest is not.

O may, of course, avoid this general rule and create an executory interest in B if he does so clearly. See the note on the chart at the beginning of this chapter under the "Life Estate on Executory Limitation" and the anticipatory note after Example 92 in chapter four. Consider:

Example 119

O → H for life, but if H should remarry, then to B and his heirs.

Here, O seems to have intended that B is to take only in the circumstance that H remarries. We would classify this grant as follows:

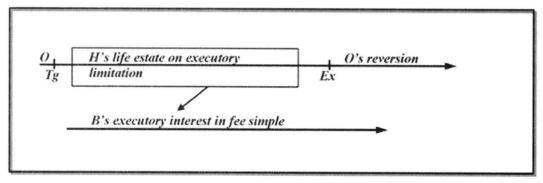

What do you make of the following grant?

Example 120

O → My widow for life, as long as she remains unmarried, then to my children and their heirs.

If this grant is in O's will, then there is no problem. At O's death, his widow is either identifiable or not. If she is, then she takes a life estate determinable and the children have a shared vested remainder in fee simple. If O is not survived by a widow, then that gift fails and the land goes immediately to the children in a shared fee simple absolute. We will further address shared present estates later in this chapter.

But suppose the grant is made while O is still alive. In that case, O's widow is an unknown person. His present wife **might** become his widow, but there is no guarantee of that; she must survive him while still married to be a "widow." Thus, O has retained the present estate, which would be a fee simple on executory limitation. The as-yet unidentifiable widow has a springing executory interest in a life estate determinable. We guess that a court would still call the children's interest a remainder, but now it would be a vested remainder subject to open, assuming that one child has already been born and that O is still alive. Compare this example to Review Problem 12 at the end of chapter five. Unlike that problem, the children's interest does not violate the Rule Against Perpetuities. Do you understand why? Hint: when O dies, the class of children closes because, subject to the gestation period discussed in chapter three after Example 73, he can have no more.

B. SOME COMPLEX CONVEYANCES

What is B's interest in the following example?

Example 121

O → A for life, then if B is still living, to B for life, then to C and his heirs.

Perhaps you would say B has a contingent remainder in a life estate because of the condition precedent. Look again. The phrase "if B is still living" is surplusage. Of course B has to be living at A's death for B to get possession for life. B's life estate cannot take effect if B is not alive at A's death. Therefore, you should ignore the surplus words and recognize that B has a vested remainder in a life estate. Although B may never take possession, because she may predecease A, the remainder is vested, because no meaningful condition precedent is stated. In this case, the common law exercised a thoughtful pragmatism.

Now compare this example to Example 121:

Example 122

O → A for life, then if B is still living, to B and his heirs.

Here the "if" clause is not surplusage. But for this survivorship condition, B would not have to survive A. Remember, remainders in fee simple are inheritable. Thus, the condition stays and B has a contingent remainder in fee simple. O has a reversion.

Consider:

Example 123

O → A for life and, after A's death, to B and his heirs.

How do you interpret the words "after A's death"? Are they surplusage, since we know that a remainder is to take effect on A's death? If so, then the surplusage would be ignored and B's remainder is vested. But are the words, "after A's death," meaningful? Do they imply that B must survive A to take the remainder? If so, then the remainder is contingent on A's predeceasing B. Having spotted and stated the issue, much of your work is done. The next step is to determine the state of the law in the relevant jurisdiction, because courts are split on the question. *See* John A. Borron, Jr., *Simes & Smith, The Law of Future Interests* § 585 & cases cited at n.2, 70 (3d ed. 2011).

What if the grant had been from O "to A for life, and, after A's funeral, to B and his heirs"? O keeps an interest here, but how much of an interest? Does B's interest violate the RAP? Think about remote possibilities, such as the possibility that the funeral may not occur within the lives in being, plus 21 years. You might call this the Tortoise Funeral Parlor problem!

Consider:

Example 124

O → A for life, then to the heirs of B and their heirs, but if at A's death B is still living, then to D and his heirs.

If you too quickly apply the rules you have learned, then you may have decided that D has an executory interest in fee simple. Look again. A has a life estate, of course. The next interest is a contingent remainder in the heirs of B, assuming that B is living at the time of the grant. Why contingent? Because B's heirs are unidentifiable and will be until B's death. Note, then, that the "but if" clause on D's interest is the condition opposite to the contingency of the first remainder. Therefore, D's and B's heirs have alternative contingent remainders. O has a reversion.

Consider:

Example 125

O → O for life, then to O's three children and their heirs if any of them are then living, but if any of O's children are then deceased, then the children of that deceased child shall receive the share of his or her parent, but if any of O's children are then dead without leaving any surviving children, then O's deceased child's share shall go to O's other children.

This grant is essentially the situation in *Spiegel's Estate v. United States*, 335 U.S. 701 (1949). If you analyze this example carefully, then you will notice that O has left himself a very limited reversion: he will take the property only if he outlives all of his children and grandchildren. The property transferred by O was worth about $1,000,000. Based on O's life expectancy, his reversion was worth less than $70. But the estate tax laws in effect at that time required that the entire $1,000,000 be included in O's estate on his death due to O's probably inadvertent retention of a reversion. The conveyance might have been construed otherwise if certain rules of construction were applied liberally. Read on to find out about some of the most famous construction rules at common law.

C. SOME RULES OF LAW AND SOME RULES OF CONSTRUCTION

Previously you read about *Pells v. Brown* and to *Purefoy v. Rogers*. *Pells* is a rule of law, stating an attribute of all executory interests: they are indestructible. The grantor's intent is not a relevant consideration when applying a rule of law.

Purefoy is considered a rule of construction. If the grantor had created an interest that was capable of taking effect as a remainder, then that interest is construed as a remainder. In other words, the rule was used as an aid to determine the grantor's intent, essentially presuming that grantors prefer or generally intend to create remainders. The consequence of *Purefoy v. Rogers* was that interests capable of being contingent remainders could fall victim to the destructibility doctrine. The issue of whether a particular interest was destructible or indestructible was resolved by a rule of law, which is applied independently of the grantor's intent.

The following provides an introduction to some of the most familiar rules of law and rules of construction that were received as part of the American common law.

1. The Rule in *Shelley's Case*

The origin of the Rule in *Shelley's Case*, 1 Co. Rep. 93b, 76 Eng. Rep. 206 (1581), actually predates the case. *See* 1-13 Richard R. Powell, *Powell on Real Property* § 13.04[3] (Michael Allan Wolf ed., LexisNexis 2011). The Rule in *Shelley's Case* is a rule of law and thus applies regardless of the grantor's intent. In its most classic form, the Rule provided: If an instrument creates a life estate in A and purports to create a remainder in the heirs of A, then the future interest becomes a remainder in fee simple in A.

Try to make some sense of the Rule in *Shelley's Case* as stated by Lord Coke: "[W]hen the ancestor by any gift or conveyance takes an estate of freehold and in the same gift or conveyance an estate is limited either mediately or immediately to his heirs in fee or in fee tail; that always in such cases 'the heirs' are words of limitation of the estate, and not words of purchase." I *Coke's Reports* 104a, 76 Eng. Rep. 234 (1581) (footnotes omitted).

Hint: All the present interests of which we have spoken are freeholds. Your introduction to non-freeholds will come when you study landlord-tenant law.

Consider the following:

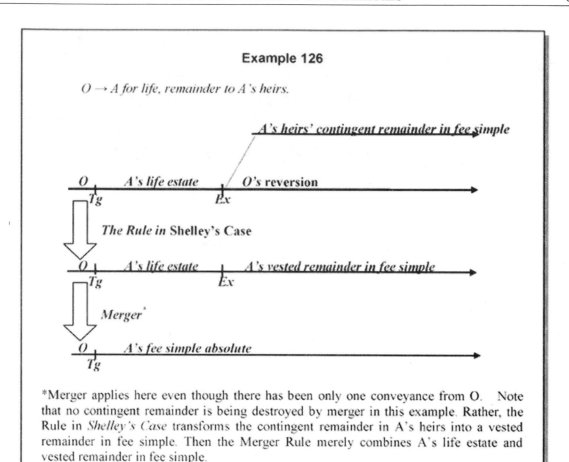

Example 126

$O \rightarrow A$ *for life, remainder to A's heirs.*

A's heirs' contingent remainder in fee simple

O A's life estate   O's reversion
Tg   Ex

The Rule in Shelley's Case

O A's life estate   A's vested remainder in fee simple
Tg   Ex

Merger*

O A's fee simple absolute
Tg

*Merger applies here even though there has been only one conveyance from O. Note that no contingent remainder is being destroyed by merger in this example. Rather, the Rule in *Shelley's Case* transforms the contingent remainder in A's heirs into a vested remainder in fee simple. Then the Merger Rule merely combines A's life estate and vested remainder in fee simple.

Why would this conveyance appeal to O? Why isn't it the same as $O \rightarrow A$ *and his heirs*? Remember that in $O \rightarrow A$ *and his heirs*, A may sell all of Blackacre, leaving his heirs-to-be with nothing. In $O \rightarrow A$ *for life, then to A's heirs*, as written, A may sell only his life estate. *See* Example 40 in chapter two. However, the Rule in *Shelley's Case* changes "then to A's heirs" into "A and his heirs," notwithstanding the fact that this does not appear to be what O intended.

Let's consider several additional examples:

Example 127

O → A for life, then to the heirs of A's body.

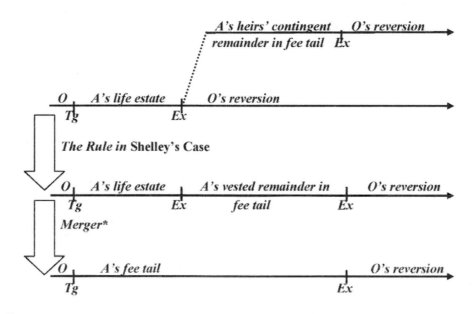

The Rule in **Shelley's Case**

*Merger**

* Merger applies here even though there has been only one conveyance from O. Note that no contingent remainder is being destroyed by merger in this example. Rather, the Rule in *Shelley's Case* transforms the contingent remainder in A's heirs into a vested remainder in fee tail. Then the Merger Rule merely combines A's life estate and vested remainder in fee tail.

Example 128

O → A for life, then to B for life, remainder to A's heirs.

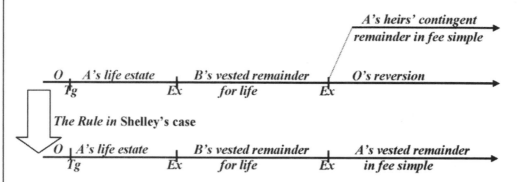

Merger does not occur because A does not own the next vested interest after her possessory life estate.

Example 129

O → A for life, and one day after A's death, to A's heirs.

The Rule in *Shelley's Case* does not apply because the Rule applies only to remainders, not to executory interests.

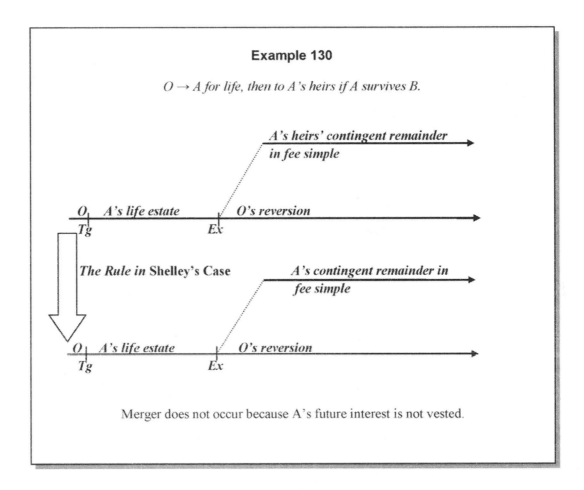

Example 130

O → A for life, then to A's heirs if A survives B.

A's heirs' contingent remainder in fee simple

O ┤ A's life estate   O's reversion
Tg   Ex

The Rule in Shelley's Case   *A's contingent remainder in fee simple*

O ┤ A's life estate   O's reversion
Tg   Ex

Merger does not occur because A's future interest is not vested.

2. The Doctrine of Worthier Title

The Doctrine of Worthier Title is similar to the Rule in *Shelley's Case.* The Doctrine is invoked by a grant of a remainder to the heirs of someone. The Rule in *Shelley's Case* is invoked upon the grant of a remainder to the heirs of the life tenant. The Doctrine of Worthier Title is invoked upon the grant of a remainder to the heirs of the grantor. The Doctrine of Worthier Title converts the future interest in the heirs of the grantor into a future interest in the grantor. For example, consider:

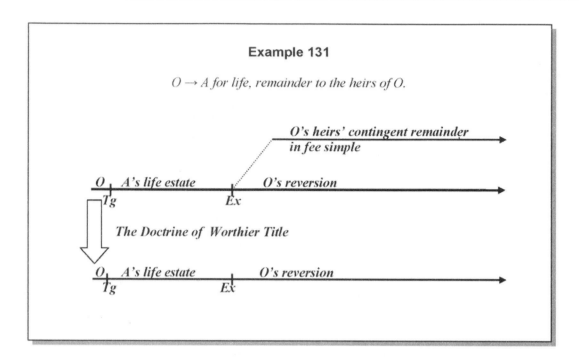

Example 131

O → A for life, remainder to the heirs of O.

The fact that the reversion existed in the grant before the Doctrine operates helps explain the name of the Doctrine. O's heirs would take either directly through the remainder or indirectly through the reversion. The latter was considered "worthier." However, note that, due to the Doctrine, O could change his mind while alive and convey his reversion to anyone, thereby preventing his heirs from getting the property. Unlike the Rule in *Shelley's Case*, the Doctrine of Worthier Title may have applied to executory interests as well as to remainders.

Initially, the Doctrine of Worthier Title was a rule of law, not a rule of construction; however, in the development of American common law, the Doctrine became a rule of construction. *See Doctor v. Hughes*, 225 N.Y. 305, 122 N.E. 221 (1919). As a rule of construction, sufficient evidence of the grantor's intent to the contrary would overcome the Doctrine. As a rule of law, evidence of the grantor's intent would be irrelevant.

3. The Rule in *Edwards v. Hammond*

The rule in *Edwards v. Hammond*, 3 Lev. 132, 83 Eng. Rep. 614 (1684), deals with grants in the form of alternative contingent remainders:

(a)   Where the condition precedent to the first remainder follows, grammatically, the words of purchase, and

(b)   where the only condition precedent to the first remainder is survival to a certain age.

Before describing how the Rule in *Edwards v. Hammond* applies to such a grant, let's consider the type of grant that invokes the Rule:

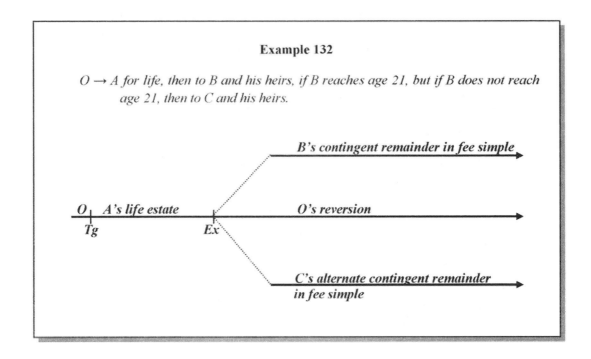

Example 132

*O → A for life, then to B and his heirs, if B reaches age 21, but if B does not reach
age 21, then to C and his heirs.*

The Rule in *Edwards v. Hammond* decrees that the condition precedent to the first remainder is
surplusage. Once you ignore the condition precedent, "if B reaches age 21," the first remainder is now vested
— specifically, vested subject to divestment. As a result, the second "remainder" must be an executory
interest. This further results in no reversion in O.

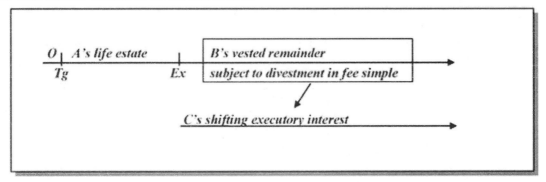

Note that no contingent remainders are left to be destroyed. In addition, in the days when contingent
remainders were inalienable, the grant as originally written restricted the property's alienability much more
than the grant as construed under the Rule in *Edwards v. Hammond*. Finally, the result in *Spiegel's Estate
v. United States* (see Example 125, above) would change if the Rule were applied.

The Rule in *Edwards v. Hammond* is a rule of construction rather than a rule of law and represents a
constructional preference in favor of a vested remainder over a contingent remainder.

4. The Rule in *Wild's Case*

Under the Rule in *Wild's Case*, 6 Co. Rep. 16b, 77 Eng. Rep. 277 (1599), a **devise** by O to *A and his children* should be construed as follows:

(a)   If A has no children on O's death [*O's death is important because the grant must be found in O's will; gifts in a will take effect at the testator's death, not when the will is written*], then A gets a fee tail; *i.e.*, the words "and his children" are read as "and the heirs of his body," and they are words of limitation.

(b)   If A has children on O's death, then A and the children take equal shares, *i.e.*, "and his children" are words of purchase.

The Rule in *Wild's Case* was a rule of construction. Part (a) suggests that a fee tail was a common — perhaps preferred — estate planning choice. Part (b) makes A and his children concurrent owners of the property. Briefly consider the different kinds of concurrent interests:

> You have considered concurrent interests before in this guide, including class gifts, such as vested remainders subject to open. You may also recall that, under the Canons of Descent, sisters inherited concurrently if they had no brother.

Example 133

$O \rightarrow A$ and B and their heirs.

Note that O has granted Blackacre to both A and B, presently and concurrently. Possession of Blackacre is shared and undivided.

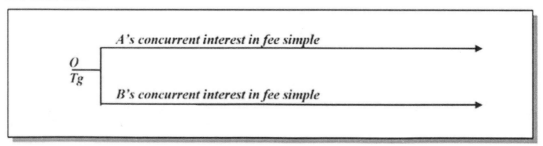

5. Concurrent Ownership

Our purpose here is to only briefly describe concurrent ownership of property. You will learn much more about concurrent ownership and about marital property in your property course. For our purposes, just be aware that the concurrent sharing or ownership of an interest in Blackacre by two or more parties is not unusual. At common law, A and B may own Blackacre concurrently in three principal ways: tenancy in common, joint tenancy, and tenancy by the entirety:

Tenancy in Common. As tenants in common, A ***and*** B each own an undivided 1/2 interest in Blackacre. That is not to say that A owns a particular half of Blackacre and B owns the other half. Short of consensual or judicial partition of the estate, neither A nor B can point to certain acreage owned individually. Each owns every square foot of Blackacre in common with the other. The interest of each is alienable and inheritable. If A transfers her interest to C, then B and C are tenants in common. Instead, if A transfers half of her undivided 1/2 interest to C and D, then A, B, C, and D would be tenants in common, but B would own 1/2, A would own 1/4, and C and D would each own 1/8. In each of these examples, the parties own "undivided" fractional interests in the whole.

Tenancy in common is the preferred estate at modern common law. That is, a tenancy in common is presumed unless the wording of the grant indicates otherwise.

Joint Tenancy. Joint tenants have a right of survivorship. Assume A and B each own an undivided half interest in Blackacre in joint tenancy. When one of them dies, the survivor takes the whole of the property automatically by operation of law. The property does not pass to the decedent's heirs and is unaffected by his will.

What happens if A transfers her interest in Blackacre to C? Then the joint tenancy is "severed" and B and C became tenants in common. The right of survivorship is a tenuous one, because an attribute of joint tenancy is that any joint tenant may sever her interest into a tenancy in common. If only two individuals are joint tenants, then a conveyance by one party of her interest would sever the entire joint tenancy into a tenancy in common, thereby terminating the other party's right of survivorship.

However, if A, B, and C are joint tenants, and if A conveys her interest to D, then D would be a tenant in common with B and C, who in turn would be tenants in common with D, but B and C would still hold in joint tenancy as to each other. Instead, if A conveyed her interest to C, then B and C would be joint tenants regarding their original interest, but B and C would be tenants in common regarding the interest that A conveyed to C.

At early common law, this was the preferred concurrent estate. That is, a joint tenancy would be presumed unless the wording of the grant indicated otherwise.

Tenancy by the Entirety. The law has long given the property of married persons a special status for the benefit of the surviving or divorcing spouse. The common law's creation was the "estate" known as tenancy by the entirety. A tenancy by the entirety is similar to a joint tenancy with its right of survivorship, but the tenancy by the entirety could exist only between a husband and wife, and the survivorship right could not be severed by one spouse acting alone.

Tenancy by the entirety was the preferred estate at common law for married couples. Today, tenancy by the entirety is recognized in about twenty states.

D. CONCLUDING THOUGHTS

The foregoing complexities should serve to remind you that the system we have presented to this point is much simplified. Our presentation provides a solid base on which to build later understanding, but do not lose sight of the fact that our presentation has been an oversimplification of the law of estates in land and future interests. The cases, treatises, and courses in real property and in wills and estates will continue to expand this presentation and enrich your understanding.

E.   REVIEW CHART

THE ESTATES
• **PRESENT ESTATES**
• Fee Simple
• Fee Tail

• Life Estate
      Life Estate *Pur Autre Vie*
      Life Estate Determinable

• Fee Simple Determinable
• Fee Simple on Condition Subsequent
• Fee Simple on Executory Limitation
• **FUTURE INTERESTS**

• Reversion
      Following an expirable estate
      Following a contingent remainder
      Following alternative contingent remainders
      Preceding some executory interests
      Following a life estate determinable

• Possibility of Reverter
• Right of Entry

• Remainder
      Indefeasibly Vested
      Vested subject to divestment
      Vested subject to open
      Contingent
      Alternative contingent

• Executory Interests
RULES OF CONSTRUCTION AND RULES OF LAW
• The Rule Against Perpetuities
• The Rule in *Shelley's Case*
• Doctrine of Worthier Title
• The Rule in *Edwards v. Hammond*
• The Rule in *Wild's Case*
• Concurrent Interests

F. OUR ANALYTICAL APPROACH (FINAL MODIFICATIONS)

We now make final modifications to our analytical approach by adding some additional matters covered in this chapter, which we **bold** so you may easily identify the additions. **We consider this approach advanced learning. You or your teacher may prefer that you use the approach that appears at the end of chapter five or only use parts of this approach.**

First Determinations:

1. What did O have before making the grant?

    Assume O begins with a fee simple absolute unless otherwise stated.

2. What does A have?

    Fee simple absolute?

    Fee tail?

    Beware a *devise* **to "A and his children." The Rule of** *Wild's Case* **converts a** *devise* **to A and his children into a fee tail if A has no children when O dies. But if A has children when O dies, then A and the children take a concurrent interest.**

    Life estate?

    Life estate determinable?

    Fee simple determinable?

    Fee simple on condition subsequent?

3. If there are no further grants, what has O retained, if anything?

    Nothing if A has a fee simple absolute.

    Reversion if A has a life estate, **life estate determinable**, or a fee tail.

    Possibility of reverter if A has a fee simple determinable.

    Right of entry if A has a fee simple on condition subsequent.

Second Determinations:

If there are further grants, then ask, as to each one:

4. Is the interest a remainder?

    Remember to construe future interests in grantees as remainders, if possible.

    Beware remainders in the heirs of the grantor. The Doctrine of Worthier Title converts a remainder in the heirs of the grantor into a reversion in the grantor.

    a. [Rule 1] Does the interest follow an expirable estate?

        i.   If no, then the interest is not a remainder. Proceed to Third Determinations, below.

        ii. If yes, then the interest may be a remainder. Proceed to b, immediately below.

    b. [Rule 2] Will the interest take effect immediately upon the expiration of the preceding estate?

        i.   If no, then the interest is not a remainder. Proceed to Third Determinations, below.

        ii. If yes, then the interest may be a remainder. Proceed to c, immediately below.

    c. [Rule 3] Can the interest take effect before the expiration of the preceding estate?

i.   If yes, then the interest is not a remainder. Proceed to Third Determinations, below.

ii. If no, then the interest is a remainder. Proceed to 5, immediately below.

5.   Since the interest is a remainder, what will the remainder be when it becomes possessory?

Fee simple absolute?

Fee tail?

Life estate?

Life estate determinable?

Fee simple determinable?

Fee simple on condition subsequent?

6.   Is the remainder vested or contingent?

a.   Is the holder of the remainder born and ascertainable?

i.   If yes, then the remainder may be vested.

ii. If no, then the remainder is contingent, unless some extraneous facts show that the remainder has become vested.

iii. In either case, proceed to b. immediately below.

b.   Is there a condition precedent to possession other than the expiration of the preceding interest?

i.   If no (and if the holder of the remainder is born and ascertainable — answered under 6.a, above), then the remainder is vested.

ii. If yes (or if the holder of the remainder is unborn or unascertainable — answered under 6.a, above), then the remainder is contingent.

Ignore true "surplusage" language that masks what is really a vested remainder.

Beware remainders in "heirs" of a grantee. The Rule in *Shelley's Case* converts a remainder in the heirs of a grantee where the grantee holds a life estate into a vested remainder in the grantee. Then consider whether the Merger Rule merges the grantee's life estate and remainder.

c.   Note: If a contingent remainder in one party (*e.g.*, B) is immediately followed by another remainder in another party (*e.g.*, C) that can become possessory only in exactly those circumstances in which the first party's (B's) remainder cannot, then both parties (B and C) have alternative contingent remainders.

Consider the Rule of *Edwards v. Hammonds*: if the condition precedent to the first remainder follows, grammatically, the words of purchase, and if the condition precedent to the first remainder is only survivorship to a certain age, then the first remainder is a vested remainder on executory limitation and the next interest is an executory interest.

7.   If the remainder is vested, is the remainder a "class gift"?

a.   If no, then the remainder is a vested remainder.

b.   If yes, then the remainder is a vested remainder subject to open unless the class has closed by facts extraneous to the grant. Is the class closed?

i.   If yes, then the class has closed and the remainder is a vested remainder.

   ii.   If no, then the remainder is a vested remainder subject to open unless extraneous facts have made the remainder a present possessory interest.

   iii.   Does the vested remainder subject to open violate the RAP? See Fourth Determinations, below.

8.   If the remainder is contingent, has it been destroyed?

   a.   Has the contingent remainder been destroyed because the remainder failed to vest in time — at or before the expiration of the preceding estate that supported the remainder?

      i.   If yes, then the remainder should be deleted from the grant and the state of the title should then be determined from what is left of the grant.

      ii.   If no, then proceed immediately to b., below.

   b.   Has the contingent remainder been destroyed by merger — by merging the preceding estate that supported the remainder with the next vested interest — arising from more than the original grant?

      i.   If yes, then the remainder should be deleted from the grant and the state of the title should then be determined from what is left of the grant.

      ii.   If no, then proceed immediately to c., below.

   c.   Has the contingent remainder been destroyed by termination (forfeiture or renunciation) of the preceding estate before its expiration?

      i.   If yes, then the remainder should be deleted from the grant and the state of the title should then be determined from what is left of the grant.

      ii.   If no, then proceed to 9., below

9.   If the remainder is contingent, does O retain a reversion?

   Yes, unless O has otherwise accounted for the full fee simple absolute.

10.   Is the contingent remainder void under RAP? See Fourth Determinations, below.

Third Determinations:

11.   Since the interest is not a remainder, consider the new interests that are possible after the Statute of Uses (1536).

   a.   Reclassify the interest that was invalid prior to 1536 as an "executory interest" in fee or as one of the five possessory estates, as appropriate.

      i.   If this interest can become possessory immediately following the interest of a prior grantee, then the interest is a "shifting executory interest."

      ii.   If this interest can become possessory immediately from the grantor, then the interest is a "springing executory interest."

   b.   Next classify the present or future interest that immediately precedes the executory interest:

      i.   If the immediately preceding interest is only implicit, due to a gap in possession between the expiration of the preceding estate and the executory interest, then the grantor retains a "reversion" and the executory interest is then a "springing" one.

   c.   When the reversion becomes possessory, it will be a present estate "on executory limitation" — most likely a "fee simple on executory limitation."

i.   If the immediately preceding future interest will become possessory, but might thereafter be lost due to a condition subsequent expressed in the grant, then the immediately preceding interest is "on executory limitation."

ii. If the executory interest does not fall under i, immediately above, then the interest is "subject to divestment."

iii. Caution: In making this analysis, be sure that the two future interests are not alternative contingent remainders. Remember the distinction between conditions precedent and conditions subsequent.

12. Is the executory interest void under RAP? See Fourth Determinations, below.

Fourth Determinations (RAP):

Note: You should have already classified the interests without regard to the RAP.

13. Identify the interests that are subject to the RAP: executory interests, contingent remainders, and vested remainders subject to open.

14. As to each interest that is subject to the RAP, will the interest vest soon enough, if the interest ever does vest, within the lives in being plus 21 years?

Basic vesting inquiry:

If the interest is certain to vest in time, then the interest is valid (*i.e.* does not violate RAP). If there is any possibility that the interest may not vest in time, then the interest violates RAP. Note: the fact that an interest may never vest is irrelevant for purposes of RAP. The key is that, if the interest ever does vest, the interest must vest in time.

The other keys to RAP are "Measuring Lives" and "Vesting Rules."

Measuring lives:

Measuring lives are the relevant lives in being at the time of the grant, that is, the lives to consider for purposes of applying the "lives in being plus 21-year" RAP period. Consider extraneous facts, such as whether a particular person is alive at the time of the grant, *e.g.*, a testator is not alive at the time of the grant because a will takes effect on the testator's death. Sometimes, measuring lives are implied from the language of the grant.

RAP Vesting Rules:

Contingent remainders vest when they become either vested remainders or present estates.

Executory interests vest when they become present estates and, in the case of shifting executory interests, also when they become vested remainders.

Vested remainders subject to open vest for RAP purposes when no more members of the class can be added, *i.e.*, when the class closes. If the class might not close within the RAP period, then the entire class gift is void.

15. If the interest is void, then strike the offending interest by using the "cross-out rule." Strike the words of the offending interest back to where the remaining words, if any, can stand alone and still make sense.

16. Then reclassify the interests by reconsidering the first three Determinations, above.

Concurrent Interests: A present or future interest may be held by two or more parties.

17. **Co-tenancy: Each party holds a fractional undivided interest in Blackacre. Co-tenancy is the default concurrent interest at *modern* common law. A co-tenancy interest is alienable inter**

vivos, inheritable, and devisable unless it was an interest that lacked one or more of these attributes.

18. **Joint Tenancy: Each party holds an equal interest in Blackacre but the ultimate survivor will get the whole interest, at which time the interest is no longer a concurrent interest. A joint tenancy is the default estate at common law. A joint tenancy interest is not inheritable or devisable, since the interest passes to the surviving joint tenant(s). The ultimate surviving joint tenant, however, ends up with an individual interest that is alienable, inheritable, and devisable unless the joint tenancy was in an interest that lacked one or more of these attributes. A joint tenancy interest in an alienable interest may be unilaterally alienated inter vivos by any one joint tenant, in which case the alienated interest becomes a co-tenancy interest with the other concurrent interest(s). Once severed, the co-tenancy interest will gain nothing by survivorship nor lose by failing to survive.**

19. **Tenancy by the Entirety: This concurrent estate may exist only between spouses. This interest is recognized in only a minority of states today, but where recognized, the tenancy by the entirety may be the default estate for married co-owners. The tenancy by the entirety has the same survivorship characteristics as a joint tenancy, but, unlike the joint tenancy, a tenancy by the entirety cannot be unilaterally alienated or severed into tenancy in common. In other words, the tenancy by the entirety can only be alienated inter vivos by both spouses acting together.**

Summary of Estates and Future Interests Attributes:

		Alienable	Devisable	Inheritable
1.	Fee Simple Absolute No Future Interest (FI)	Yes	Yes	Yes
2.	Fee Tail	Limited	No	Lineal
3.	Life Estate	Yes	No	No
4.	Life Estate *Pur Autre Vie*	Yes	Yes (ltd.)	Yes (ltd.)
5.	Life Estate Determinable	Yes	No	No
	FI: Reversion	Yes	Yes	Yes
	FI: Remainder			
	Vested	Yes	Yes*	Yes*
	Vested Subject to Open	Yes	Yes*	Yes*
	Vested Subject to Divestment	Yes	Yes*	Yes*
	Contingent "Destructible"	No	Yes*	Yes*
	Alternative Contingent	No	Yes*	Yes*
6.	Life estate on Executory Limitation	Yes	No	No
	FI: Reversion	Yes	Yes	Yes
	FI: Executory Interest	No	Yes*	Yes*
7.	Fee Simple Determinable	Yes	Yes	Yes
	FI: Possibility of Reverter	No	Not likely	Yes
8.	Fee Simple Upon Condition Subsequent	Yes	Yes	Yes
	FI: Right of Entry	No	No	Yes
9.	Fee Simple on Executory Limitation	Yes	Yes	Yes
	FI: Reversion	Yes	Yes	Yes
	FI: Executory Interest	No	Yes*	Yes*

* If the interest is otherwise inheritable/devisable.

G.   REVIEW PROBLEMS

In each of the following, please give the state of the title at the common law in 1700. Assume that O has a fee simple absolute prior to the conveyance. You must give the state of the title for each of the separate fact situations. All fact patterns are to be treated cumulatively.

1.   O →   *A for life, as long as she practices law.*

        (a)   A is alive and practicing law.

        (b)   A is disbarred and forbidden to practice law ever again.

2.   O →   *A for life, then to A's children and their heirs.*

        (a)   A is living and has 2 children, B and C.

        (b)   A dies.

3.   O →   *A for life, then to the heirs of O.*

            Assume A and O are living.

4.   O →   *A for life, then one year after A's death to the heirs of O.*

5.   O →   *A for life, then to B for life, then to A's heirs.*

        (a)   A and B are living.

        (b)   A dies, intestate, leaving as his only heir, X.

        (c)   B dies.

6.   O →   *A and his heirs thirty years from the date of A's birth.*

        (a)   O is living. A is 10 years old.

        (b)   A dies on his 29th birthday, leaving as his only heir B.

        (c)   One year passes.

7.   O →   *A for life, then to the first son of B who reaches age 21 and his heirs, but if no son of B reaches age 21, to A's heirs.*

        (a)   A and B are alive. C, B's only son, is 19.

        (b)   O conveys his interest to C.

        (c)   C dies at 20, leaving E as his heir.

    (d)   B dies.

8. $O \rightarrow$ *A for life, then to the first child of A to graduate from law school and her heirs.*

    (a)   A is living. A has two children, S and D, who are both enrolled in law school.

    (b)   D drops out of law school and enrolls in med school.

    (c)   O conveys his reversion to A.

9. $O \rightarrow$ *A for life, then to the children of B who survive B and their heirs.*

    (a)   A and B are alive. B has no children.

    (b)   B has a child, X.

    (c)   A renounces the life estate.

10. $O \rightarrow$ *A for the life of O, then to B for life if B survives O.*

    (a)   A and B are living.

    (b)   O dies, leaving a will in favor of X.

11. $O \rightarrow$ *A for life, then to B for life, then if C survives A and B, to C and his heirs.*

    (a)   A, B and C are living.

    (b)   O conveys his reversion to A.

    (c)   B dies.

12. $O \rightarrow$ *O for the life of W, then to S and his heirs if S reaches age 21, but if S does not reach age 21, then to D and her heirs.*

    (a)   W, S, and D are alive.

    (b)   W dies. S is 19.

    (c)   S celebrates his 21st birthday.

13. $O \rightarrow$ *D and her children by A.* Assume the conveyance is by will.

    (a)   D and A are alive. D and A have no children.

    (b)   D and A have a son.

Answers to Review Problems

In each of the following, please give the state of the title as it would be at the common law in 1700. Assume that O has a fee simple absolute prior to the conveyance. You must give the state of the title for each of the separate fact situations. All fact patterns are to be treated cumulatively.

1.   O →   *A for life, as long as she practices law.*
   (a)   A is alive and practicing law.
         A has a life estate determinable.
         O has a reversion.
   (b)   A is disbarred and forbidden to practice law ever again.
         O has a fee simple absolute.

2.   O →   *A for life, then to A's children and their heirs.*
   (a)   A is living and has 2 children, B and C.
         A has a life estate.
         B and C have a vested remainder subject to open in fee simple.

> The Rule in *Shelley's Case* does not apply in this situation because the conveyance does not create a remainder in the heirs of A. The conveyance creates a remainder in A's children. While A's children are often the heirs of A, they are not the only possible heirs of A. If B and C were to predecease A, without wills, they would not be her heirs and their heirs would inherit the vested remainder.

   (b)   A dies.
         B and C have a fee simple, as joint tenants.

3.   O →   *A for life, then to the heirs of O.*
         Assume A and O are living.
         A has a life estate.
         O has a reversion due to the Doctrine of Worthier Title.

4.   O →   *A for life, then one year after A's death to the heirs of O.*
         A has a life estate.
         O has a reversion and an executory interest.

> Before applying the Doctrine of Worthier Title, the state of the title is: A has a life estate; the heirs of O have a springing executory interest; and O has a reversion. We have applied the Doctrine because it may have been applied to executory interests. We have not applied the doctrine of merger, because we are not sure an executory interest should be considered "vested" for purposes of merger.

5.   O →   *A for life, then to B for life, then to A's heirs.*
   (a)   A and B are living.
         A has a life estate and a vested remainder in fee simple. Merger does not occur here because A's interests are separated by a vested remainder.

B has a vested remainder in a life estate.

(b)   A dies, intestate, leaving as his only heir, X.

B has a life estate.

X has a vested remainder in fee simple.

(c)   B dies.

X has a fee simple.

6. $O \rightarrow$ *A and his heirs thirty years from the date of A's birth.*

(a)   O is living. A is 10 years old.

O has a fee simple on executory limitation.

A has a springing executory interest in fee simple.

(b)   A dies on his 29th birthday, leaving as his only heir B.

No change except B has A's executory interest.

(c)   One year passes.

B has a fee simple.

7. $O \rightarrow$ *A for life, then to the first son of B who reaches age 21 and his heirs, but if no son of B reaches age 21, to A's heirs.*

(a)   A and B are alive. C, B's only son, is 19.

A has a life estate.

The first son of B who reaches age 21 has contingent remainder in fee simple. *Edwards v. Hammond* does not apply because, in this example, the common law judges thought the age contingency was not surplus, but was in fact an essential part of the description of the remainderman.

A has an alternative contingent remainder in fee simple due to the Rule in *Shelley's Case*.

O has a reversion.

(b)   O conveys his interest to C.

No change except C has O's reversion.

(c)   C dies at 20, leaving E as his heir.

No change except that E has the reversion that was C's. The contingent remainder is not destroyed because it is still possible that B will have a son who will reach age 21 before A dies.

(d)   B dies.

B's only son C has died and C can have no more children.

A has a fee simple absolute. The first contingent remainder is destroyed, A's alternative contingent remainder vests, eliminating the reversion. A's life estate and vested remainder merge into a fee simple.

8. $O \rightarrow$ *A for life, then to the first child of A to graduate from law school and her heirs.*

(a)   A is living. A has two children, S and D, who are both enrolled in law school.

A has a life estate.

First child who graduates has a contingent remainder in fee simple.

O has a reversion.

(b)   D drops out of school and enrolls in med school.

No change.

(c)   O conveys his reversion to A.

A has a fee simple absolute. A's life estate and reversion are no longer separated by a vested remainder, so they merge.

9. $O \rightarrow$ *A for life, then to the children of B who survive B and their heirs.*

(a)   A and B are alive. B has no children.

A has a life estate.

The children of B who survive B have a contingent remainder in fee simple.

O has a reversion.

(a) B has a child, X.

No change.

(c) A renounces the life estate.

O has a fee simple absolute because the contingent remainders are destroyed and the reversion becomes possessory.

10. $O \rightarrow$ *A for the life of O, then to B for life if B survives O.*

(a) A and B are living.

A has a life estate *pur autre vie.*

B has a vested remainder in a life estate, because the condition on the life estate is surplusage.

O has a reversion.

(b) O dies, leaving a will in favor of X.

B has a life estate.

X has a reversion.

11. $O \rightarrow$ *A for life, then to B for life, then if C survives A and B, to C and his heirs.*

(a) A, B and C are living.

A has a life estate.

B has a vested remainder in a life estate.

C has a contingent remainder in fee simple.

O has a reversion.

(b) O conveys his reversion to A.

A has a life estate and a reversion.

B has a vested remainder in a life estate.

C has a contingent remainder in fee simple.

(c) B dies.

A has a fee simple absolute. A's life estate and reversion are no longer separated by a vested remainder, so they merge.

12. $O \rightarrow$ *O for the life of W, then to S and his heirs if S reaches age 21, but if S does not reach age 21, then to D and her heirs.*

(a) W, S, and D are alive.

O has a life estate *pur autre vie.*

S has a vested remainder subject to divestment in fee due to the Rule in *Edwards v. Hammond.*

D has a shifting executory interest in fee simple.

(b) W dies. S is 19.

S has a fee simple on executory limitation.

D has a shifting executory interest in fee simple.

(c) S celebrates his 21st birthday.

S has a fee simple absolute.

Did you get all of this correct? Under *Edwards v. Hammond*, the first condition precedent, "if S reaches 21," is ignored because this condition follows the words of purchase, "to S and his heirs." The "but if" survivorship clause remains. When W dies, S takes the property at age 19, thus having a present possessory interest, but S might lose the land if he does not reach age 21. Thus, after W dies, S has a present interest in fee simple on executory limitation. If S dies before reaching 21, then D and his heirs will take in fee simple. If S reaches age 21, then S will have a fee simple absolute.

13. $O \rightarrow$ *D and her children by A.* Assume the conveyance is by will.
       (a)   D and A are alive. D and A have no children.
              D has a fee tail special.
              The beneficiaries of O's will have a reversion.
       (b)   D and A have a son.
              No change.

Chapter 7

STATUTORY MODIFICATIONS

A. INTRODUCTION

You now have mastered a simplified system that represents the common law of estates in land and future interests as of 1700. When you are asked in this chapter or the appendices to analyze a grant under the common law, you should apply the basic system you learned in the preceding chapters.

But what of the more modern law? England enacted statutes that reformed the common law system and made much of it obsolete. Modern simplification of property law in England occurred in the early twentieth century with a series of laws. Much of the reform legislation was enacted in 1925, effective January 1, 1926. *See* C. Moynihan, *Introduction to the Law of Real Property* 23 (4th ed. 2005). The reform legislation was both technical and comprehensive. For example, the 1925 legislation includes:

(1)   Law of Property Act of 1925 (15 Geo. V, c. 20)

(2)   Settled Land Act of 1925 (15 Geo. V, c. 18)

(3)   The Trustees Act of 1925 (15 Geo. V, c. 19)

(4)   The Land Charges Act of 1925 (15 Geo. V, c. 22)

(5)   The Administration of Estates Act of 1925 (15 Geo. V, c. 23)

(6)   Land Registration Act of 1925 (15 Geo. V, c. 21)

The legislation was designed to honor the grantor's intent and obtain the greatest freedom of alienability of land for commercial purposes. *See* J. Cribbett, *Principles of the Law of Property* 38, 342-343 (3d ed. 1989).

In the United States, however, such a sweeping reform has never occurred. Modification of the common law system has been piecemeal — state by state, statute by statute, and case by case. In making changes, state legislatures and courts often have used the vocabulary of the common law. Because changes have been piecemeal and have relied on common law terms, sometimes incorrectly used, you are likely to find that understanding a change made in your jurisdiction will require you to recall or determine the common law result that the legislature or court was trying to change or perhaps even incorrectly restate, as well as to use the vocabulary you have acquired. The good news is that not many changes have been made, and many of the more common changes are similar from state to state. In this chapter, you are given the opportunity to test your new vocabulary and analytical skills on state statutes that codify, modify, or wholly reform various aspects of what you have learned.

In addition, this chapter suggests the kinds of changes you might expect to find in the statutes that govern your jurisdiction. You will have an easier time reading those statutes if you approach them with a mental checklist of typical statutory changes. Once you have that checklist, we think you will have a good foundation from which to begin to study how American case law has occasionally modified what you have learned and, in particular, the law of the jurisdiction in which you will practice.

Below we survey typical statutory changes in the common law of estates in land and future interests. We will also mention a few court decisions that modify the common law. The survey includes text, examples, problems, and answers. An appendix to this text includes selected statutes from several jurisdictions. We will quote or cite some of these statutes. We hope that this presentation will help you identify and study the relevant statutes and cases in your state.

At the end of this chapter, we will not present a modified analytical approach; however, you may wish to create one for the jurisdiction of your choice or of your professor's choice. If you do so, then you will need to consider whether case law and statutes for the chosen state have modified the common law.

We do not address the many examples of case law where the courts have misapplied the common law. Presenting a number of examples would only serve to confuse you; however we will provide one illustrative example. Your professor may wish to provide other examples. In *Williams v. Watt*, 668 P.2d 620 (Wyo. 1983), the Supreme Court of Wyoming considered a conveyance of land where the grantor, O, conveyed Blackacre to A, "reserving an undivided one-half interest in all oil, gas, and mineral rights . . . for a period of 20 years . . . and as long thereafter as oil, gas, or other minerals continue to be produced . . ." The court held that O had reserved a fee simple determinable in this ½ interest and that A had received a vested remainder in fee in this ½ interest. We have not provided examples of a grantor expressly reserving an interest, although with regard to this ½ interest, we think you understand that O conveyed a springing executory interest and kept a fee simple on executory limitation. However, the springing executory interest is void under RAP, leaving O with a fee simple absolute. Courts often try to construe instruments to avoid a RAP violation, but few have done so as creatively as Wyoming in this example. Because O did not <u>intend</u> for the RAP to void A's future interest, perhaps we should forgive the Wyoming court for this creative classification of interests; however, the court could have avoided the RAP problem, as some other courts have done, by construing the grant somewhat differently. *See, e.g., Walker v. Foss*, 930 S.W.2d 701 (Tex. App. 1996), and *Bagby v. Bredthauer*, 627 S.W.2d 190 (Tex. App. 1981). Note that O conveyed Blackacre to A and then reserved an interest. What if we construed this grant as if O had conveyed the full fee simple to A and that A had then conveyed back to O the undivided ½ mineral interest? Voilà! A conveyed a fee simple determinable to O, keeping a possibility of reverter. This avoids RAP because RAP does not apply to a possibility of reverter, which is considered vested for RAP purposes, and this construction also avoids a wholesale change in the common law of classifying estates in land and future interests.

B. ENGLISH COMMON LAW ESTATES IN LAND AND FUTURE INTERESTS AS MODIFIED BY AMERICAN STATUTES

In many if not all states, you will encounter statutes that affect the common law rules governing the creation of the present estate. For example, in nearly all states you will find a court decision or a statute similar to Cal. Civ. Code § 1072 or N.D. Cent. Code § 47-09-15. The California statute provides that "[w]ords of inheritance or succession are not requisite to transfer a fee in real property." Actually, you have already learned this change, so this is just review. This type of statute or court decision essentially provides that the fee simple absolute is the preferred estate — something that we have asked you to presume all along. See discussion following Example 1 in chapter one. At common law, the preferred estate was the life estate. See discussion following Example 8 in chapter one.

What does this preference mean?

Example 134: *O → A*.

At common law, O has conveyed a life estate. But thanks to the statute, O has conveyed a fee simple absolute or has *purported* to do so. Thus, the magic words, "and his heirs," are not necessary to convey a fee simple absolute. You might ask whether any statutes clearly say what A has. Yes, in California, North Dakota, and elsewhere. Cal. Civ. Code § 1105 provides that "[a] fee simple title is presumed to be intended to pass by a grant of real property, unless it appears from the grant that a lesser estate was intended." N.D. Cent. Code § 47-10-13 is virtually identical.

What do you think about the following statutory provision?

Every estate in lands which shall be granted, conveyed or bequeathed, although other words heretofore necessary to transfer an estate of inheritance is not added, shall be deemed a fee simple estate of inheritance, if a less estate is not limited by express words, or do not appear to have been granted, conveyed or bequeathed by construction or operation of law.

See 765 Ill. Comp. Stat 5/13. This single statute accomplishes two goals. Can you identify both, based on the legislation in California and North Dakota quoted above? That's right. The legislature has provided that the phrase "and her heirs" is unnecessary to the creation of a fee interest. The legislature also has also answered the central question: What did the creator of the conveyance or devise intend to convey? The answer is that the creator is presumed to have transferred a fee simple absolute. N.M. Stat. Ann. § 47-1-33 is similar.

Consider the following:

Example 135. *O → A as long as she remains unmarried.*

Does A have a life estate determinable or a fee simple determinable? The answer — it depends. Under the statutes mentioned above, the presumption would be a fee simple determinable. However, in real life, conveyances and devises are made in documents that contain many words. Additional words may indicate that O intended a life estate determinable. *See, e.g., Lewis v. Searles,* 452 S.W.2d 153 (Mo. 1970). Thus, the ultimate answer to the question of what A has as a result of O's conveyance will depend upon how the document is construed, which may turn on what other evidence of O's intent is available and admissible. The bottom line is that the statutory preference for a fee simple and the elimination of the need for words of inheritance gives rise to new construction problems — problems the common law rules largely avoid.

Given the possibility of other evidence, you might question whether the vocabulary that you learned is very helpful and whether the simple examples in this book, sometimes called "skeleton grants," are meaningful. Well, we think that you now have a basic skill that will help you both in locating and understanding statutes, in reading and analyzing cases, and in construing instruments. We think that the facility you have acquired with "skeleton grants" gives you the power to reduce the language of statutes, cases, and instruments to simpler forms and, having reduced them, to identify the range of possible meanings. This ability will then allow you to search for persuasive or controlling authorities and to argue policy. Whether you are litigating, trying to settle a case, or drafting instruments, your facility with "skeleton grants" and the knowledge of the common law should be helpful.

By the way, in the above example, why did we say that O conveyed or *purported* to convey a fee simple absolute? In this book, we ask you to assume that O begins with a fee simple. What if O had only a life estate? Then O could convey only what he owned. But he could purport to convey more, which has important ramifications that you will study in your property class but which are beyond this presentation.

In many if not all states, you will find a statute that modifies the common law fee tail. Suppose you encounter this conveyance in Illinois:

Example 136. *O → A and the heirs of his body.*

At common law, A had a fee tail, and O had a reversion. But Illinois has the following statutory provision:

In cases where, by the common law, any person or persons might hereafter become the owner of, without applying the rule of property known as the rule in Shelley's Case, in fee tail, of any lands, tenements or hereditaments, by virtue of any legacy, gift, grant or other conveyance, hereafter to be made, or by any other means whatsoever, such person or persons, instead of being or becoming the owner thereof in fee tail, shall be deemed and adjudged to be, and become the owner thereof, for his or her natural life only, and the remainder shall pass in fee simple absolute, to the person or persons to whom the estate tail would, on the death of the first grantee, legatee or donee in tail, first pass according to the course of the common law, by virtue of such legacy, gift, grant or conveyance.

See 765 Ill. Comp. Stat. 5/6.

How does this statute change the common law result? Take your time. Think of the "skeleton grant" and determine, first, what the legislature has said A will have.

The statute gives A a life estate. How about A's children? They have a remainder. What kind of a remainder do they have? The answer depends on whether A has any children. If A has a child, then the child has a vested remainder subject to open in fee simple. If A does not have a child, then A's unborn children have a contingent remainder in fee simple, and O has a reversion.

Case authority in Illinois supports this result. *Doney v. Clipson*, 120 N.E. 571, 571 (Ill. 1918), explains the result:

> A granting clause in a deed substantially in the language 'to A and the heirs of his body' defines the estate granted as a fee tail at common law, which . . . our Conveyance Act has turned into a life estate in A with a remainder in fee to his children, contingent until their birth if he has none, but vested if he has a child, subject to open and let in after-born children.

Henry v. Metz, 46 N.E.2d 945, 949 (Ill. 1943), describes the statute set out above as creating a "remainder vested in the children, which opens up to let in after-born children of a life tenant."

Other states have taken a different approach. Suppose you encounter Example 136 in California, which has the following statutory provision:

> Estates tail are abolished, and every estate which would be at common law adjudged to be a fee tail is a fee simple, and if no valid remainder is limited thereon, is a fee simple absolute.

See CAL. CIV. CODE § 763. What do you think? The statute seems pretty straightforward, doesn't it? A has a fee simple. O has nothing.

Now, suppose you encounter the following conveyance in California:

Example 137. *O → A and the heirs of his body, then to B and his heirs.*

California has the following additional statutory provision:

> Where a remainder in fee is limited upon any estate, which would by the common law be adjudged a fee tail, such remainder is valid as a contingent limitation upon a fee, and vests in possession on the death of the first taker, without issue living at the time of his death.

See CAL. CIV. CODE § 764.

Now, what do you think? Determining what O has given A is a little harder. However, the statute refers to a "contingent limitation upon a fee." Further, California has a statute that prefers a fee when construing an instrument. *See* CAL. CIV. CODE § 1105. Based on these legislative signals, we think the state of the title is that A has a fee simple on executory limitation, and B has an executory interest in fee.

What happens if A dies, leaving a child, X? The statute seems to provide that A's interest will terminate only if he dies without leaving any surviving issue. If X is A's only heir, then, like the fee tail, X would acquire title; however, under the statute, X would acquire a fee simple absolute — an interest that can be sold or devised or inherited by someone other than a lineal descendant. On the other hand, if A dies without a lineal heir, then B or his heir would hold a fee simple absolute.

In addition to the modification of the common law rule governing the creation of a fee simple and the statutory substitution of interests for the common law estate of fee tail, other modifications of the common law have been made. Let's consider two examples.

Example 138:   *O →   A and her heirs as long as the land is farmed.*
Example 139:   *O →   A and her heirs, but if the land ceases to be farmed, then O and his heirs may reenter and claim the land.*

The good news is that in most states, the classification scheme you have learned is alive and well. In Example 138, A has a fee simple determinable, and O has a possibility of reverter. In Example 139, A has a fee simple on condition subsequent, and O has a right of entry, or if you your professor prefers, a power of termination.

California, however, has the following statute:

> Every estate that would be at common law a fee simple determinable is deemed to be a fee simple subject to a restriction in the form of a condition subsequent. Every interest that would be at common law a possibility of reverter is deemed to be and is enforceable as a power of termination.

See CAL. CIV. CODE § 885.020.

How would you apply this statute to the two examples above? The statute does not change the common law result in the second example. However, in the first example, the statute appears to substitute a new interest for a fee simple determinable — "a fee simple subject to a restriction in the form of a condition subsequent," which seems to be a wordy way of saying fee simple on condition subsequent. Further, the statute substitutes the term "power of termination" for the possibility of reverter. Thus, in both examples, A has a fee simple on condition subsequent, and O has a right of entry, or as the California legislature prefers, power of termination. For other, related changes, *see* CAL. CIV. CODE §§ 885.010, .030, .040.

Now let's suppose that these examples were in instruments executed many years ago, say the 1930s. Suppose further that these examples concern land located in Minnesota, which has the following statute:

> Subd. 2a. Except for any right to reenter or to repossess as provided in subdivision 3, all private covenants, conditions, or restrictions created by which the title or use of real property is affected, cease to be valid and operative 30 years after the date of the deed, or other instrument, or the date of the probate of the will, creating them, and may be disregarded . . . .

> Subd. 3. Hereafter any right to reenter or to repossess land on account of breach made in a condition subsequent shall be barred unless such right is asserted by entry or action within six years after the happening of the breach upon which such right is predicated.

See MINN. STAT. ANN. § 500.20(2a).

What does this statute mean? The statute appears to restrict the duration of certain deed restrictions. Note that the right of entry for breach of a condition subsequent is not subject to the durational limit but is subject to lapse if not exercised within six years of a breach of the condition. But what about the fee simple determinable? Is its duration *as a future interest* limited to 30 years? We think so. Of course, if it becomes possessory within 30 years of the date of instrument or probate of the will that created it, then it would be effective indefinitely, assuming the possibility of reverter was in fee simple. *See Hiller v. County of Atoka*, 529 N.W.2d 426 (Minn. Ct. App. 1995). California has a similar provision. *See* CAL. CIV. CODE § 885.030.

In adopting statutes that modify the common law, legislatures are expressing changing views about property. In substituting something different for the common law fee tail and in modifying other common law rules, legislatures often limit the control an owner may retain over his grantees. As you will learn in all of your law-school courses, efforts to change the common law are ongoing.

You have already met one form of limitation at common law, the Rule Against Perpetuities (RAP). The RAP restricts, as you know, the creation of future interests. A majority of states have modified and a few states have repealed the RAP. One of the more popular recent modifications is the Uniform Statutory Rule Against Perpetuities, adopted by more than half the states. *See, e.g.,* CAL. PROB. CODE §§ 21200 to 21231; MINN. STAT. ANN. §§ 501A.01 to -.07; N.M. STAT. ANN. §§ 45-2-901 to -906; N.D. CENT. CODE §§ 47-02-27.1 to -27.5. Among other modifications, the Uniform Statutory Rule provides a flat 90-year vesting period in lieu of using measuring lives plus 21 years and also exempts commercial transactions in contrast to donative transfers.

Other states have adopted different modifications. *See, e.g.*, 765 ILL. COMP. STAT. 305/1 to 305/5. A few states have repealed the RAP as applied to trusts. *See, e.g.*, 25 DEL. CODE ANN. tit. 25 § 503; N.J. STAT. ANN. § 46:24-9; S.D. CODIFIED LAWS § 43-6-3; IDAHO CODE § 55-111. Yet others have retained the common law RAP, some because the RAP, or some part of it, is ensconced in the state constitution, as in Oklahoma and Texas. *See, e.g.*, OKLA. CONST., Art. 2, § 32; TEX. CONST., Art. 1, § 26. Several states, including Oklahoma and Texas, have adopted *cy pres* statutes, allowing courts some latitude to reform instruments that, as written, violate the RAP in order to avoid the violation. *See, e.g.*, 60 OKLA. STAT. ANN. §§ 75-78; TEX. PROP. CODE ANN. § 5.043. We will not attempt to illustrate or describe these statutory modifications in this presentation. However, the statutory appendix includes some excerpts from both the Uniform Statutory Rule and from other statutory modifications. You may find it interesting to consider these excerpts.

Because we believe you are equipped to understand these excerpts, we think you now have a foundation for a study of wills and trusts and estate planning. You now know that statutory modifications are common and that they need to be taken into account when you draft or construe an instrument.

Let's consider another kind of statutory restriction on an owner's power to control his property after it has been transferred to another.

> Example 140: *O → A and his heirs, but if A marries, then to B and his heirs.*

How does the following North Dakota statutory provision affect this example?

> Conditions imposing restraints upon marriage, except upon the marriage of a minor, or of the widow of the person by whom the condition is imposed, are void. This does not affect limitations when the intent was not to forbid marriage but only to give the use until marriage.

See N.D. CENT. CODE § 47-02-25.

In attempting to apply the statute to the skeleton grant, you need to know more about (1) O's relationship to A, (2) A's age, and (3) O's purpose in making the conveyance. Assuming that the conveyance expresses an intent to forbid marriage and that A is not a minor and is not O's widow, we think that A would have a fee simple.

You probably noticed that, in describing statutory modifications for the rules governing present estates, we described, at least implicitly and sometimes expressly, modifications to the correlative future interests. For example, we implied that the possible existence of a reversion after a fee tail disappears in those jurisdictions that replace the fee tail with a fee simple or a fee simple on executory limitation. *See, e.g.*, CAL. CIV. CODE § 763. We also mentioned statutory modifications to the Rule Against Perpetuities and other statutory expressions of public policy that may directly affect the creation of future interests and indirectly the present estates upon which the future interests depend.

Here are two other statutory modifications affecting future interests. First, interests that were inalienable at common law, by deed or will, tend to become freely alienable by statute. For example, N.D. CENT. CODE § 47-02-18 provides that "[f]uture interests pass by succession, will or transfer in the same manner as present interests." N.M. STAT. ANN. § 47-1-4 is comparable, but it refers to conveyances only.

Second, we want to address one aspect of the common law that might best be characterized as an attribute of some future interests rather than as a rule. That aspect is the common law doctrine of destructibility. You learned in chapter three that a contingent remainder was destroyed at common law if it failed to vest before the termination of the prior estate on which it depended.

Again, let's take an example and consider a statute. Consider the following example:

> Example 141: *O → A for life, then to the first son of A who reaches age 21 and his heirs.*

Suppose O and A are living, A has a son S, age 10, and then A dies, survived by S, who is still age 10. At common law, you will remember, O had a fee simple absolute. S's contingent remainder was "destroyed" when A's life estate ended at a time when S could not satisfy the condition. Now, assuming the same facts, suppose this conveyance occurs in a state that has the following statute:

> No future interest shall fail or be defeated by the determination of any precedent estate or interest prior to the happening of the event or contingency on which the future interest is limited to take effect.

See 765 ILL. COMP. STAT. 340/1. The statute provides that "[n]o future interest shall fail . . . ." What does that mean?

Is the following statute more clear?

> No future interest, valid in its creation, is defeated by the determination of the precedent interest before the happening of the contingency on which the future interest is limited to take effect, but should such contingency afterwards happen, the future interest takes effect in the same manner and to the same extent as if the precedent interest had continued to the same period.

See N.D. CENT. CODE § 47-02-32.

Under both statutes, the legislature appears to have intended to abolish the doctrine of destructibility. If the doctrine has been abolished, then the state of the title in the above example after A's death is: O has a fee simple on executory limitation. S has an executory interest in fee. Suppose S dies before reaching age 21? We think that O has a fee simple absolute. Do you understand why? We believe that the two statutes actually modify the doctrine of destructibility rather than completely eliminate the doctrine. That is, if an owner imposes an otherwise valid condition, whether in connection with a contingent remainder or an executory interest, then the beneficiary must satisfy the condition to acquire title. In addition to statutes that modify the common law doctrine of destructibility, at least one court has done so without the blessing of a statute. *See ABO Petroleum Corp. v. Amstutz*, 93 N.M. 332, 606 P.2d 278 (1979).

We turn now to other rules and doctrines that are often modified by statute, in particular, the Rule in *Shelley's Case* and the Doctrine of Worthier Title.

C.   SELECTED COMMON LAW RULES AS MODIFIED BY AMERICAN STATUTES

In the course of the reception of the common law in this country, the venerable Rule in *Shelley's Case* was abolished by many state legislatures. Some of these statues are included in the statutory appendix. You may like the effort of the Illinois legislature best: "The rule of property known as the rule in *Shelley's Case* is abolished." *See* 765 ILL. COMP. STAT. 345/1.

If the Rule in *Shelley's Case* is not uppermost in your mind, then this example will help.

Example 142: *O → B for life, then to the heirs of B.*

At common law, the phrase "the heirs of B" was construed as providing words of limitation rather than words of purchase. That is, under the Rule in *Shelley's Case*, these words were construed as meaning, "then to B and her heirs." As a consequence, B's vested remainder in fee merged with her life estate to create a fee simple absolute.

If the Rule in *Shelley's Case* has been abolished, what is the state of the title? To aid you in answering this question, consider the following statute:

> When a remainder is limited to the heirs, or heirs of the body, of a person to whom a life estate in the same property is given, the persons who, on the termination of the life estate are the successors or heirs of the body of the owner for life, are entitled to take by virtue of the remainder so limited to them and not as mere successors of the owner for life.

See N.D. CENT. CODE § 47-04-20.

Under such a statute, a conveyance to "the heirs of B" is now viewed as creating an interest in B's heirs, because the statute treats the phrase "the heirs of B" as words of purchase, which identify a grantee rather than describe the estate granted. This result might even be bolstered by the modern statutory constructional preference for a fee interest. Therefore, after the rule has been abolished, the state of the title is: B has a life estate. The heirs of B have a contingent remainder. O has a reversion.

Statutes abolishing the Doctrine of Worthier Title are less common in the jurisdictions represented in the appendix — perhaps because, as discussed in chapter six, the rule became a rule of construction in American case law, not a rule of law. However, CAL. PROB. CODE § 21108 provides:

> The law of this state does not include (a) the common law rule of worthier title that a transferor cannot devise an interest to his or her own heirs or (b) a presumption or rule of interpretation that a transferor does not intend, by a transfer to his or her own heirs or next of kin, to transfer an interest to them. The meaning of a transfer of a legal or equitable interest to a transferor's own heirs or next of kin, however designated, shall be determined by the general rules applicable to the interpretation of instruments.

Similarly, 765 ILL. COMP. STAT. 350/1 provides:

> Where a deed, will or other instrument purports to create any present or future interest in real or personal property in the heirs of the maker of the instrument, the heirs shall take, by purchase and not by descent, the interest that the instrument purports to create. The doctrine of worthier title and the rule of the common law that a grantor cannot create a limitation in favor of his own heirs are abolished.

The California provision might be a little clearer than the Illinois provision as it addresses both the English common law principle and the American common law modification. The Illinois statute changes the common law in terms that reflect a similarity between this rule and the Rule in *Shelley's Case*. The Illinois statute expressly describes "the heirs of O" as taking "by purchase," rather than "by descent." In other words, the Illinois legislature treats the phrase "the heirs of O" as words of purchase, rather than as words of limitation. Notice, however, that both statutes modify the common law. Consider:

Example 143: *O → B for life, then to the heirs of O.*

Under the Doctrine of Worthier Title, the phrase "heirs of O" described an interest O retained rather than an interest O created. Once the Doctrine of Worthier Title is eliminated, then the state of the title is: B has a life estate.The heirs of O have a contingent remainder in fee simple. O has a reversion. Although both the Illinois and California statutory approach modify the common law rule, would the result be the same in all cases to which these statutes might be applied? We'll let you ponder that question.

Let's review one more common law rule: the rule that preferred a joint tenancy rather than a tenancy in common.

Example 144: *O → A and B.*

At common law, A and B held jointly with right of survivorship. By virtue of the deed from O, the survivor of A and B will get a fee simple absolute in his sole name.

How might the following statute alter this common law preference?

> All interest in any real estate, either granted or bequeathed to two or more persons other than executors or trustees, shall be held in common, unless it be clearly expressed in said grant or bequest that it shall be held by both parties.

N.M. STAT. ANN. § 47-1-15. Under this statute, the common law presumption in favor of a joint tenancy, with right of survivorship, is replaced by a statutory preference for a tenancy in common. Accordingly, when A dies, his interest will pass to his heirs and devisees, not to B by right of survivorship. If B predeceases A, then his interest will likewise pass to his heirs and devisees, not to A by right of survivorship. However, by expressing his intent sufficiently, a grantor may create a joint tenancy, with right of survivorship.

On a related point, you should recall that in chapter six we mentioned that the tenancy by the entirety is recognized in about twenty states. In states where the tenancy by the entirety is not recognized, an attempt to create one might be construed as creating a joint tenancy, tenancy in common, or community property, depending upon each state's particular preference.

Let's review what we have learned. What follows is based on an original text prepared by Lynn Cianci Eby, University of New Mexico, Class of 1978, for the 1976-77 academic year. Subsequent revisions and expansions were made by the authors. The late Professor W. Garrett Flickinger of the University of New Mexico School of Law graciously reviewed some early drafts and made helpful comments. The section should serve as a review of the common law as well as an overview of modern statutory modifications.

D. REVIEW OUTLINE

1. The Present Estates at English Common Law (About 1700)

a. Fee Simple Absolute
Problem: O → *A and his heirs*
Facts: A is living
Answer: A — fee simple absolute

b. Fee Tail
Problem: O → *A and the heirs of her body*
Facts: A is living
Answer: A — fee tail
O — reversion

c. Life Estate
Problem: O → *A for life*
Facts: A is living
Answer: A — life estate
O — reversion

Life Estate *Pur Autre Vie*
Problem: O → *A for the life of B*
Facts: A and B are living
Answer: A — life estate *pur autre vie*
O — reversion

d. Fee Simple Determinable
Problem: O → *A and her heirs as long as the land is farmed*
Facts: A is living. The land is being farmed
Answer: A — fee simple determinable
O — possibility of reverter

e. Fee Simple on Condition Subsequent
Problem: O → *A and her heirs, but if the land ceases to be farmed, then O and his heirs may reenter and claim the land*
Facts: O and A are living. The land is being farmed
Answer: A — fee simple on condition subsequent
O — right of entry or power of termination

f. Fee Simple on Executory Limitation
Problem: O → *A and her heirs, but if B returns from Rome, to B and his heirs*
Facts: A and B are living. B is still in Rome
Answer: A — fee simple on executory limitation
B — shifting executory interest in fee simple

2. The Present Estates as Modified by American Statutes

In the course of the reception of the English common law in this country and in the course of statutory modification over the succeeding years, most of the present estates have remained intact. The exceptions lie:

a. in the preference for a life estate at common law in the absence of words of inheritance such as "and his heirs." Most jurisdictions now have a statute that provides a constructional preference in favor of a fee simple.

b. in some states, the fee simple determinable and the fee simple on condition subsequent are affected by limitations on the correlative future interests. *See* 4(c), *infra.*

c. in the modification of the fee tail by statute. States vary in the way in which the fee tail is treated. Some examples follow.

> CAL. CIV. CODE § 763
> ***Problem:***   *O → A and the heirs of her body*
> ***Facts:***   A is living
> ***Answer:***   A — fee simple
>   O — nothing
>
> 765 ILL.COMP. STAT. 5/6
> ***Problem:***   *O → A and the heirs of her body*
> ***Facts:***   A is living
> ***Answer:***   A — life estate
>   (1)   Children of A (if born) — vested remainder subject to open in fee simple
>   (2)   Children of A (if not born) — contingent remainder in fee simple. O has a reversion.

"The estate in fee simple defeasible is a present interest that terminates upon the happening of a stated event that might or might not occur. The subcategories historically known as the fee simple determinable, the fee simple subject to a condition subsequent, and the fee simple subject to an executory limitation are no longer recognized but are absorbed under the term fee simple defeasible."

RESTATEMENT (THIRD) PROPERTY § 24.3.

---

3. Future Interests at English Common Law (About 1700)

a. **Reversion**
    (1) **Following an Expirable Estate**
       Problem: *O → A while she lives*
       Facts: A is living
       Answer: A — life estate
                    O — reversion
       Problem: *O → A and the heirs of his body*
       Facts: A is living
       Answer: A — fee tail
                    O — reversion
    (2) **Following a Contingent Remainder**
       Problem: *O → A for life, then to B and his heirs if B survives A*
       Facts: A and B are living
       Answer: A — life estate
                    B — contingent remainder in fee simple

                                O — reversion

(3) Following Alternative Contingent Remainders

Problem: *O → A for life, then if B marries C, to B and his heirs, but if B does not marry C, then to C and his heirs*

Facts: A, B, and C are living

Answer: A — life estate

B — contingent remainder in fee simple

C — alternative contingent remainder in fee simple

O — reversion

(4) Preceding Springing Executory Interest

Problem: *O → A for life, and one day after A's funeral to B and his heirs*

Facts: O, A, and B are living

Answer: A — life estate

B — executory interest in fee simple

O — reversion (in fee simple on executory limitation)

> The material in parentheses after O's reversion frequently is omitted.

---

b. Possibility of Reverter

Problem: *O → A and his heirs until the wind no longer blows through the trees*

Facts: O and A are living

Answer: A — fee simple determinable

O — possibility of reverter

Problem: *O → A and her heirs while she remains married to H*

Facts: O, A, and H are living. A and H have married

Answer: A — fee simple determinable

O — possibility of reverter

c. Right of Entry (Power of Termination)

Problem: *O → A and his heirs, provided that if the land is not farmed, then O or his heirs may enter and reclaim the land*

Facts: O and A are living. The land is being farmed

Answer: A — fee simple on condition subsequent

O — right of entry (power of termination)

Problem: *O → A and her heirs on the condition that if the land is not used for library purposes, then O and his heirs may enter and reclaim the land*

Facts: O and A are living. The land is being used as a library

Answer: A — fee simple on condition subsequent

O — right of entry (power of termination)

d. Remainders

(1) Vested Remainder

Problem: *O → A for life, then to B and his heirs*

Facts: *A and B are living*

Answer: A — life estate
                   B — vested remainder in fee simple

> B's remainder is vested indefeasibly and not
> susceptible to any diminution or loss.

(2) **Contingent Remainder**
Problem: $O \rightarrow$ *A for life, then if B reaches age 21, to B and her heirs*
Facts: A and B are living. B is 15
Answer: A — life estate
                    B — contingent remainder in fee simple
                    O — reversion
Problem: $O \rightarrow$ *A for life, then if B survives A, to B and his heirs*
Facts: A and B are living
Answer: A — life estate
                    B — contingent remainder in fee simple
                    O — reversion

> Because the condition of survival must be satisfied before
> B can take the land, the remainder is contingent. A
> reversion always follows a contingent remainder in fee.

Problem: $O \rightarrow$ *A for life, then to A's youngest child living at the time of
                    A's death and that child's heirs*
Facts: A is living
Answer: A — life estate
                    Child of A — contingent remainder in fee simple
                    O — reversion

> The child's remainder is contingent because we cannot determine the
> youngest child living, if any, until after A dies. Suppose A is 92 and
> has two children, P and Q, and that Q is the younger. We cannot be
> sure that Q will be alive or that Q might not have a younger sibling
> when A dies. Thus, the remainder is contingent.

Problem: $O \rightarrow$ *A for life, then to whoever is dean of the Law School and
                    her heirs*
Facts: A is living
Answer: A — life estate
                    The person who is dean when A dies has a contingent remain-
                    der in fee simple
                    O — reversion

> The dean's remainder is contingent because the identity of the dean who will take the property is unknown until A dies. A reversion always follows a contingent remainder in fee.

(3) **Alternative Contingent Remainder**

Problem: *O → A for life, then if B has married W, to B and his heirs, but if B has not married W, then to C and his heirs*

Facts: A, B, W, and C are living. B has not married

Answer: A — life estate

B — contingent remainder in fee simple

C — alternative contingent remainder in fee simple

O — reversion (this always follows contingent remainders, even alternative contingent remainders)

(4) **Vested Remainder Subject to Divestment**

Problem: *A → B for life, then to C and her heirs, but if C dies without issue surviving her, then to D and his heirs*

Facts: B, C, and D are living

Answer: B — life estate

C — vested remainder subject to divestment in fee

D — shifting executory interest in fee simple

(5) **Vested Remainder Subject to Open**

Problem: *A → B for life, then to the children of B and their heirs*

Facts: B is alive and has two children, C and D

Answer: B — life estate

C & D — vested remainder subject to open in fee simple (this is sometimes also called a vested remainder subject to partial divestment)

e. **Executory Interests**

    (1) **Shifting Executory Interest**

Problem: *O → A and her heirs, but if A changes her name, then to B and his heirs*

Facts: A and B are living. A is known as "A"

Answer: A — fee simple on executory limitation

B — shifting executory interest in fee simple

    (2) **Springing Executory Interest**

Problem: *O → S and his heirs upon S's marriage*

Facts: O and S are living. S has not married

Answer: O — fee simple on executory limitation

S — springing executory interest in fee simple

> Here, O is keeping present possession of the land until S marries. S has only a future interest. This "freehold" to commence in the future could not be accomplished before 1536; after 1536 it could be accomplished by creating an executory interest.

4. Future Interests as Modified by American Statutes

In the course of the reception of English common law and the subsequent statutory modification, the law of future interests has been modified, generally, as follows:

a.   The inalienable interests and interests that were not devisable tend to become freely alienable. *See, e.g.*, N.M. Stat. Ann. § 47-1-4; N.D. Cent. Code § 47-02-18.

b.   The reversion after a fee tail disappears in those jurisdictions in which the fee tail is replaced by a fee simple. For example,

Problem: O →   *A and the heirs of his body*

Facts: A is living

Cal. Civ. Code § 763:

Answer: A — fee simple

Compare, on the other hand,765 Ill. Comp. Stat. 5/6:

Answer: A — life estate

Children of A (if born) — vested remainder subject to open in fee simple.

Children of A (if not born) — contingent remainder in fee simple. In this case, O has a reversion.

c.   In some jurisdictions statutes may limit the duration of a possibility of reverter, a right of entry, or both.

"A future interest is either a reversion or a remainder. A future interest is a reversion if it was retained by the transferor. A future interest is a remainder if it was created in a transferee."
RESTATEMENT (THIRD) PROPERTY § 25.2.

"A future interest is either contingent or vested. A future interest is contingent if it might not take effect in possession or enjoyment. A future interest is vested if it is certain to take effect in possession or enjoyment. A contingent or a vested future interest may additionally be classified according to the present interest into which the future interest will ripen once and if it takes effect in possession or enjoyment — as a fee simple absolute (or absolute ownership), a fee simple defeasible, a life estate, or a term of years."
Id. § 25.3.

Section 25.2 simplifies the classification of future interests into two categories — reversions or remainders — and abolishes the distinction between remainders, executory interests, reversions, possibilities of reverter, and rights of entry. Section 25.3 abolishes the previous vesting terms and simplifies them into two categories — contingent or vested. Classifying future interests as being subject to open applies to both vested and contingent interests.
Id. § 25.4

d.   A number of jurisdictions have enacted statutory modifications of the RAP.

Problem: $O \rightarrow$ *A and his heirs, but if the land is used for a farm, then to B and his heirs*

Facts: O, A, and B are living

At English common Law:

Answer: A — fee simple
              O — nothing
              B — nothing

The gift to B is an executory interest which will not "vest" for purposes of the RAP until the time comes for B or his successors to take possession. That time may come too remotely; i.e., more than 21 years after O, A and B die. Therefore, B's interest is void under the RAP.

Problem: $O \rightarrow$ *A and his heirs, but if the land is used for a farm during A's lifetime, then to B for life*

Facts: O, A, and B are living

At English common law:

Answer: A — fee simple on executory limitation
B — executory interest in a life estate
O — reversion

> B's interest, being a life estate, will come into possession, if at all, within B's own lifetime. Therefore, B's interest does not violate the RAP.

Problem: $O \rightarrow$ *A and his heirs, but if the land is used for a farm, then to B and his heirs if B is then living*

Facts: O, A, and B are living

At English common law:

Answer: A — fee simple on executory limitation
B — executory interest in fee
O — nothing

> By the terms of the grant, B's interest will come into possession or fail during his lifetime. The presence of the express condition of survival saves B's grant from violating the RAP.

By statute, such as, *e.g.*, CAL. CIV. CODE §§ 21200, 21201 and 765 ILL. COMP. STAT. 305/2, the common law may have been superseded or modified. Although these statutes do not appear to change the basic principles illustrated by these examples, you should consider the combined effect of such statutes as CAL. CIV. CODE §§ 885.010, .030, and CAL. PROB. CODE § 21205.

The Restatement (Third) of Property does not use traditional lives in being, plus 21 years. Instead, typically, the measuring lives are the two generations younger than the transferor. The distinction between vested and contingent remainders is no longer significant because a new termination rule is substituted for the concept of remoteness in vesting, which applies only to contingent remainders. The 21-year period is also abolished. If the generations-based perpetuity period has expired, but a beneficiary is to receive a share upon reaching a specific age and if that beneficiary is younger than the earlier of the specified age or age 30, then that share may be retained in trust until the beneficiary reaches, or dies before reaching, the earlier of the specified age or age 30. RESTATEMENT (THIRD) PROPERTY §§ 27.1 and 26.6. The Restatement also excludes commercial transactions and donations for charitable purposes from the perpetuities rule. *Id.* at § 27.3.

The Restatement (Second) of Property, § 1.3, adopted a "wait and see" rule, which does not void a future interest that *actually* vests for RAP purposes within the RAP period.

e. Some jurisdictions have enacted other specific restrictions on the control a grantor may exercise on his grantees.

f. The doctrine of destructibility of contingent remainders has been modified by statute.

Problem: O → *A for life, then to the first son of A who reaches age 21 and his heirs*

Facts: (i) O and A are living. A has a son, S, age 10
(ii) A dies when S is 16

At English common law:

Answer: (i) A — life estate

First son who reaches age 21 — contingent remainder in fee simple

O — reversion

(ii) O — fee simple absolute

By statute, such as, *e.g.*, CAL. CIV. CODE §§ 741, 742, 765 ILL. COMP. STAT. 340/1, MINN. STAT. ANN. § 500.15 and N.D. CENT. CODE § 47-02-32:

Answer: (i) A — life estate

First son who reaches age 21 — contingent remainder in fee simple

O — reversion

(ii) O — fee simple on executory limitation

First son who reaches age 21 — springing executory interest in fee simple

> S will take if and when he becomes 21. If S does not reach 21, but A has another son who does reach 21, then that son will take.

5. Selected Rules of Law and Rules of Construction

a. **The Rule in** *Shelley's Case*
   Problem: O → B for life, then to C and her heirs if C survives B, but if she does not survive B, then to the heirs of B
   Facts: B and C are living
   At English common law:
   Answer: B — life estate
                C — contingent remainder in fee simple
                B — alternative contingent remainder in fee simple
                O — reversion

   By statute, such as, *e.g.*, CAL. CIV. CODE § 779, 765 ILL. COMP. STAT. 345/1, MINN. STAT. ANN. § 500.14(4), N.M. STAT. ANN. § 47-1-19 and N.D. CENT. CODE § 47-04-20:
   Answer: B — life estate
                C — contingent remainder in fee simple
                Heirs of B — alternative contingent remainder in fee simple
                O — reversion

b. **Doctrine of Worthier Title**
   Problem: O → B for life, then to the heirs of O
   Facts: O and B are living
   At English common law:
   Answer: B — life estate
                O — reversion

   > O's heirs may inherit the estate by descent upon O's death intestate.

   By statute, such as, *e.g.*, CAL. PROB. CODE § 21108 and 765 ILL. COMP. STAT. 350/1:
   Answer: B — life estate
                Heirs of O — contingent remainder in fee simple
                O — reversion

c. **Doctrine of** *Edwards v. Hammond*
   Problem: O → A for life, then to B and his heirs if B reaches age 21, and if B fails to reach age 21, to C and his heirs
   Facts: O, A, and B are living. B is 19
   At English common law:
   Answer: A — life estate
                B — vested remainder subject to divestment, in fee

C — executory interest in fee

> Generally, this constructional preference has not been changed by statute, but whether a modern court would adhere to it is hard to say. The doctrine was cited and discussed in *Shackley v. Homer*, 127 N.W. 145, 155 (Neb. 1910).

d. **Concurrent Estates**
   Problem: O → *A and B and their heirs*
   Facts: (1)   O, A, and B are living
                 (2)   A dies, leaving as his only heir X
   At English common law:
   Answer: (1)   A and B — fee simple as joint tenants
                 (2)   B — fee simple absolute
   By statute, such as, *e.g.*, Cal. Civ. Code § 686, 765 Ill. Comp. Stat. 1005/1, Minn. Stat. Ann. § 500.19(2), N.M. Stat. Ann. § 47-1-15 and N.D. Cent. Code § 47-02-08:
   Answer: (1)   A and B — fee simple as tenants in common
                 (2)   X and B — fee simple as tenants in common

e. **Rule in *Wild's Case***
   Problem: O → *A and his children.* Assume the conveyance is by will.
   Facts: (1)   O is dead. A is living and has no children.
                 (2)   O is dead. A is living and has one child, C.
   At English common law:
   Answer: (1)   A has a fee tail.
                 (2)   A and C have a fee simple as joint tenants.

(1) illustrates the first resolution in *Wild's Case* and represents a constructional preference for a fee tail to accomplish the testator's intent.

(2) illustrates a class gift and the common law constructional preference for a joint tenancy.

The Rule in *Wild's Case* generally has not been changed by statute. The case results are too diverse to discuss here.

A common modern result in (1) is that A is recognized as having a life estate and there is a contingent remainder in A's unborn children. O's successors have a reversion. A common modern result in (2) is that A and C are recognized as having a fee simple as tenants in common. Both results seem consistent with the statutory modifications you have learned.

E.   A FINAL PROBLEM AND ANSWER: "DIE WITHOUT ISSUE"

> **Problem**: $O \rightarrow$ *A and her heirs, but if A dies without issue, then to B and his*
> *heirs*
>
> **Facts**:   O, A, and B are living

At common law, the phrase "die without issue" was interpreted as meaning indefinite failure of issue, with the result that A in this example is understood to have a fee tail. B has a vested remainder in fee simple.

Suppose this conveyance takes place in a jurisdiction that has the following statute:

> A condition in a transfer of a present or future interest that refers to a person's death "with" or "without" issue, or to a person's "having" or "leaving" issue or no issue, or a condition based on words of similar import, is construed to refer to that person's being dead at the time the transfer takes effect in enjoyment and to that person either having or not having, as the case may be, issue who are alive at the time of enjoyment.

See CAL. PROB. CODE § 21112.

What did the legislature intend by this statute? When this statute is applied to the problem, what is the state of the title? If you aren't sure, then read MINN. STAT. ANN. § 500.14(1), N.M. STAT. ANN. § 47-1-18 and N.D. CENT. CODE § 47-09-14, in the statutory appendix.

> **Answer:**   A —
> B —
> O —

Answer to Final Problem

Problem: $O \rightarrow$ *A and his heirs, but if A dies without issue, then to B and his heirs.*
CAL. PROB. CODE § 21112:

Answer: A — fee simple on executory limitation
               B — executory interest in fee
               O — nothing

By statute in many states, the phrase "dies without issue" is to be interpreted or construed as meaning "definite" failure of issue. That is to say, in the example, B is viewed as being given a gift that will take effect only if, at A's death, A is not survived by issue. If A is survived by issue at his death, then A's estate includes a fee simple absolute. That fee will pass pursuant to A's will or, if A dies without a will, to A's heirs under the laws of intestate succession.

> In Illinois, the answer probably would be the same in that the existing case law seems to permit the common law construction to be overcome with only slight evidence of contrary intent. *See* John A. Borron, Jr., *Simes & Smith, The Law of Future Interests* § 527 & n. 10 (3d ed. 2011); *see also Strain v. Sweeney*, 163 Ill. 603 (1896), in which the Illinois court applied the "definite" failure of issue construction as a matter of following the testator's implied intent.

> The appendices provide two additional problem sets. Answer the set in Appendix I by applying common law. Answer the set in Appendix II by first applying the common law and then by applying the statutory schemes represented in Appendix III. Answers are included for both sets of problems.

Appendix I

PROBLEMS WITH ANSWERS

Part I

Give the state of the title in 1530.

1. *O →* *A for life, then if B marries C, to B and his heirs.*

   a. Everyone is alive. B is unmarried.

      A has a life estate. B has a contingent remainder in fee. O has a reversion.

   b. *A → X.*

      X has a life estate *pur autre vie.* The rest is unchanged.

   c. *O → X.*

      Through application of the doctrine of merger, X has a fee simple.

2. Same Grant.

   a. *A → X.*

      X has a life estate *pur autre vie.* B has a contingent remainder in fee. O has a reversion.

   b. B marries C.

      X has a life estate *pur autre vie.* B has a vested remainder in fee simple. O has nothing.

3. *O →* *A for life, then to A's widow for life.*

   A has a life estate. Whoever becomes A's widow, if anyone does, has a contingent remainder for life. O has a reversion.

4. *O →* *A for life, then to A's present wife for life.*

   A has a life estate. If A has a "present wife," which is a legitimate assumption, given O's words, A's wife has a vested remainder for life. O has a reversion.

5. *O →* *A for life, then to W for life.*

A has a life estate. W has a vested remainder for life. O has a reversion.

6.   *O → A for life, then to A's wife for life.*

A has a life estate. Assuming A is unmarried, which is our convention, then A's wife, if any, has a contingent remainder for life. O has a reversion.

The difference between Problem 4 and Problem 6 is really an artificial one based on exam-taking convention.

In the real world, the question would be, "What did O intend?"

In Problem 6, if A was actually married at the time of the grant, then the wife would have a vested remainder for life. (To see why it matters whether her remainder is vested or contingent, see Problem 1(c) above.)

In Problem 4, if A was unmarried at the time of the grant, then we, and the court, would be confused about what O meant. In that event, we guess that the court would turn Problem 4 into Problem 6.

---

7.   *O → A for life, then to A's widow for life, then to B and his heirs.*

A has a life estate. The woman, if any, who becomes A's widow has a contingent remainder for life. B has a vested remainder in fee. O has nothing.

8.   *O → A for life, then to A's children and their heirs.*

a.   O and A are alive. A has no children.

A has a life estate. The nonexistent children have a contingent remainder in fee. O has a reversion.

b.   S is born.

A has a life estate. S has a vested remainder subject to open in fee. O has nothing.

c.   D is born.

No change, except that D now shares in the vested remainder subject to open in fee.

d.   A dies.

The class closes naturally. S and D share a fee simple as joint tenants with right of survivorship.

9.   *O →   A for life, then to A's grandchildren and their heirs.*

   a.   O and A are alive. A has no grandchildren.

           A has a life estate The grandchildren have a contingent remainder in fee. O has a reversion.

   b.   GS is born.

           A has a life estate. GS has a vested remainder subject to open in fee simple. O has nothing.

   c.   GD is born.

           No change, except that GD now shares the vested remainder subject to open with GS.

   d.   A dies.

           "Naturally" the class is still open, because more grandchildren could be born. But the "Rule of Convenience" closes the class "artificially." GS and GD share a fee simple as joint tenants with right of survivorship.

10.   *O →   A for life, then to B's children for life.*

   Assuming no children, as is our convention, unless told otherwise, A has a life estate. B's future children, if any, have a contingent remainder for their collective lives. O has a reversion. If B has many children before A dies, then those childres alive at A's death will take, collectively, a life estate, which will endure until the last child dies.

11.   *O →   A for life, then to B's heirs.*

   A has a life estate. Assuming B is alive, which is our convention, B's heirs have a contingent remainder in fee. The phrase "to B's heirs" is read "to B's heir and his heirs." O has a reversion. Note that B must be dead when A dies. If B is alive when A dies, then B would have no heirs.

12.   *O →   A for life, then to A's widow for life, then to A's grandchildren and their heirs.*

   A has a life estate. A's widow has a contingent remainder for life. The grandchildren have a contingent remainder in fee. O has a reversion. We are using the convention that A is alive and has no children, since we're not told otherwise. **But, see the box, below.**

   Suppose A is married to W. No change, as we won't know if W will be the "widow" until A dies.

   Suppose a grandchild GD is born. Now A has a life estate, the contingent remainder is the same, and GD has a vested remainder subject to open in fee. O has nothing.

This vested remainder might stay open for a long time. It will not close "naturally" until the death of the last of A's children. Because A is still alive, A might have more children, and we cannot even be sure that all of A's children — let alone the **grandchildren** — have been born. Even with the "Rule of Convenience," the remainder will not close until distribution is required, at the death of A's "widow," assuming a widow exists at A's death. The common law was willing to imagine that the woman who will eventually become A's widow might herself not be born at the *Tg*. Thus, we cannot be **certain** that the remainder will close until after the deaths of people who may not even be born at the *Tg*.

The RAP will evolve to destroy this very patient remainder because the courts could not be certain that A would not marry a woman not born at the *Tg* who might survive all lives in being at the *Tg* for more than 21 years. In 1700, then, the state of the title is: A has a life estate. A's widow has a contingent remainder for life. O has a reversion. This works to control O's "dead hand," because relatively "soon" the reversion will go to O's heirs or assigns who then will control the disposition of the property. They can send it to A's grandchildren if they wish, but the dead O will have no say in the matter.

If GD was alive at the *Tg*, RAP would even destroy the vested remainder subject to open, as it must be able to vest in all members of the class within the RAP period. Today, however, some states would not apply the RAP if GD was alive at the *Tg*.

Part II

Give the state of the title in 1550:

1. *O → A and his heirs, but if the land is ever used for commercial purposes, then O may re-enter and claim the land.*

    A has a fee simple on condition subsequent. O has a right of entry.

2. *O → A and his heirs as long as the land is not used for commercial purposes.*

    A has a fee simple determinable. O has a possibility of reverter.

3. *O → A and his heirs, but if the land is ever used for commercial purposes, then to B and his heirs.*

    A has a fee simple on executory limitation. B has a shifting executory interest in fee. O has nothing.

4. *O → A and his heirs, then to B and his heirs.*

    A has a fee simple absolute. B and O have nothing.

5. $O \rightarrow$ *A for life, and if B is still solvent one year after A's death, to B and his heirs.*

     A has a life estate. B has a springing executory interest in fee. O has a reversion.

6. $O \rightarrow$ *A for life, then, if B is still solvent, to B and his heirs.*

     A has a life estate. B has a contingent remainder in fee simple. O has a reversion.

7. $O \rightarrow$ *A for life, then, if B is still solvent, to B and his heirs.*

     A has a life estate. B has a vested remainder subject to divestment in fee simple.

     C has a shifting executory interest in fee simple. O has nothing. You may call B's interest a vested remainder in fee simple on executory limitation.

8. $O \rightarrow$ *A for life, then to B and his heirs as long as B and his heirs remain solvent, but if any of them become insolvent, to C and his heirs.*

     A has a life estate. B has a vested remainder subject to divestment in fee simple. C has a shifting executory interest in fee. O has nothing. You may call B's interest a vested remainder in fee simple on executory limitation.

9. $O \rightarrow$ *A for life, then to B and his heirs if B is solvent, but if B is insolvent, to C and his heirs.*

     A has a life estate. B has a contingent remainder in fee simple. C has an alternative contingent remainder in fee. O has a reversion.

10. $O \rightarrow$ *A for life, but if A leaves the Church, to the Church forever.*

     A has a life estate subject to an executory interest. The Church has a shifting executory interest in fee. O has a reversion.

11. $O \rightarrow$ *A for life, then to B and his heirs, but if B uses the land for commercial purposes, to C and his heirs.*

     A has a life estate. B has a vested remainder in fee simple on executory limitation. C has a shifting executory interest in fee. O has nothing.

12. $O \rightarrow$ *A for life, then to B and his heirs, but if the land is used for commercial purposes, to C and his heirs.*

     Except for the application of the Rule against Perpetuities, this grant is the same as the previous one.

13. $O \rightarrow$ *A for life, then to B and his heirs, but if A becomes a priest, to the Church forever.*

14. $O \rightarrow$ *A for life, then to B and his heirs, but if B becomes a priest, to the Church forever.*

15. $O \rightarrow$ *A for life, then to B and his heirs, but if B uses the land for commercial purposes, then to the Church forever.*

The "standard" classification of the state of the title in Problems 13 and 14 is exactly the same. A has a life estate. B has a vested remainder subject to divestment in fee simple. The Church has a shifting executory interest in fee. O has nothing.

The "advanced" classification would make B's interest in Problem 13 a vested remainder subject to divestment in fee simple, because B's interest can be lost only during A's life, while B's interest is still a non-possessory remainder. In Problem 15 (which is similar to Problem 11), B's interest is a vested remainder in fee simple on executory limitation, because B cannot lose his interest in Blackacre until after he comes into possession. B's interest in Problem 14 could be lost either before or after he takes possession and could be called, most formally, a vested remainder subject to divestment in fee simple on executory limitation, to indicate that B could lose his interest either before or after taking possession. Most courts don't have the patience for such a long term and would call it a vested remainder subject to divestment in fee simple.

What would be the state of the title for the grants in Part II in 1700, *i.e.*, after the Rule Against Perpetuities is in place?

The RAP would void the executory interest in Examples 3, 8, and 12.

Look carefully at Examples 3, 8, and 12. In each, the owner of the executory interest may have to wait, broadly speaking, a long time to come into possession: In Grants 3 and 12, until the land is used for commercial purposes. In Grant 8, until any one of B's descendants goes broke.

Of course, either of those eventualities **might** happen in the next week or the next year after **Tg**. But the common law RAP does not wait to see how the world actually turns out. Rather, the validity of the grant must be tested under the RAP at the **Tg**. The RAP requires **certainty** that all interests, subject to the RAP, will vest within the period. No matter what period might have been chosen, no such certainty exists for the conditions in grants 3, 8, and 12. Those conditions might still be around and unmet centuries from now. The Statute of Uses may have accepted such extreme flexibility, but the courts, in crafting the RAP, were not willing to give O the power to leave the state of the title so uncertain for centuries, not knowing in whom the interests might vest. So, the RAP destroys the executory interests in grants 3, 8, and 12.

Determine the state of the title by using the "cross out rule."

Grant 3: A has a fee simple absolute. No one else has anything.

Grant 8: A has a life estate. B has a vested remainder in fee simple determinable. O has a possibility of reverter.

Grant 12: A has a life estate. B has a vested remainder in fee simple absolute.

Appendix II

PROBLEMS WITH ANSWERS

Instructions:

In each of the hypotheticals, give the state of the title for each of the fact situations as it would exist in England in 1700, and then give the state of the title based on the statutes for one of the jurisdictions represented in Appendix III. In each case, the grantor had a fee simple absolute. For each problem, treat each set of fact situations as cumulative.

1. $O \rightarrow$ *A for life, remainder to B and his heirs if B marries C.*

    (a) O, A, B, and C are living. B has not married.

    (b) B marries C.

    (c) O conveys all his interest to A and her heirs.

2. $O \rightarrow$ *A for life, then if B has reached age 21, to B and his heirs.*

    (a) O, A, and B are all alive. B is 16.

    (b) A dies one year later.

3. $O \rightarrow$ *A for life, then to A's heirs if A survives B.*

    (a) O, A, and B are living.

4. $O \rightarrow$ *B for life, and one year after B's death to the heirs of B.*

    (a) O and B are living.

5. $O \rightarrow$ *A for life, remainder to B and her heirs if B marries C, and if B does not marry C, to D and his heirs.*

    (a) O, A, B, C, and D are living. B has not married.

    (b) B marries C.

    (c) A renounces her life estate.

6. $O \rightarrow$ *H for life, then to C and his heirs so long as liquor is not sold on the premises.*

    (a) O, H, and C are living.

7.   *O →*   *A for life, then to B and the heirs of his body.*

   (a)   O, A, and B are living.

8.   *O →*   *A.*

   (a)   O and A are living.

9.   *O →*   *A for life, then to A's children and their heirs.*

   (a)   O and A are living. A has no children.

   (b)   One child, C, is born to A.

10.   *O →*   *A for life, then to B's heirs.*

   (a)   O and A are living.

11.   *O →*   *A until she dies.*

   (a)   O and A are living.

12.   *O →*   *A and the heirs of his body, then to the children of B and their heirs.*

   (a)   O, A, and B are living. A and B have no children. A is married, and B is married.

   (b)   A has a child, C.

   (c)   B has a child, D.

   (d)   B dies.

   (e)   A dies with a will leaving all his property to F and his heirs.

13.   *O →*   *C for life, remainder to B for life, then to the heirs of B.*

   (a)   O, B, and C are all alive.

14.   *O →*   *B for life, remainder to C for life, then to the heirs of B.*

   (a)   O, B, and C are all alive.

   (b)   C dies.

15.   *O →*   *A and his heirs upon A's marriage.*

   (a)   O and A are living. A is unmarried.

16.　　$O \rightarrow$　*B for life, then to C for life, remainder to the heirs of C.*

　　(a)　　B and C are living.

17.　　$O \rightarrow$　*A for life as long as A remains Catholic, then to B and his heirs.*

　　(a)　　A and B are living. A is Catholic.

　　(b)　　A dies.

18.　　$O \rightarrow$　*A for life, then to B and his heirs as long as the land is farmed.*

　　(a)　　O, A, and B are living. The land is being farmed.

19.　　$O \rightarrow$　*A for life, then to A's firstborn child and that child's heirs.*

　　(a)　　O and A are living. A has no children.

　　(b)　　A child is born to A.

20.　　$O \rightarrow$　*A for life, then to B and his heirs, but if B does not marry, then to C and his heirs.*

　　(a)　　A, B, and C are living. B is unmarried.

21.　　$O \rightarrow$　*A for life thirty years from the date of this conveyance.*

　　(a)　　O and A are living.

　　(b)　　A dies 29 years later, leaving B as his only heir.

　　(c)　　One year passes.

22.　　$O \rightarrow$　*A for life, then to B for life, then if C has married W, to C and his heirs.*

　　(a)　　O, A, B, C, and W are living. C has not married.

23.　　$O \rightarrow$　*B for life, then if C marries D, to C and her heirs unless C serves liquor on the premises, in which case to E and his heirs.*

　　(a)　　O, B, C, D, and E are living. C is unmarried.

24.　　$O \rightarrow$　*B for life, and after B's death, to the heirs of B.*

　　(a)　　O and B are living.

25.　　$O \rightarrow$　*A for life, then to B and his heirs, but if B dies younger than age 21, then to C and his heirs.*

(a)   O, A, B, and C are living. B is 19.

26.   *O → A for life, then to B and his heirs, but if B dies without children surviving him, then to C and his heirs.*

(a)   O, A, B, and C are living. B has five children.

27.   *O → A and his heirs, but if A should marry B, to C and his heirs.*

(a)   A, B, and C are living. A has not married B.

28.   *O → B for life or until she remarries, then to the heirs of B.*

(a)   The conveyance is in O's will. O is dead. B, O's widow, is living, and has not remarried

29.   *O → A for life, then to W for life, then if Z is still alive, to C for life, otherwise to B and his heirs.*

(a)   O, A, W, Z, C, and B are living.

30.   *O → B for life, remainder to such of B's children as survive B and their heirs.*

(a)   O and B are living. B has no children.

(b)   Triplets, E, F, and G, are born to B.

31.   *O → A for life, then to B's heir and his heirs.*

(a)   O, A, and B are living.

32.   *O → A for life, remainder to B and his heirs, but if B fails to live to 50, then to C and his heirs.*

(a)   A, B, and C are living. B is 30.

33.   *O → W for life, then to A and his heirs if A survives W, and if A fails to survive W, then to B and his heirs.*

(a)   O, W, A, and B are all living.

(b)   B dies, without a will, leaving D as his heir.

(c)   W dies.

(d)   A dies, without a will, leaving E as his heir.

34.   *O → A for life, then if B has married C, to B and his heirs.*

(a)   O, A, B, and C are living. B has not married.

35. *O → A for life, then to B and her heirs if B has married C.*

(a)   O, A, B, and C are living. B has not married.

36. *O → A for life, then if B marries C, to B and her heirs.*

(a)   O, A, B, and C are living. B has not married.

37. *O → A for life, and one year after A's death to B and her heirs.*

(a)   O, A, and B are living.

38. *O → A for life, then to B and his heirs if B writes a complete biography of A's life.*

(a)   O, A, and B are living.

39. *O → A for life, then to B and her heirs after one year.*

(a)   O, A, and B are living.

ANSWER KEY

1. ***Problem:***   *O → A for life, remainder to B and his heirs if B marries C.*

    Facts: (a)   O, A, B, and C are living. B has not married.

                       (b)   B marries C.

                       (c)   O conveys all his interest to A and her heirs.

    Answer: **Common Law** and **California, Illinois, Minnesota, New Mexico & North Dakota**

                       (a)   A — life estate

                               B — contingent remainder in fee simple

                               O — reversion

                       (b)   A — life estate

                               B — vested remainder in fee simple

                       (c)   No change (O has no reversion to convey to A)

2. ***Problem:***   *O → A for life, then if B has reached age 21, to B and his heirs.*

Facts: (a)   O, A, and B are all alive. B is 16.

        (b)   A dies one year later.

Answer: **Common Law**

        (a)   A — life estate

                B — contingent remainder in fee simple

                O — reversion

        (b)   O — fee simple (B's contingent remainder is destroyed because the supporting estate has expired before his remainder vested)

Answer: **California** (CAL. CIV. CODE § 742)

        Illinois (765 ILL. COMP. STAT. 340/1)

        Minnesota (MINN. STAT. ANN. § 500.15(3))

        North Dakota (N.D. CENT. CODE § 47-02-32)

        (a)   A — life estate

                B — contingent remainder in fee simple

                O — reversion

        (b)   O — fee simple on executory limitation

                B — springing executory interest in fee simple

> Because the doctrine of destructibility of contingent remainders has been abolished, in this example, B's interest is not destroyed. For an illustration of a case abolishing the doctrine, see *ABO Petroleum Corp. v. Amstutz*, 93 N.M. 332, 600 P.2d 278 (1979).

3.   *Problem:*   *O → A for life, then to A's heirs if A survives B.*

        Facts: O, A, and B are living.

        Answer: **Common Law**

A — life estate and contingent remainder in fee simple

O — reversion

The Rule in *Shelley's Case* gives A the remainder, not the heirs of A.
Merger does not apply because A's remainder is not vested. Merger only
occurs when both interests are vested.

Answer: **California** (CAL. CIV. CODE § 779)

Illinois (765 ILL. COMP. STAT. 345/1)

Minnesota (MINN. STAT. ANN. § 500.14(4))

New Mexico (N.M. STAT. ANN. § 47-1-19)

North Dakota (N.D. CENT. CODE § 47-04-20)

A — life estate

Heirs of A — contingent remainder in fee simple

O — reversion

Because the Rule in *Shelley's Case* has been abolished, the heirs of A will take
the remainder.

---

4.   *Problem:*   O → *B for life, and one year after B's death to the heirs of B.*

    Facts: O and B are living.

    Answer: **Common Law** and **California, Illinois, Minnesota, New Mexico & North Dakota**

B — life estate

O — reversion in fee simple on executory limitation

Heirs of B — springing executory interest in fee simple

> The Rule in *Shelley's Case* does not apply to executory interests, only to remainders.

5. **Problem:** $O \rightarrow$ *A for life, remainder to B and her heirs if B marries C, and if B does not marry C, to D and his heirs.*

    Facts: (a)   O, A, B, C, and D are living. B has not married.

    (b)   B marries C.

    (c)   A renounces her life estate.

    Answer: **Common Law** and **California, Illinois, Minnesota, New Mexico & North Dakota**

    (a)   A — life estate

    B — contingent remainder in fee simple

    D — alternative contingent remainder in fee simple

    O — reversion

    (b)   A — life estate

    B — vested remainder in fee simple

    (c)   B — fee simple absolute

> A's renunciation has the same effect as her death would have had. Here, B had a vested remainder, so there is no question of destruction.

6. **Problem:** $O \rightarrow$ *H for life, then to C and his heirs so long as liquor is not sold on the premises.*

    Facts: O, H, and C are living.

    Answer: **Common Law** and **Illinois, Minnesota, New Mexico & North Dakota**

    H — life estate

C — vested remainder in fee simple determinable

O — possibility of reverter

California (CAL. CIV. CODE § 885.020)

H — life estate

C — vested remainder in fee simple subject to a restriction in the form of a condition subsequent

O — power of termination

MINN. STAT. ANN. § 500.20(1) provides that a limitation must not be or become merely nominal, and § 500.20(1) provides that the condition may be disregarded 30 years after its creation, § 500.20(2). *Cf.* CAL. CIV. CODE § 885.030, which provides expiration dates for powers of termination.

7. *Problem:*   *O → A for life, then to B and the heirs of his body.*

    Facts: O, A, and B are living.

    Answer: **Common Law**

                     A — life estate

                     B — vested remainder in fee tail

                     O — reversion

    Answer: **California** (CAL. CIV. CODE § 763)

                     Minnesota (MINN. STAT. ANN. §§ 500.03)

                     North Dakota (N.D. CENT. CODE § 47-04-05)

                     A — life estate

                     B — vested remainder in fee simple

                     O — nothing

> The fee tail has been abolished under these statutes and converted into a fee simple.

Answer: **Illinois** (765 ILL. COMP. STAT. 5/6)

New Mexico (N.M. STAT. ANN. § 47-1-17)

A — life estate

B — vested remainder in a life estate

Children of B (if born) — vested remainder subject to open, in fee simple

Children of B (if not born) — contingent remainder in fee simple

O — reversion

> The fee tail has been abolished under these statutes and converted into a life estate and remainder in fee.

8.   *Problem:* $O \rightarrow$ A.

Facts: O and A are living.

Answer: **Common Law**

A — life estate

O — reversion

California (CAL. CIV. CODE § 1105)

Illinois (765 ILL. COMP. STAT. 5/13)

Minnesota (MINN. STAT. ANN. § 500.02)

New Mexico (N.M. STAT. ANN. § 47-1-33)

North Dakota (N.D. CENT. CODE § 47-10-13)

A — fee simple

> The preferred estate at modern law is the fee simple absolute. Thus, words of inheritance are unnecessary to create a fee simple absolute.

9. **Problem:**   *O → A for life, then to A's children and their heirs.*

    Facts: (a)   O and A are living. A has no children.

    (b)   One child, C, is born to A.

    Answer: **Common Law and California, Illinois, Minnesota, New Mexico & North Dakota**

    (a)   A — life estate

    Children of A — contingent remainder in fee simple

    O — reversion

    (b)   A — life estate

    C — vested remainder subject to open in fee simple

10. **Problem:**   *O → A for life, then to B's heirs.*

    Facts: O, A, and B are living.

    Answer: **Common Law and California, Illinois, Minnesota, New Mexico & North Dakota**

    A — life estate

    Heirs of B — contingent remainder in fee simple

    O — reversion

> The phrase "to B's heirs" is read "to B's heir and his heirs." Even if B has children, the remainder is contingent because no one knows who B's heirs will be until B dies. Heirs are determined at the time of B's death.
>
> The Rule in *Shelley's Case* does not apply because the grant of a remainder is not to the heirs of the life tenant.

11. ***Problem:*** $O \rightarrow$ A until she dies.

     Facts: O and A are living.

     Answer: **Common Law** and **California, Illinois, Minnesota, New Mexico & North Dakota**

                          A — life estate

                          O — reversion

12. ***Problem:*** $O \rightarrow$ *A and the heirs of his body, then to the children of B and their heirs.*

     Facts: (a)   O, A, and B are living. A and B have no children. A is married, and B is married.

                    (b)   A has a child, C.

                    (c)   B has a child, D.

                    (d)   B dies.

                    (e)   A dies with a will leaving all his property to F and his heirs.

     Answer: **Common Law**

                    (a)   A — fee tail

                          Children of B — contingent remainder in fee simple

                          O — reversion

                    (b)   no change

                    (c)   A — fee tail

                          D — vested remainder subject to open in fee simple

(d)   A — fee tail

       D — vested remainder in fee simple (no longer subject to open)

(e)   C — fee tail

       D — vested remainder in fee simple

Answer: **California** (CAL. CIV. CODE §§ 763, 764)

       North Dakota (N.D. CENT. CODE §§ 47-04-05, 06)

(a)   A — fee simple on executory limitation

       Children of B — executory interest in fee

(b)   no change

(c)   A — fee simple on executory limitation

       D — executory interest in fee

(d)   A — fee simple on executory limitation

       D — executory interest in fee

(e)   F — fee simple

This future interest is created by statute. We substituted the common law terms that seem most consistent with the statutory description.

Answer: **Illinois** (765 ILL. COMP. STAT. 5/6)

       New Mexico (N.M. STAT. ANN. § 47-1-17)

(a)   A — life estate

       Children of A — contingent remainder in fee simple

       Children of B — alternative contingent remainder in fee simple

       O — reversion

(b)   A — life estate

C — vested remainder subject to open in fee simple

(c)   no change

(d)   no change

(e)   C — fee simple

Answer: **Minnesota** (Minn. Stat. Ann. §§ 500.03, 04)

(a)   A — fee simple absolute

(b)   no change

(c)   no change

(d)   no change

(e)   F — fee simple absolute

But see Buel v. Southwick, 70 N.Y. 581 (1877) (holding that a similar statute, clear on its face, was held not to destroy a remainder following the "fee tail").

---

13.   *Problem:*   *O → C for life, remainder to B for life, then to the heirs of B.*

Facts: (a)   O, B, and C are all alive.

Answer: **Common Law**

C — life estate

B — vested remainder in fee simple

O — nothing

The Rule in Shelley's Case vests the second remainder in B. The two vested remainders then merge.

Answer: **California** (Cal. Civ. Code § 779)

Illinois (765 Ill. Comp. Stat. 345/1)

Minnesota (Minn. Stat. Ann. § 500.14(4))

New Mexico (N.M. Stat. Ann. § 47-1-19)

North Dakota (N.D. Cent. Code § 47-04-20)

C — life estate

B — vested remainder in a life estate

Heirs of B — contingent remainder in fee simple

O — reversion

The Rule in *Shelley's Case* has been abolished.

---

14.   **Problem:**   O → B for life, remainder to C for life, then to the heirs of B.

      Facts: (a)   O, B, and C are all alive.

                       (b)   C dies.

      Answer: **Common Law**

                       (a)   B — life estate and a vested remainder in fee simple

                              C — vested remainder in a life estate

---

The Rule in *Shelley's Case* applies. Merger does not apply because of the intervening vested remainder.

                       (b)   B — fee simple absolute.

> C's remainder was vested, but only for life, so it has expired. B's interests then merge.

Answer: **California** (CAL. CIV. CODE § 779)

Illinois (765 ILL. COMP. STAT. 345/1)

Minnesota (MINN. STAT. ANN. § 500.14(4))

New Mexico (N.M. STAT. ANN. § 47-1-19)

North Dakota (N.D. CENT. CODE § 47-04-20)

(a)   B — life estate

C — vested remainder in a life estate

Heirs of B — contingent remainder in fee simple

O — reversion

(b)   B — life estate

Heirs of B — contingent remainder in fee simple

O — reversion

> The Rule in *Shelley's Case* has been abolished.

15.   *Problem:*   *O → A and his heirs upon A's marriage.*

Facts: O and A are living. A is unmarried.

Answer   **Common Law** and **California, Illinois, Minnesota, New Mexico & North Dakota**

O — fee simple on executory limitation

A — springing executory interest in fee simple

You may have erroneously concluded that A had a fee simple determinable. Notice, however, that A does not have a present interest. The present interest is held by O, who will not give it up until A is married. In fact, if A never marries, O retains a fee simple. A has only a future interest. If you thought O had a fee simple determinable, then you have correctly understood the practical aspect of O's interest, but the form is not correct for a fee simple determinable.

16.   *Problem:*   *O → B for life, then to C for life, remainder to the heirs of C.*

    Facts: B and C are living.

    Answer: **Common Law**

    B — life estate

    C — vested remainder in fee simple

The Rule in *Shelley's Case* applies even though C's interest is a future interest, not a present possessory interest. Merger then occurs to give C a vested remainder in fee simple.

    Answer: **California** (CAL. CIV. CODE § 779)

    Illinois (765 ILL. COMP. STAT. 345/1)

    Minnesota (MINN. STAT. ANN. § 500.14(4))

    New Mexico (N.M. STAT. ANN. § 47-1-19)

    North Dakota (N.D. CENT. CODE §§ 47-04-20)

    B — life estate

    C — vested remainder in life estate

    Heirs of C — contingent remainder in fee simple

O — reversion

> The Rule in *Shelley's Case* has been abolished.

17.   *Problem:* $O \rightarrow$ *A for life as long as A remains Catholic, then to B and his heirs.*

   Facts: (a)   A and B are living. A is Catholic.

            (b)   A dies.

   Answer: **Common Law** and **California, Illinois, Minnesota, New Mexico & North Dakota**

            (a)   A — life estate determinable

                  B — vested remainder in fee simple

> Authorities are not in full agreement on this answer. See the explanatory note to Problem 28, below.

            (b)   B — fee simple

18.   *Problem:* $O \rightarrow$ *A for life, then to B and his heirs as long as the land is farmed.*

   Facts: O, A, and B are living. The land is being farmed.

   Answer: **Common Law** and **Illinois, Minnesota, New Mexico & North Dakota**

            A — life estate

            B — vested remainder in fee simple determinable

            O — possibility of reverter

> Why vested? B takes when A dies, and B can only lose the land if he subsequently fails to farm the land. Note that no condition prevents B from taking possession upon A's death. In fact, even if A didn't farm the land, B gets it. *Cf.* Problem 6, above.

California (CAL. CIV. CODE § 885.020)

A — life estate

B — vested remainder in fee simple subject to a restriction in the form of a condition subsequent

O — power of termination

> MINN. STAT. ANN. § 500.20(1) provides that a possibility of reverter must not be or become merely nominal. Moreover, even if not nominal, it may be disregarded after 30 years from its creation. *Id.* § 500.20(2a). *Cf.* CAL. CIV. CODE § 885.030, which provides expiration dates for powers of termination.

19. **Problem:** O → *A for life, then to A's firstborn child and that child's heirs.*

    Facts: (a) O and A are living. A has no children.

    (b) A child is born to A.

    Answer: **Common Law** and **California, Illinois, Minnesota, New Mexico & North Dakota**

    (a) A — life estate

    Firstborn child of A — contingent remainder in fee simple

    O — reversion

    (b) A — life estate

    1st child of A — vested remainder in fee simple

> Once A's first child is born, the remainder becomes vested.

20.   **Problem:**   *O →   A for life, then to B and his heirs, but if B does not marry, then to C and his heirs.*

   Facts: A, B, and C are living. B is unmarried.

   Answer: **Common Law** and **California, Illinois, Minnesota, New Mexico & North Dakota**

   A — life estate

   B — vested remainder subject to divestment in fee

   C — shifting executory interest in fee simple

> See the answer to review Problem 4, at the end of chapter four, above.

21.   **Problem:**   *O →   A for life thirty years from the date of this conveyance.*

   Facts: (a)   O and A are living.

   (b)   A dies 29 years later, leaving B as his only heir.

   (c)   One year passes.

   Answer: **Common Law** and **California, Illinois, Minnesota, New Mexico & North Dakota**

   (a)   O — fee simple on executory limitation and a reversion in fee

   A — springing executory interest in a life estate

   (b)   O — fee simple

   (c)   No change

22. *Problem:* O → *A for life, then to B for life, then if C has married W, to C and his heirs.*

Facts: O, A, B, C, and W are living. C has not married.

Answer: **Common Law** and **California, Illinois, Minnesota, New Mexico & North Dakota**

A — life estate

B — vested remainder in life estate

C — contingent remainder in fee simple

O — reversion

23. *Problem:* O → *B for life, then if C marries D, to C and his heirs unless C serves liquor on the premises, in which case to E and his heirs.*

Facts: O, B, C, D, and E are living. C is unmarried.

Answer: **Common Law** and **Illinois, Minnesota, New Mexico & North Dakota**

B — life estate

C — contingent remainder in fee simple on executory limitation

E — shifting executory interest in fee simple

O — reversion

If C does not marry D, then the land reverts to O.

California (CAL. CIV. CODE § 885.10(a)(2))

We think the answer would be the same under California law. However, because the statutory definition of a power of termination to enforce a restriction encompasses an executory interest created in a transferee, E's interest could also be called a power of termination.

24. *Problem:* O → *B for life, and after B's death, to the heirs of B.*

Facts: O and B are living.

Answer: **Common Law**

B — fee simple absolute

In this example, because of the Rule in *Shelley's Case*, B's heirs do not have a contingent remainder in fee simple. Rather, B has a life estate and a vested remainder in fee simple. Then, under the doctrine of merger, B's life estate and remainder became a present fee simple.

Answer: **California** (CAL. CIV. CODE § 779)

Illinois (765 ILL. COMP. STAT. 345/1)

Minnesota (MINN. STAT. ANN. § 500.14(4))

New Mexico (N.M. STAT. ANN. § 47-1-19)

North Dakota (N.D. CENT. CODE § 47-04-20)

B — life estate

Heirs of B — contingent remainder in fee simple

O — reversion

The Rule in *Shelley's Case* has been abolished.

---

25.   *Problem:*   O → *A for life, then to B and his heirs, but if B dies younger than age 21, then to C and his heirs.*

Facts: O, A, B, and C are living. B is 19.

Answer: **Common Law** and **California, Illinois, Minnesota, New Mexico & North Dakota**

A — life estate

B — vested remainder subject to divestment in fee

C — shifting executory interest in fee simple

See the answer to Review Problem 4, at the end of chapter four, above. *Cf.* Problem 20, above.

26.   *Problem:*   *O → A for life, then to B and his heirs, but if B dies without children surviving him, then to C and his heirs.*

       Facts: O, A, B, and C are living. B has 5 children.

       Answer: **Common Law** and **California, Illinois, Minnesota, New Mexico & North Dakota**

                    A — life estate

                    B — vested remainder subject to divestment in fee

                    C — shifting executory interest in fee simple

See the answer to Review Problem 4, at the end of chapter four, above. *Cf.* Problem 20, above.

27.   *Problem:*   *O → A and his heirs, but if A should marry B, to C and his heirs.*

       Facts: A, B, and C are living. A has not married B.

       Answer: **Common Law** and **California, Illinois, Minnesota, New Mexico**

                    A — fee simple on executory limitation

                    C — shifting executory interest in fee simple

C's interest does not satisfy the requirements of a remainder because it may, if A marries B, cut short A's interest.

North Dakota (N.D. Cent. Code § 47-02-25)

A — fee simple (You might have added that if there was more evidence of O's intent, the grant might have been valid under the statute. If so, A would have a fee simple on executory limitation and C would have a shifting executory interest in fee.)

28. *Problem:* $O \rightarrow$ *B for life or until she remarries, then to the heirs of B.*

Facts: The conveyance is in O's will. O is dead. B, O's widow, is living, and has not remarried.

Answer: **Common Law**

B — fee simple

The Rule in *Shelley's Case* gives B both a life estate determinable and a vested remainder in fee simple. Merger then converts these into a present fee simple.

Answer: **California** (Cal. Civ. Code § 779)

Illinois (765 Ill. Comp. Stat. 345/1)

Minnesota (Minn. Stat. Ann. § 500.14(4))

New Mexico (N.M. Stat. Ann. § 47-1-19)

North Dakota (N.D. Cent. Code §§ 47-02-25, 47-04-20)

B — life estate determinable

Heirs of B — contingent remainder in fee simple

O — reversion

John A. Borron, Jr., *Simes & Smith, The Law of Future Interests* § 107, citing 2 Restatement of Property § 156, Illustration 6, citing dicta in *Seay v. Seay*, 384 S.W.2d 466, 238 Ark. 808 (1964), and in *Conger v. Conger*, 494 P.2d 1081, 208 Kan. 823 (1972).

Compare: *O → B for life, but if she remarries, then to the heirs of B.*

> [Assume the conveyance is in O's will, O is dead, and B, O's widow, is living, and has not remarried.]

> B — life estate on executory limitation

> Heirs of B — shifting executory interest in fee simple

> O — reversion

The Rule in *Shelley's Case* has been abolished, so the phrase "to the heirs of B" is not rewritten. Those heirs will not be determined until B's death. Hence, their remainder is contingent in Problem 28. We explained why their interest is a remainder in chapter six.

Our authority for this answer is John A. Borron, Jr., *Simes & Smith, The Law of Future Interests* § 107 (3d ed. 2011), which cites 2 Restatement of Property § 156, Illustration 6. However, the case authority cited is dicta: *Seay v. Seay*, 384 S.W.2d 466, 238 Ark. 808 (1964), *Conger v. Conger*, 494 P.2d 1081, 208 Kan. 823 (1972).

In the compare example, the "but if" language threatens to cut short B's life estate. Thus, we conclude that B has a life estate on executory limitation and that the heirs of B have a shifting executory interest in fee simple.

Compare the following examples:

1. O → A for life until he fails to farm, then to B and his heirs.

   Here A has a life estate determinable.

2. O → A for life, but if A fails to farm, then to B and his heirs.

   Here A has a life estate on executory limitation.

Note that the life estate determinable naturally expires when the condition is broken. The life estate on executory limitation may be cut short by the "but if . . ." language. Hence, a remainder follows the former, and an executory interest follows the latter.

29. **Problem:**   *O → A for life, then to W for life, then if Z is still alive, to C for life, otherwise to B and his heirs.*

Facts: O, A, W, Z, C, and B are living.

Answer: **Common Law** and **California, Illinois, Minnesota, New Mexico & North Dakota**

A — life estate

W — vested remainder in life estate

C — contingent remainder in life estate

C's life estate is not *pur autre vie* (for the life of Z). C's life estate is contingent on Z being alive at the time of W's death. But C's life estate is measured by C's life.

B — alternative contingent remainder in fee simple

O — reversion

30. **Problem:**   *O → B for life, remainder to such of B's children as survive B and their heirs.*

Facts: (a)   O and B are living. B has no children.

(b)   Triplets, E, F, and G, are born to B.

Answer: **Common Law** and **California, Illinois, Minnesota, New Mexico & North Dakota**

(a)   B — life estate

Children of B who survive B — contingent remainder in fee simple

O — reversion

(b)   Same as (a).

Even though E, F, and G are alive now, they must fulfill the condition of being alive when B dies, so their remainder is still contingent.

31. *Problem:*   *O → A for life, then to B's heir and his heirs.*

       Facts: O, A, and B are living.

       Answer: **Common Law** and **California, Illinois, Minnesota, New Mexico & North Dakota**

                A — life estate

                Heir of B — contingent remainder in fee simple

                O — reversion

The remainder is contingent because a living person has no heir.

The Rule in *Shelley's Case* does not apply, and its abolition is not relevant, because the remainder was not granted to the life tenant's heirs.

32. *Problem:*   *O → A for life, remainder to B and his heirs, but if B fails to live to 50, then to C and his heirs.*

       Facts: A, B, and C are living. B is 30.

       Answer: **Common Law** and **California, Illinois, Minnesota, New Mexico &North Dakota**

                A — life estate

                B — vested remainder subject to divestment in fee

                C — shifting executory interest in fee simple

> See the answer to review Problem 4, at the end of chapter two, above. *Cf.* Problem 20, above.

33. **Problem:** $O \rightarrow$ *W for life, then to A and his heirs if A survives W, and if A fails to survive W, then to B and his heirs.*

Facts:

(a) O, W, A, and B are all living.

(b) B dies, without a will, leaving D as his heir.

(c) W dies.

(d) A dies, without a will, leaving E as his heir.

Answer: **Common Law** and **California, Illinois, Minnesota, New Mexico & North Dakota**

(a) W — life estate

A — contingent remainder in fee simple

B — alternative contingent remainder in fee simple

O — reversion

(b) same as (a) except D has B's alternative contingent remainder

(c) A — fee simple absolute

> Because A has met the condition of surviving W, A has a fee simple.

(d) E — fee simple absolute

34. **Problem:** $O \rightarrow$ *A for life, then if B has married C, to B and his heirs.*

Facts: O, A, B, and C are living. B has not married.

Answer: **Common Law** and **California, Illinois, Minnesota, New Mexico & North Dakota**

A — life estate

B — contingent remainder in fee simple

O — reversion

35. *Problem:* $O \rightarrow$ *A for life, then to B and her heirs if B has married C.*

Facts: O, A, B, and C are living. B has not married.

Answer: **Common Law** and **California, Illinois, Minnesota, New Mexico & North Dakota**

A — life estate

B — contingent remainder in fee simple

O — reversion

Cf. Problem 34, above. The difference in language does not change the classification. The "if B has married C" clause is still a condition precedent. If B marries C before A dies, A's life estate is not cut off. B's interest would merely become vested.

36. *Problem:* $O \rightarrow$ *A for life, then if B marries C, to B and her heirs.*

Facts: O, A, B, and C are living. B has not married.

Answer: **Common Law** and **California, Illinois, Minnesota, New Mexico & North Dakota**

A — life estate

B — contingent remainder in fee simple

O — reversion

Case law (*Purefoy v. Rogers*, discussed in connection with the Statute of Uses in chapter five) interprets "if B marries C" to mean "if B has married C." Thus, the marriage can take place before A's death and still meet the condition. In fact, if B marries C before A's death, B's contingent remainder becomes vested.

Even after the Statute of Uses, an interest was construed as a contingent remainder rather than an executory interest if the interest had the capacity to operate as a contingent remainder.

Thus, suppose that A dies before B marries C. In 1700, B's contingent remainder would be destroyed.

37. **Problem:** *O → A for life, and one year after A's death, to B and her heirs.*

Facts: O, A, and B are living.

Answer: **Common Law** and **California, Illinois, Minnesota, New Mexico & North Dakota**

A — life estate

O — reversion (in fee simple on executory limitation)

B — springing executory interest in fee simple

The material in parentheses frequently is omitted.

38. **Problem:** *O → A for life, then to B and his heirs if B writes a complete biography of A's life.*

Facts: O, A, and B are living. B has not started a biography.

Answer: **Common Law** and **California, Illinois, Minnesota, New Mexico & North Dakota**

A — life estate

O — reversion (in fee simple on executory limitation)

B — springing executory interest in fee simple

Why doesn't B have a contingent remainder? Since a *complete* biography would necessarily include an account of A's death, B couldn't be ready to take immediately upon A's death.

The RAP is not violated, because B will write the biography, if ever, during his lifetime.

---

39. **Problem:** $O \rightarrow$ *A for life, then to B and her heirs after one year.*

Facts: O, A, and B are living.

Answer: **Common Law** and **California, Illinois, Minnesota, New Mexico & North Dakota**

A — life estate

O — reversion (in fee simple on executory limitation)

B — springing executory interest in fee simple

O's future interest is in a possessory estate for one year and is subject to an executory interest. B's interest was not possible before 1536. After 1536, it could be created as an executory interest.

Appendix III

SELECTED STATUTES

A. CALIFORNIA

1. Civil Code

§ 683. *Joint tenancy; definition; method of creation*

(a) A joint interest is one owned by two or more persons in equal shares, by a title created by a single will or transfer, when expressly declared in the will or transfer to be a joint tenancy, or by transfer from a sole owner to himself or herself and others, or from tenants in common or joint tenants to themselves or some of them, or to themselves or any of them and others, or from a husband and wife, when holding title as community property or otherwise to themselves or to themselves and others or to one of them and to another or others, when expressly declared in the transfer to be a joint tenancy, or when granted or devised to executors or trustees as joint tenants. A joint tenancy in personal property may be created by a written transfer, instrument or agreement.

(b) Provisions of this section do not apply to a joint account in a financial institution if Part 2 (commencing with Section 5100) of Division 5 of the Probate Code applies to such account.

§ 686. *Interest in common; interests excluded*

Every interest created in favor of several persons in their own right is an interest in common, unless acquired by them in partnership, for partnership purposes, or unless declared in its creation to be a joint interest, as provided in Section 683, or unless acquired as community property.

§ 741. *Future interests; alienation or loss of precedent interest*

No future interest can be defeated or barred by any alienation or other act of the owner of the intermediate or precedent interest, nor by any destruction of such precedent interest by forfeiture, surrender, merger, or otherwise, except as provided by the next section, or where a forfeiture is imposed by statute as a penalty for the violation thereof.

§ 742. *Future interests; premature determination of precedent interest*

No future interest, valid in its creation, is defeated by the determination of the precedent interest before the happening of the contingency on which the future interest is limited to take effect; but should such contingency afterwards happen, the future interest takes effect in the same manner and to the same extent as if the precedent interest had continued to the same period.

§ 763. *Estates tail abolished; fee simple and fee simple absolute*

Estates tail are abolished, and every estate which would be at common law adjudged to be a fee tail is a fee simple; and if no valid remainder is limited thereon, is a fee simple absolute.

§ 764. *Fee tails as contingent remainders*

Where a remainder in fee is limited upon any estate, which would by the common law be adjudged a fee tail, such remainder is valid as a contingent limitation upon a fee, and vests in possession on the death of the first taker, without issue living at the time of his death.

§ 779. *Heirs of life purchasers; taking as purchasers*

When a remainder is limited to the heirs, or heirs of the body, of a person to whom a life estate in the same property is given, the persons who, on the termination of the life estate, are the successors or heirs of the body of the owner for life, are entitled to take by virtue of the remainder so limited to them, and not as mere successors of the owner for life.

§ 885.010. *Definitions*

(a) As used in this chapter

(1) "Power of termination" means the power to terminate a fee simple estate in real property to enforce a restriction in the form of a condition subsequent to which the fee simple estate is subject, whether the power is characterized in the instrument that creates or evidences it as a power of termination, right of entry or reentry, right of possession or repossession, reserved power of revocation, or otherwise, and includes a possibility of reverter that is deemed to be and is enforceable as a power of termination pursuant to Section 885.020.

(2) "Power of termination" includes the power created in a transferee to terminate a fee simple estate in real property to enforce a restriction on the use of the real property in the form of a limitation or condition subsequent to which the fee simple estate is subject, whether the power is characterized in the instrument that creates or evidences it as an executory interest, executory limitation, or otherwise, and includes the interest known at common law as an executory interest preceded by a fee simple determinable.

(b) A power of termination is an interest in the real property.

(c) For the purpose of applying this chapter to other statutes relating to powers of termination, the terms "right of reentry," "right of repossession for a breach of condition subsequent," and comparable terms used in the other statutes mean "power of termination" as defined in this section.

§ 885.020. *Fees simple determinable and possibilities of reverter abolished*

Fees simple determinable and possibilities of reverter are abolished. Every estate that would be at common law a fee simple determinable is deemed to be a fee simple subject to a restriction in the form of a condition subsequent. Every interest that would be at common law a possibility of reverter is deemed to be and is enforceable as a power of termination.

§ 885.030. *Expiration dates; recorded instruments; contrary provisions*

(a) A power of termination of record expires at the later of the following times:

(1) Thirty years after the date the instrument reserving, transferring, or otherwise evidencing the power of termination is recorded.

(2) Thirty years after the date a notice of intent to preserve the power of termination is recorded, if the notice is recorded within the time prescribed in paragraph (1).

(3) Thirty years after the date an instrument reserving, transferring or otherwise evidencing the power of termination or a notice of intent to preserve the power of termination is recorded, if the instrument or notice is recorded within 30 years after the date such an instrument or notice was last recorded.

(b) This section applies notwithstanding any provision to the contrary in the instrument reserving, transferring or otherwise evidencing the power of termination or in another recorded document unless the instrument or other recorded document provides an earlier expiration date.

§ 885.040. *Obsolete powers; expiration; grants to public entities, etc.*

(a) If a power of termination becomes obsolete, the power expires.

(b) As used in this section, a power of termination is obsolete if any of the following circumstances applies:

(1) The restriction to which the fee simple estate is subject is of no actual and substantial benefit to the holder of the power.

(2) Enforcement of the power would not effectuate the purpose of the restriction to which the fee simple estate is subject.

(3) It would be otherwise inequitable to enforce the power because of changed conditions or circumstances.

(c) No power of termination shall expire under this section during the life of the grantor if it arises from a grant by a natural person without consideration to a public entity or to a society, corporation, institution, or association exempt by the laws of this state from taxation.

§ 1072. *Words of inheritance or succession*

Words of inheritance or succession are not requisite to transfer a fee in real property.

§ 1105. *Fee simple title; presumption*

A fee simple title is presumed to pass by a grant of real property, unless it appears from the grant that a lesser estate was intended.

2. *Probate Code*

§ 21108. *Common law rule of worthier title; interest transferred to transferor's own heirs or next of kin*

The law of this state does not include (a) the common law rule of worthier title that a transferor cannot devise an interest to his or her own heirs or (b) a presumption or rule of interpretation that a transferor does not intend, by a transfer to his or her own heirs or next of kin, to transfer an interest to them. The meaning of a transfer of a legal or equitable interest to a transferor's own heirs or next of kin, however designated, shall be determined by the general rules applicable to the interpretation of instruments.

§ 21109. *Transferees; failure to survive*

(a) A transferee who fails to survive the transferor of an at-death transfer or until any future time required by the instrument does not take under the instrument.

(b) If it cannot be determined by clear and convincing evidence that the transferee survived until a future time required by the instrument, it is deemed that the transferee did not survive until the required future time.

§ 21112. *Issue; conditions*

A condition in a transfer of a present or future interest that refers to a person's death "with" or "without" issue, or to a person's "having" or "leaving" issue or no issue, or a condition based on words of similar import, is construed to refer to that person's being dead at the time the transfer takes effect in enjoyment and to that person either having or not having, as the case may be, issue who are alive at the time of enjoyment.

§ 21200. *Short title*

This chapter shall be known and may be cited as the Uniform Statutory Rule Against Perpetuities.

§ 21201. *Common law rule superseded*

This chapter supersedes the common law rule against perpetuities.

§ 21202. *Application of part*

(a) Except as provided in subdivision (b), this part applies to nonvested property interests and unexercised powers of appointment regardless of whether they were created before, on, or after January 1, 1992.

(b) This part does not apply to any property interest or power of appointment the validity of which has been determined in a judicial proceeding or by a settlement among interested persons.

§ 21205. *Nonvested property interests; validity; conditions*

A nonvested property interest is invalid unless one of the following conditions is satisfied:

(a) When the interest is created, it is certain to vest or terminate no later than 21 years after the death of an individual then alive.

(b) The interest either vests or terminates within 90 years after its creation.

§ 21206. *General power of appointment; condition precedent; validity; conditions*

A general power of appointment not presently exercisable because of a condition precedent is invalid unless one of the following conditions is satisfied:

(a) When the power is created, the condition precedent is certain to be satisfied or become impossible to satisfy no later than 21 years after the death of an individual then alive.

(b) The condition precedent either is satisfied or becomes impossible to satisfy within 90 years after its creation.

§ 21207. *Nongeneral power of appointment; general testamentary power of appointment; validity; conditions*

A nongeneral power of appointment or a general testamentary power of appointment is invalid unless one of the following conditions is satisfied:

(a) When the power is created, it is certain to be irrevocably exercised or otherwise to terminate no later than 21 years after the death of an individual then alive.

(b) The power is irrevocably exercised or otherwise terminates within 90 years after its creation.

§ 21208. *Posthumous births*

In determining whether a nonvested property interest or a power of appointment is valid under this article, the possibility that a child will be born to an individual after the individual's death is disregarded.

§ 21209. *Construction of "later of" language in perpetuity saving clause; application of section*

(a) If, in measuring a period from the creation of a trust or other property arrangement, language in a governing instrument (1) seeks to disallow the vesting or termination of any interest or trust beyond, (2) seeks to postpone the vesting or termination of any interest or trust until, or (3) seeks to operate in effect in any similar fashion upon, the later of (A) the expiration of a period of time not exceeding 21 years after the death of the survivor of specified lives in being at the creation of the trust or other property arrangement or (B) the expiration of a period of time that exceeds or might exceed 21 years after the death of the survivor of lives in being at the creation of the trust or other property arrangement, that language is inoperative to the extent it produces a period that exceeds 21 years after the death of the survivor of the specified lives.

(b) Notwithstanding Section 21202, this section applies only to governing instruments, including instruments exercising powers of appointment, executed on or after January 1, 1992.

§ 21210.   *Nonvested property interests or powers of appointment*

Except as provided in Sections 21211 and 21212, the time of creation of a nonvested property interest or a power of appointment is determined by other applicable statutes or, if none, under general principles of property law.

§ 21211.   *Powers exercisable by one person alone*

For purposes of this chapter:

(a) If there is a person who alone can exercise a power created by a governing instrument to become the unqualified beneficial owner of (1) a nonvested property interest or (2) a property interest subject to a power of appointment described in Section 21206 or 21207, the nonvested property interest or power of appointment is created when the power to become the unqualified beneficial owner terminates.

(b) A joint power with respect to community property held by individuals married to each other is a power exercisable by one person alone.

§ 21212.   *Interests or powers arising from transfer of property; previously funded trusts; other existing property arrangement*

For purposes of this chapter, a nonvested property interest or a power of appointment arising from a transfer of property to a previously funded trust or other existing property arrangement is created when the nonvested property interest or power of appointment in the original contribution was created.

§ 21220.   *Petition; conditions*

On petition of an interested party, a court shall reform a disposition in the manner that most closely approximates the transferor's manifested plan of distribution and is within the 90 years allowed by the applicable provision in Article 2 (commencing with Section 21205), if any of the following conditions is satisfied:

(a) A nonvested property interest or a power of appointment becomes invalid under the statutory rule against perpetuities provided in Article 2 (commencing with Section 21205).

(b) A class gift is not but might become invalid under the statutory rule against perpetuities provided in Article 2 (commencing with Section 21205), and the time has arrived when the share of any class member is to take effect in possession or enjoyment.

(c) A nonvested property interest that is not validated by subdivision (a) of Section 21205 can vest but not with 90 years after its creation.

§ 21225.   *Application of chapter*

Article 2 (commencing with Section 21205) does not apply to any of the following:

(a) A nonvested property interest or a power of appointment arising out of a nondonative transfer, except a nonvested property interest or a power of appointment arising out of (1) a premarital or postmarital agreement, (2) a separation or divorce settlement, (3) a spouse's election, (4) or a similar arrangement arising out of a prospective, existing, or previous marital relationship between the parties, (5) a contract to make or not to revoke a will or trust, (6) a contract to exercise or not to exercise a power of appointment, (7) a transfer in satisfaction of a duty of support, or (8) a reciprocal transfer.

(b) A fiduciary's power relating to the administration or management of assets, including the power of a fiduciary to sell, lease, or mortgage property, and the power of a fiduciary to determine principal and income.

(c) A power to appoint a fiduciary.

(d) A discretionary power of a trustee to distribute principal before termination of a trust to a beneficiary having an indefeasibly vested interest in the income and principal.

(e) A nonvested property interest held by charity, government, or governmental agency or subdivision, if the nonvested property interest is preceded by an interest held by another charity, government, or governmental agency or subdivision.

(f) A nonvested property interest in or a power of appointment with respect to a trust or other property arrangement forming part of a pension, profit sharing, stock bonus, health, disability, death benefit, income deferral, or other current or deferred benefit plan for one or more employees, independent contractors, or their beneficiaries or spouses, to which contributions are made for the purpose of distributing to or for the benefit of the participants or their beneficiaries or spouses the property, income, or principal in the trust or other property arrangement, except a nonvested property interest or a power of appointment that is created by an election of a participant or a beneficiary or spouse.

(g) A property interest, power of appointment, or arrangement that was not subject to the common law rule against perpetuities or is excluded by another statute of this state.

(h) A trust created for the purpose of providing for its beneficiaries under hospital service contracts, group life insurance, group disability insurance, group annuities, or any combination of such insurance, as defined in the Insurance Code.

§ 21230.   *Validating lives*

The lives of individuals selected to govern the time of vesting pursuant to Article 2 (commencing with Section 21205) of Chapter 1 may not be so numerous or so situated that evidence of their deaths is likely to be unreasonably difficult to obtain.

§ 21231.   *Spouse as life in being*

In determining the validity of a nonvested property interest pursuant to Article 2 (commencing with Section 21205) of chapter 1, an individual described as the spouse of an individual alive at the commencement of the perpetuities period shall be deemed to be an individual alive when the interest is created, whether or not the individual so described was then alive.

B. ILLINOIS

1.   Chapter 765

5/6. *Entailment*

§ 6. In cases where, by the common law, any person or persons might hereafter become the owner of, without applying the rule of property known as the rule in Shelley's Case, in fee tail, of any lands, tenements or hereditaments, by virtue of any legacy, gift, grant or other conveyance, hereafter to be made, or by any other means whatsoever, such person or persons, instead of being or becoming the owner thereof in fee tail, shall be deemed and adjudged to be, and become the owner thereof, for his or her natural life only, and the remainder shall pass in fee simple absolute, to the person or persons to whom the estate tail would, on the death of the first grantee, legatee or donee in tail, first pass, according to the course of the common law, by virtue of such legacy, gift, grant or conveyance.

5/13. *What estate conveyed*

§ 13. Every estate in lands which shall be granted, conveyed or bequeathed, although other words heretofore necessary to transfer an estate of inheritance is not added, shall be deemed a fee simple estate of inheritance, if a less estate is not limited by express words, or do not appear to have been granted, conveyed or bequeathed by construction or operation of law.

305/1. *Title*

Title. This Act shall be known and may be cited as the "Statute Concerning Perpetuities".

305/2. *Purpose*

Purpose. This Act modifies the common law rule of property known as the rule against perpetuities, which, except as modified by statutes in force at the effective date of this Act and by this Act, shall remain in full force and effect.

305/3. *Definitions and Terms*

Definitions and Terms. As used in this Act unless the context otherwise requires:

(a) "Trust" means any trust created by any written instrument, including, without limitation, a trust created by the exercise of a power of appointment.

(a-5) "Qualified perpetual trust" means any trust created by any written instrument executed on or after January 1, 1998, including an amendment to an instrument in existence prior to that date and the exercise of a power of appointment granted by an instrument executed or amended on or after that date:

(i) to which, by the specific terms governing the trust, the rule against perpetuities does not apply; and

(ii) the power of the trustee (or other person to whom the power is properly granted or delegated) to sell property of which is not limited by the governing trust instrument or any provision of law for any period of time beyond the period of the rule against perpetuities.

(b) "Trustee" includes the original trustee of any trust and also any succeeding or added trustee.

(c) "Instrument" means any writing pursuant to which any legal or equitable interest in property or in the income therefrom is affected, disposed of or created.

(d) "Beneficiary" includes any person to whom any interest, whether vested or contingent, is given by an instrument.

(e) Any reference in this Act to income to be "paid" or to income "payments" or to "receiving" income includes income payable or distributable to or applicable for the benefit of a beneficiary.

305/4. *Application of the Rule Against Perpetuities*

(a) [Omitted]

(b) The period of the rule against perpetuities shall not commence to run in connection with any disposition of property or interest therein, and no instrument shall be regarded as becoming effective for purposes of the rule against perpetuities, and no interest or power shall be deemed to be created for purposes of the rule against perpetuities as long as, by the terms of the instrument, the maker of the instrument has the power to revoke the instrument or to transfer or direct to be transferred to himself the entire legal and equitable ownership of the property or interest therein.

(c) In determining whether an interest violates the rule against perpetuities:

(1) It shall be presumed (A) that the interest was intended to be valid, (B) in the case of an interest conditioned upon the probate of a will, the appointment of an executor, administrator or trustee, the completion of the administration of an estate, the payment of debts, the sale or distribution of property, the determination of federal or state tax liabilities or the happening of any administrative contingency, that the contingency must occur, if at all, within the period of the rule against perpetuities, and (C) where the instrument creates an interest in the "widow," "widower," or "spouse" of another person, that the maker of the instrument intended to refer to a person who was living at the date that the period of the rule against perpetuities commences to run;

(2) where any interest, but for this subparagraph (c) (2), would be invalid because it is made to depend upon any person attaining or 3 failing to attain an age in excess of 21 years, the age specified shall be reduced to 21 years as to every person to whom the age contingency applies;

(3) if, notwithstanding the provisions of subparagraphs (c) (1) and (2) of this Section, the validity of any interest depends upon the possibility of the birth or adoption of a child, (A) no person shall be deemed capable of having a child until he has attained the age of 13 years, (B) any person who has attained the age of 65 years shall be deemed incapable of having a child, (C) evidence shall be admissible as to the incapacity of having a child by a living person who has not attained the age of 65 years, and (D) the possibility of having a child or more remote descendant by adoption shall be disregarded.

(d) Subparagraphs (a) (2), (3) and (6) and paragraph (b) of this Section shall be deemed to be declaratory of the law prevailing in this State at the effective date of this Act.

305/5. *Trusts.*

(a) Subject to the provisions of paragraphs (e) and (f) of this Section, a trust containing any limitation which, but for this paragraph (a), would violate the rule against perpetuities (as modified by Section 4) shall terminate at the expiration of a period of (A) 21 years after the death of the last to die of all of the beneficiaries of the instrument who were living at the date when the period of the rule against perpetuities commenced to run or (B) 21 years after that date if no beneficiary of the instrument was then living, unless events occur which cause an earlier termination in accordance with the terms of the instrument and then the principal shall be distributed as provided by the instrument.

(b) Subject to the provisions of paragraphs (c), (d) and (e) of this Section, when a trust terminates because of the application of paragraph (a) of this Section, the trustee shall distribute the principal to those persons who would be the heirs at law of the maker of the instrument if he died at the expiration of the period specified in paragraph (a) of this Section and in the proportions then specified by statute, unless the trust was created by the exercise of a power of appointment and then the principal shall be distributed to the person who would have received it if the power had not been exercised.

(c) Before any distribution of principal is made pursuant to paragraph (b) of this Section, the trustee shall distribute, out of principal, to each living beneficiary who, but for termination of the trust because of the application of paragraph (a) of this Section, would have been entitled to be paid income after the expiration of the period specified in paragraph (a) of this Section, an amount equal to the present value (determined as provided in paragraph (d) of this Section) of the income which the beneficiary would have been entitled to be paid after the expiration of that period.

(d) [Omitted]

(e) [Omitted]

(f) [Omitted]

330/4. *Duration of possibility of reverter or rights of entry or re-entry for breach of condition*

§ 4. Neither possibilities of reverter nor rights of entry or re-entry for breach of condition subsequent, whether heretofore or hereafter created, where the condition has not been broken, shall be valid for a longer period than 40 years from the date of the creation of the condition or possibility of reverter. If such a possibility of reverter or right of entry or re-entry is created to endure for a longer period than 40 years, it shall be valid for 40 years.

335/1. *Surrender or merger of reversion*

§ 1. When the reversion expectant on a lease, made either before or after the passing of this act, of tenements or hereditaments of any tenure, shall be surrendered or merged, the estate, which shall for the time being confer as against the tenant under the same lease the next vested right to the same tenements or hereditaments, shall, to the extent and for the purpose of preserving such incidents to, and obligations on the same reversion, as but for the surrender or merger thereof, would have subsisted, be deemed the reversion expectant on the same lease.

340/1. *When not defeated*

§ 1. No future interest shall fail or be defeated by the determination of any precedent estate or interest prior to the happening of the event or contingency on which the future interest is limited to take effect.

345/1. *Abolition of rule*

§ 1. The rule of property known as the rule in Shelley's Case is abolished.

350/1. *Abolition of worthier title and of rule that grantor cannot create limitations in favor of own heirs*

§ 1. Where a deed, will or other instrument purports to create any present or future interest in real or personal property in the heirs of the maker of the instrument, the heirs shall take, by purchase and not by descent, the interest that the instrument purports to create. The doctrine of worthier title and the rule of the common law that a grantor cannot create a limitation in favor of his own heirs are abolished.

1005/1. *Joint tenancy defined — Presumption of tenancy in common — Survivorship rights*

§ 1. No estate in joint tenancy in any lands, tenements or hereditaments, or in any parts thereof or interest therein, shall be held or claimed under any grant, legacy or conveyance whatsoever heretofore or hereafter made, other than to executors and trustees, unless the premises therein mentioned shall expressly be thereby declared to pass not in tenancy in common but in joint tenancy; and every such estate other than to executors and trustees (unless otherwise expressly declared as aforesaid, or unless, as to a devise or conveyance of homestead property, expressly declared to pass to a husband and wife as tenants by the entirety in the manner provided by Section 1c), shall be deemed to be in tenancy in common and all conveyances heretofore made, or which hereafter may be made, wherein the premises therein mentioned were or shall be expressly declared to pass not in tenancy in common but in joint tenancy, are hereby declared to have created an estate in joint tenancy with the accompanying right of survivorship the same as it existed prior to the passage of "An Act to amend Section 1 of an Act entitled: 'An Act to revise the law in relation to joint rights and obligations,' approved February 25, 1874, in force July 1, 1874," approved June 26, 1917.

C. MINNESOTA

§ 500.02. *Estates of inheritance*

Every estate of inheritance shall continue to be termed a fee simple, or fee; and every such estate, when not defeasible or conditional, shall be a fee simple absolute or an absolute fee.

§ 500.03. *Effect of conveyance to grantee in fee tail*

In all cases where any person, if this chapter had not been passed, would at any time hereafter become seized in fee tail of any lands, tenements, or hereditaments by virtue of any devise, gift, grant, or other conveyance heretofore made, or hereafter to be made, or by any other means, such person, instead of becoming seized thereof in fee tail, shall be deemed and adjudged to be seized thereof as in fee simple.

§ 500.04. *Conveyance by owner of fee tail estate*

Where lands, tenements, or hereditaments heretofore have been devised, granted, or otherwise conveyed by a tenant in tail, and the person to whom such devise, grant, or other conveyance has been made, or that person's heirs or assigns, have from the time such devise took effect, or from the time such grant or conveyance was made, to the day of passing this chapter, been in the uninterrupted possession of such lands, tenements, or hereditaments, and claiming and holding the same under or by virtue of such devise, grant, or other conveyance, they shall be deemed as good and legal to all intents and purposes as if such tenant in tail had, at the time of making such devise, grant, or other conveyance, been seized in fee simple of such lands, tenements, or hereditaments, any law to the contrary notwithstanding.

§ 500.14. *Future estates construed; validity;creating instruments*

Subdivision 1. Failure of heirs or issue. Unless a different intent is effectively manifested, whenever property is limited upon the death of any person without "heirs" or "heirs of the body" or "issue" general or special, or "descendants" or "offspring" or "children" or any such relative described by other terms, the limitation is to take effect only when that person dies not having such relative living at the time of the person's death, or in gestation and born alive thereafter, and is not a limitation to take effect upon the indefinite failure of such relatives; nor, unless a different intent is effectively manifested, does the limitation mean that death without such relative is restricted in time to the lifetime of the creator of the interest.

Subdivision 2. Alternative future estates. Two or more future estates may also be created, to take effect in the alternative, so that if the first in order fails to vest the next in succession shall be substituted for it, and take effect accordingly.

Subdivision 3. Probability of contingency. No future estate, otherwise valid, shall be void on the ground of the probability or improbability of the contingency on which it is limited to take effect.

Subdivision 4. Certain remainders vest by purchase. When a remainder is limited to the heirs, or heirs of the body, of a person to whom a life estate in the same premises is given, the persons who, on the termination of the life estate, are the heirs or heirs of the body of such tenant for life shall be entitled to take as purchasers, by virtue of the remainder so limited to them. No conveyance, transfer,devise, or bequest of an interest, legal or equitable, in real or personal property, shall fail to take effect by purchase because limited to a person or persons, howsoever described, who would take the same interest by descent or distribution.

Subdivision 5. Posthumous children as remainderpersons. When a future estate is limited to heirs, or issue, or children, posthumous children shall be entitled to take in the same manner as if living at the death of their parent.

Subdivision 6. Posthumous birth averts "death without issue." A future estate, depending on the contingency of the death of any person without heirs or issue or children, shall be defeated by the birth of a posthumous child of such person capable of taking by descent.

§ 500.15. *Future estates; protection from destructibility rules*

Subdivision 1. Owner's destruction of precedent estate. No expectant estate can be defeated or barred by any alienation or other act of the owner of the intermediate or precedent estate, nor by any destruction of such precedent estate, by disseizin, forfeiture, surrender, merger, or otherwise.

Subdivision 2. Exception. Subdivision 1 shall not be construed to prevent an expectant estate from being defeated in any manner, or by any act or means, which the party creating such estate has, in the creation thereof, provided or authorized; nor shall an expectant estate thus liable to be defeated be on that ground adjudged void in its creation.

Subdivision 3. Premature determination of precedent estate. No remainder, valid in its creation, shall be defeated by the determination of the precedent estate before the happening of the contingency on which the remainder is limited to take effect; but, should such contingency afterward happen, the remainder shall take effect in the same manner and to the same extent as if the precedent estate had continued to the same period.

§ 500.19. *Division*

Subdivision 1. According to number. Estates, in respect to the number and connection of their owners, are divided into estates in severalty, in joint tenancy, and in common; the nature and properties of which, respectively, shall continue to be such as are now established by law, except so far as the same may be modified by the provisions of this chapter.

Subdivision 2. Construction of grants and devises. All grants and devises of lands, made to two or more persons, shall be construed to create estates in common, and not in joint tenancy, unless expressly declared to be in joint tenancy. This section shall not apply to mortgages, nor to devises or grants made in trust, or to executors.

Subdivision 3. Joint tenancy requirements abolished. The common law requirement for unity of time, title, interest, and possession in the creation of a joint tenancy is abolished.

Subdivision 4. Conveying interest directly. [Omitted]

Subdivision 5. Severance of estates in joint tenancy. [Omitted]

§ 500.20. *Defeasible estates*

Subdivision 1. Normal conditions and limitations. When any covenants, conditions, restrictions or extensions thereof annexed to a grant, devise or conveyance of land are, or shall become, merely nominal, and of no actual and substantial benefit to the party or parties to whom or in whose favor they are to be performed, they may be wholly disregarded; and a failure to perform the same shall in no case operate as a basis of forfeiture of the lands subject thereto.

Subdivision 2a. Restriction of duration of condition. Except for any right to reenter or to repossess as provided in subdivision 3, all private covenants, conditions, or restrictions created by which the title or use of real property is affected, cease to be valid and operative 30 years after the date of the deed, or other instrument, or the date of the probate of the will, creating them, and may be disregarded.

This subdivision does not apply to covenants, conditions or restrictions:

    (1) [Omitted];

    (2) [Omitted];

    (3) [Omitted];

    (4) [Omitted];

(5) [Omitted];

(6) [Omitted].

(7) [Omitted].

Subdivision 3. Time to assert power of termination. Hereafter any right to reenter or to repossess land on account of breach made in a condition subsequent shall be barred unless such right is asserted by entry or action within six years after the happening of the breach upon which such right is predicated.

§ 501A.01. *When nonvested interest, powers of appointment are invalid; exceptions*

(a) A nonvested property interest is invalid unless:

(1) when the interest is created, it is certain to vest or terminate no later than 21 years after the death of an individual then alive; or

(2) the interest either vests or terminates within 90 years after its creation.

(b) A general power of appointment not presently exercisable because of a condition precedent is invalid unless:

(1) when the power is created, the condition precedent is certain to be satisfied or become impossible to satisfy no later than 21 years after the death of an individual then alive; or

(2) the condition precedent either is satisfied or becomes impossible to satisfy within 90 years after its creation.

(c) A nongeneral power of appointment or a general testamentary power of appointment is invalid unless:

(1) when the power is created, it is certain to be irrevocably exercised or otherwise to terminate no later than 21 years after the death of an individual then alive; or

(2) the power is irrevocably exercised or otherwise terminates within 90 years after its creation.

(d) In determining whether a nonvested property interest or a power of appointment is valid under paragraph (a), clause (1), paragraph (b), clause (1), or paragraph (c), clause (1), the possibility that a child will be born to an individual after the individual's death is disregarded.

(e) If, in measuring a period from the creation of a trust or other property arrangement, language in a governing instrument seeks to:

(1) disallow the vesting or termination of any interest trust beyond;

(2) postpone the vesting or termination of any interest or trust until; or

(3) operate in effect in any similar fashion upon,

the later of the expiration of a period of time not exceeding 21 years after the death of the survivor of specified lives in being at the creation of the trust or other property arrangement, or the expiration of a period of time that exceeds or might exceed 21 years after the death of the survivor of lives in being at the creation of the trust or other property arrangement; that language is inoperative to the extent it produces a period of time that exceeds 21 years after the death of the survivor of the specified lives.

§ 501A.02. *When nonvested property interest or power of appointment created*

(a) Except as provided in subsections (b) and (c) and in section 501A.05, subsection (a), the time of creation of a nonvested property interest or a power of appointment is determined under general principles or property law.

(b) For purposes of sections 501A.01 to 501A.07, if there is a person who alone can exercise a power created by a governing instrument to become the unqualified beneficial owner of (i) a nonvested property interest or (ii) a property interest subject to a power of appointment described in section 501A.01, subsection (b) or (c), the nonvested property interest or power of appointment is created when the power to become the unqualified beneficial owner terminates.

(c) For purposes of sections 501A.01 to 501A.07, a nonvested property interest or a power of appointment arising from a transfer of property to a previously funded trust or other existing property arrangement is created when the nonvested property interest or power of appointment in the original contribution was created.

§ 501A.03. *Reformation*

Upon the petition of an interested person, a court shall reform a disposition in the manner that most closely approximates the transferor's manifested plan of distribution and is within the 90 years allowed by section 501A.01, subsection (a)(2), (b)(2), or (c)(2) if:

(1) a nonvested property interest or a power of appointment becomes invalid under section 501A.01 (statutory rule against perpetuities);

(2) a class gift is not but might become invalid under section 501A.01 (statutory rule against perpetuities) and the time has arrived when the share of any class member is to take effect in possession or enjoyment; or

(3) a nonvested property interest that is not validated by section 501A.01, subsection (a)(1) can vest but not within 90 years after its creation.

§ 501A.04. *Exclusions from statutory rule*

Section 501A.01 (statutory rule against perpetuities) does not apply to:

(1) a nonvested property interest or a power of appointment arising out of a nondonative transfer, except a nonvested property interest or a power of appointment arising out of (i) a premarital or postmarital agreement, (ii) a separation or divorce settlement, (iii) a spouse's election, (iv) a similar arrangement arising out of a prospective, existing, or previous marital relationship between the parties, (v) a contract to make or not to revoke a will or trust, (vi) a contract to exercise or not to exercise a power of appointment, (vii) a transfer in satisfaction of a duty of support, or (viii) a reciprocal transfer;

(2) a fiduciary's power relating to the administration or management of assets, including the power of a fiduciary to sell, lease, or mortgage property, and the power of a fiduciary to determine principal and income;

(3) a power to appoint a fiduciary;

(4) a discretionary power of a trustee to distribute principal before termination of a trust to a beneficiary having an indefeasibly vested interest in the income and principal;

(5) a nonvested property interest held by a charity, government, or governmental agency or subdivision, if the nonvested property is preceded by an interest held by another charity, government, or governmental agency or subdivision;

(6) a nonvested property interest in a power of appointment with respect to a trust or other property arrangement forming part of a pension, profit sharing, stock bonus, health, disability, death benefit, income deferral, or other current or deferred benefit plan for one or more employees, independent contractors, or their beneficiaries or spouses, to which contributions are made for the purpose of distributing to or for the benefit of the participants or their beneficiaries or spouses the property, income, or principal in the trust or other property arrangement, except a nonvested property interest or a power of appointment that is created by an election of a participant or a beneficiary or spouse; or

(7) a property interest, power of appointment, or arrangement that was not subject to the common

law rule against perpetuities or is excluded by another statute of this state.

§ 501A.05. *Prospective application*

(a) Except as extended by subsection (b), sections 501A.01 to 501A.07 apply to a nonvested property interest or a power of appointment that is created after December 31, 1991. For purposes of this section, a nonvested property interest or a power of appointment created by the exercise of a power of appointment is created when the power is irrevocably exercised or when a revocable exercise becomes irrevocable.

(b) If a nonvested property interest of a power of appointment was created before January 1, 1992, and is determined in a judicial proceeding, commenced after December 31, 1991, to violate this state's rule against perpetuities as that rule existed before January 1, 1992, a court upon the petition of an interested person may reform the disposition in the manner that most closely approximates the transferor's manifested plan of distribution and is within the limits of the rule against perpetuities applicable when the nonvested property interest or power of appointment was created.

§ 501A.06. *Supersedes common law rule*

Sections 501A.01 to 501A.07 supersede the rule of the common law known as the rule against perpetuities.

§ 501A.07. *Short title*

Sections 501A.01 to 501A.07 may be cited as the Uniform Statutory Rule Against Perpetuities.

D. NEW MEXICO

1. Chapter 42

§ 42-9-4. *[Filing complaint or statement, affidavit and bond; issuance of writ; property subject to attachment.]*

A creditor wishing to sue his debtor by attachment, may place in the clerk's office of the district court of any county in this state, having jurisdiction, a complaint, or other lawful statement of his cause of action, and shall also file an affidavit and bond; and thereupon such creditor may sue out an original attachment against the lands, tenements, goods, moneys, effects, credits and any right, title, lien or interest whether legal or equitable upon, in or to real or personal, tangible or intangible property whether present or possessory or reversionary or in remainder and all property which could be reached upon execution or upon equitable proceedings in aid of execution, of the debtor in whosesoever hands they may be except such property as is now, or may hereafter be, specifically exempted from attachment or execution by law and except interests of beneficiaries in spendthrift trusts for whom spendthrift trusts are or may be created.

2. Chapter 45

§ 45-1-201. *Definitions.*

A. As used in the Uniform Probate Code, unless the context otherwise requires:

. . . .

(12) "estate" includes the property of the decedent, trust or other person whose affairs are subject to the Uniform Probate Code as originally constituted and as it exists from time to time during administration;

(37) "property" includes both real and personal property or any interest therein and means anything that may be the subject of ownership;

. . . .

§ 45-2-101. *Intestate estate.*

A. Any part of a decedent's estate not effectively disposed of by his will passes by intestate succession to the decedent's heirs as prescribed in the Uniform Probate Code, except as modified by the decedent's will.

B. A decedent by will may expressly exclude or limit the right of an individual or class to succeed to property of the decedent passing by intestate succession. If that individual or a member of that class survives the decedent, the share of the decedent's intestate estate to which that individual or class would have succeeded passes as if that individual or each member of that class had disclaimed his intestate share.

§ 45-2-901. *Statutory rule against perpetuities.*

A. A nonvested property interest is invalid unless:

(1) when the interest is created, it is certain to vest or terminate no later than twenty-one years after the death of an individual then alive; or

(2) the interest either vests or terminates within ninety years after its creation.

B. [Omitted].

C. [Omitted].

D. In determining whether a nonvested property interest or a power of appointment is valid under each Paragraph (1) of Subsections A, B and C of this section, the possibility that a child will be born to an individual after the individual's death shall be disregarded.

E. If, in measuring a period from the creation of a trust or other property arrangement, language in a governing instrument seeks to postpone the vesting or termination of any interest or trust until, seeks to disallow the vesting or termination of any interest or trust beyond, seeks to require all interests or trusts to vest or terminate no later than, or seeks to operate in effect in any similar fashion upon the later of:

(1) the expiration of a period of time not exceeding twenty-one years after the death of the survivor of specified lives in being at the creation of the trust or other property arrangement; or

(2) the expiration of a period of time that exceeds or might exceed twenty-one years after the death of the survivor of lives in being at the creation of the trust or other property arrangement, then the portion of the language described in Paragraph (2) above is inoperative if and to the extent it produces a period of time that exceeds twenty-one years after the death of the survivor of the lives specified in Paragraph (1) above.

§ 45-2-902. *Nonvested property interest or power of appointment created*

A. Except as provided in Subsections B and C of this section and except as provided in Subsection A of Section 45-2-905 NMSA 1978, the time of creation of a nonvested property interest or a power of appointment is determined under general principles of property law.

B. Under Sections 45-2-901 through 45-2-905 NMSA 1978, if there is a person who alone can exercise a power created by a governing instrument to become the unqualified owner of either a nonvested property interest or a property interest subject to a power of appointment as described in Subsection B or C of Section 45-2-901 NMSA 1978, the nonvested property interest or power of appointment is created when the power to become the unqualified beneficial owner terminates. Under Sections 45-2-901 through 45-2-905 NMSA 1978, a joint power with respect to community property or to marital property under the Uniform Marital Property Act held by individuals married to each other is a power exercisable by one person alone.

C. Under Sections 45-2-901 through 45-2-905 NMSA 1978, a nonvested property interest or a power of appointment arising from a transfer of property to a previously funded trust or other existing property arrangement is created when the nonvested property interest or power of appointment in the original contribution was created.

§ 45-2-903. *Reformation.*

Upon the petition of an interested person, a court shall reform a disposition in the manner that most closely approximates the transferor's manifested plan of distribution and is within the ninety years allowed by each Paragraph (2) of Subsections A, B or C of Section 45-2- 901 NMSA 1978 if:

A. a nonvested property interest or a power of appointment becomes invalid under Section 45-2- 901 NMSA 1978;

B. a class gift is not but might become invalid under Section 45-2- 901 NMSA 1978 and the time has arrived when the share of any class member is to take effect in possession or enjoyment; or

C. a nonvested property interest that is not validated by Paragraph (1) of Subsection A of Section 45-2- 901 NMSA 1978 can vest but not within ninety years after its creation.

§ 45-2-904. *Exclusions.*

Section 45-2- 901 NMSA 1978 does not apply to:

A. a nonvested property interest or a power of appointment arising out of a nondonative transfer, except a nonvested property interest or a power of appointment arising out of:

(1) a premarital or postmarital agreement;

(2) a separation or divorce settlement;

(3) a spouse's election;

(4) a similar arrangement arising out of a prospective, existing or pervious marital relationship between the parties;

(5) a contract to make or not to revoke a will or trust;

(6) a contract to exercise or not to exercise a power of appointment;

(7) a transfer in satisfaction of a duty of support; or

(8) a reciprocal transfer;

B. a fiduciary's power relating to the administration or management of assets, including the power of a fiduciary to sell, lease or mortgage property and the power of a fiduciary to determine principal and income;

C. a power to appoint a fiduciary;

D. a discretionary power of a trustee to distribute principal before termination of a trust to a beneficiary having an indefeasibly vested interest in the income and principal;

E. a nonvested property interest held by a charity, government or governmental agency or subdivision if the nonvested property interest is preceded by an interest held by another charity, government or governmental agency or subdivision;

F. a nonvested property interest in or a power of appointment with respect to a trust or other property arrangement forming part of a pension, profit sharing, stock bonus, health, disability, death benefit, income deferral or other current or deferred benefit plan for one or more employees, independent contractors or their beneficiaries or spouses, to which contributions are made for the purpose of distributing to or for the benefit of the participants or their beneficiaries or spouses the property, income or principal in the trust or other property arrangement, except a nonvested property interest or a power of appointment that is created by an election of a participant or a beneficiary or spouse;

G. a property interest, power of appointment or arrangement that was not subject to the common-law rule against perpetuities or that is excluded by another statute of New Mexico; or

H. a property interest or arrangement subject to a time limit under the provisions of Section 45-2-907 NMSA 1978.

§ 45-2-905. *Prospective application.*

A. Except as extended by Subsection B of this section, Sections 45-2- 901 through 45-2- 905 NMSA 1978 apply to a nonvested property interest or a power of appointment that is created on or after July 1, 1992. For purposes of this section, a nonvested property interest or a power of appointment created by the exercise of a power of appointment is created when the power is irrevocably exercised or when a revocable exercise becomes irrevocable.

B. If a nonvested property interest or a power of appointment was created before July 1, 1992 and is determined in a judicial proceeding, commenced on or after July 1, 1992, to violate the New Mexico rule against perpetuities as that rule existed before July 1, 1992, a court, upon the petition of an interested person, may reform the disposition in the manner that most closely approximates the transferor's manifested plan of distribution and is within the limits of the rule against perpetuities applicable when the nonvested property interest or power of appointment was created.

§ 45-2-906. *Supervision.*

Sections 45-2- 901 through 45-2- 905 NMSA 1978 supersede the rule of the common law known as the rule against perpetuities.

3.   Chapter 47

§ 47-1-2. *Monopolies; entailments; primogeniture.*

Monopolies are contrary to the genius of a free government and shall never be allowed, nor shall the law of primogeniture or entailments ever be in force in this state.

§ 47-1-4. *Conveyances authorized.*

Any person or persons, or body politic, holding, or who may hold, any right or title to real estate in this state, be it absolute or limited, in possession, remainder or reversion, may convey the same in the manner and subject to the restrictions prescribed in this chapter.

§ 47-1-15.   *Joint grantees or devisees; tenancy in common.*

All interest in any real estate, either granted or bequeathed to two or more persons other than executors or trustees, shall be held in common, unless it be clearly expressed in said grant or bequest that it shall be held by both parties.

§ 47-1-16.   *[Instrument of conveyance; prima facie evidence of joint tenancy.]*

An instrument conveying or transferring title to real or personal property to two or more persons as joint tenants, to two or more persons and to the survivors of them and the heirs and assigns of the survivor, or to two or more persons with right of survivorship, shall be prima facie evidence that such property is held in a joint tenancy and shall be conclusive as to purchasers or encumbrancers for value. In any litigation involving the issue of such tenancy a preponderance of the evidence shall be sufficient to establish the same.

§ 47-1-17.   *[Entailed estates.]*

Whenever a conveyance or bequest is made wherein the conveyor or testator shall hold possession of property, be it lands or tenements, in law or equity, as under English Statute of Edward the First, styled the entail statute, [1] and said property is to be perpetuated in the family, each one of said conveyances or bequests shall only invest the conveyors or testators [2] with possession during their lifetime, who shall possess and hold the right and title to said premises, and no others the same as a tenant for life is recognized by law; and at the death of said conveyor or testator said lands and tenements shall descend to the children of said conveyor or testator, to be equally divided among them as absolute tenants in common; and if there should be but one child, it shall descend absolutely to it; and if any child should die, the part which he or she should have received shall be given to his or her successor, and if there should be no such successor, then it shall descend to his or her legal heirs.

§ 47-1-18. *Reversion; "heirs" and "successors" defined.*

When a balance or residue, in lands or tenements, goods or property, is limited by writing or otherwise to take effect after the decease of any person without heirs, or bodily heirs or succession, the words heirs and successors shall be so construed as to mean heirs or successors living, at the time of the decease of the person styled ancestor.

---

[1] This somewhat off-hand reference is to the enactment of Parliament known more commonly as De Donis Conditionalibus, 13 Edw. I, ch. 1 (1285), given short shrift by the discussion above. De Donis, as it is known by intimates, granted recognition to the fee tail as you have mastered it and protected the rights of the lineal descendants from disentailment

[2] This reference quite obviously should be to conveyees and legatees.

§ 47-1-19. *Rights of heirs of life tenant when made remaindermen.*

When the remainder of a possession is limited to the heirs or heirs of the body of a person who holds said property as a life estate, in these premises the persons who at the termination of said life estate, are to be heirs or heirs of the body of said life estate, shall be authorized to take as purchasers by virtue of the remainder of the possession so limited in them.

§ 47-1-20. *[Remainder to unborn child.]*

When any possession has been or shall be conveyed limiting the remainder of the possession to the son or. daughter of any person, born after the death of its parent, possession shall be taken the same as if he or she was born during the life of the parent, although no possession should have been conveyed to sustain the remainder of a contingent possession after his death, and after this an absolute possession or bequest may be made, commencing in the future, in writing in the same manner as by will.

§ 47-1-21. *[Future possession dependent on death without heirs; effect of birth of posthumous child.]*

A future possession depending upon the contingency of the death of a person without heirs shall be revoked by the birth of a posthumous son or daughter of said person capable of succeeding him.

§ 47-1-23. *[Transfer of reversion authorized]*

That the possibility or right of reversion for breach or violation of condition or conditions subsequent contained in any deed or other instrument conveying real estate in the state of New Mexico, is hereby made assignable, and the grantor in any such instrument heretofore or hereafter made affecting real estate in the state of New Mexico, is given the right to assign and transfer such future contingent right of reentry, forfeiture and reversion for violation or breach of such condition or conditions subsequent.

§ 47-1-24. *[Rights of transferee of reversion.]*

The assignee of or any successor to the right of reentry, forfeiture and reversion for breach or violation of condition or conditions subsequent, is hereby given upon such assignment, all of the rights and privileges of the original grantor for the enforcement of reentry, forfeiture and reversion when any such condition or conditions subsequent shall have been breached or broken, including all legal and equitable remedies for the judicial enforcement of such right or rights.

§ 47-1-33. *Unnecessary terms; construction of deeds or reservations.*

In a conveyance or reservation of real estate the terms, "heirs," "assigns" or other technical words of inheritance shall not be necessary to convey or reserve an estate in fee. A deed or reservation of real estate shall be construed to convey or reserve an estate in fee simple, unless a different intention clearly appears in the deed.

§ 47-1-35. *[Conveyance or mortgage to joint tenants.]*

In a conveyance or mortgage of real estate, the designation of two or more grantees "as joint tenants" shall be construed to mean that the conveyance is to the grantees as joint tenants, and not as tenants in common, and to the survivor of them and the heirs and assigns of the survivor.

§ 47-1-36. *Joint tenancies defined; creation.*

A joint tenancy in real property is one owned by two or more persons, each owning the whole and an equal undivided share, by a title created by a single devise or conveyance, when expressly declared in the will or conveyance to be a joint tenancy, or by conveyance from a sole owner to himself and others, or from tenants in common to themselves, or to themselves and others, or from husband and wife when holding as community property or otherwise to themselves or to themselves and others, when expressly declared in the conveyance to be a joint tenancy, or when granted or devised to executors or trustees.

E. NORTH DAKOTA

1. Title 30.1

§ 30.1-04-01 (2-101).[3] *Intestate estate.*

Any part of the estate of a decedent not effectively disposed of by his will passes to his heirs as prescribed in the following sections of this title.

§ 30.1-04-02 (2-102). *Share of the spouse.*

The intestate share of the surviving spouse is:

1. If there is no surviving issue or parent of the decedent, the entire intestate estate.

2. If there is no surviving issue but the decedent is survived by a parent or parents, the first fifty thousand dollars, plus one-half of the balance of the intestate estate.

3. If there are surviving issue all of whom are issue of the surviving spouse also, the first fifty thousand dollars, plus one-half of the balance of the intestate estate.

4. If there are surviving issue, one or more of whom are not issue of the surviving spouse, one-half of the intestate estate.

§ 30.1-04-03 (2-103). *Share of heirs other than surviving spouse.*

The part of the intestate estate not passing to the surviving spouse under section 30.1-04-02, or the entire intestate estate if there is no surviving spouse, passes as follows:

1. To the issue of the decedent. If they are all of the same degree of kinship to the decedent they take equally, but if of unequal degree, then those of more remote degree take by representation.

2. If there is no surviving issue, to his parent or parents equally.

3. If there is no surviving issue or parent, to the issue of the parents or either of them by representation.

4. If there is no surviving issue, parent, or issue of a parent, but the decedent is survived by one or more grandparents or issue of grandparents, half of the estate passes to the paternal grandparents if both survive, or to the surviving paternal grandparent, or to the issue of the paternal grandparents if both are deceased, by representation; and the other half passes to the maternal relatives in the same manner. If there be no surviving grandparent or issue of grandparent on either the paternal or the maternal side, the entire estate passes to the relatives on the other side in the same manner as the half.[4]

§ 30.1-04-03.1. *Persons related to decedent through two lines.*

A person related to the decedent through two lines of relationship is entitled to only a single share based on the relationship that would entitle him to the larger share.

§ 30.1-04-04 (2-104). *Requirement that heir survive decedent for one hundred twenty hours.*

Any person who fails to survive the decedent by one hundred twenty hours is deemed to have predeceased the decedent for purposes of homestead allowance, exempt property, and intestate succession, and the decedent's heirs are determined accordingly. If the time of death of the decedent or of the person who would

---

[3] The parenthetical references are to the corresponding Uniform Probate Code sections.

[4] You will note that this section and the preceding one define the "heirs" differently than did the common law in a number of respects: the spouse is a potential heir, male domination is gone, and the class of heirs is more limited, reaching only as far as issue of grandparents. If it cannot be established that the person who would otherwise be an heir has survived the decedent by one hundred twenty hours, it is deemed that the person failed to survive for the required period. This section is not to be applied where its application would result in a taking of intestate estate by the state under section 30.1-04-05.

otherwise be an heir, or the times of death of both, cannot be determined, and it.

§ 30.1-04-05 (2-105). *No taker.*

If there is no taker under the provisions of this title, the intestate estate passes to the state for the support of the common schools and an action for the recovery of such property and to reduce it into the possession of the state or for its sale and conveyance may be brought by the attorney general or by the state's attorney in the district court of the county in which the property is situated.[5]

§ 30.1-04-06 (2-106). *Representation.*

If representation is called for by this title, the estate is divided into as many shares as there are surviving heirs in the nearest degree of kinship and deceased persons in the same degree who left issue who survive the decedent, each surviving heir in the nearest degree receiving one share and the share of each deceased person in the same degree being divided among his issue in the same manner.

§ 30.1-04-07 (2-107). *Kindred of half blood.*

Relatives of the half blood inherit the same share they would inherit if they were of the whole blood.

§ 30.1-04-08 (2-108). *Afterborn heirs.*

Relatives of the decedent conceived before his death but born thereafter inherit as if they had been born in the lifetime of the decedent.

§ 30.1-04-09 (2-109). *Meaning of child and related terms.*

If, for purposes of intestate succession, a relationship of parent and child must be established to determine succession by, through, or from a person:

1. An adopted person is the child of an adopting parent and not of the natural parents, except that adoption of a child by the spouse of a natural parent has no effect on the relationship between the child and either natural parent.

2. In cases not covered by subsection 1, a person is the child of its parents regardless of the marital status of its parents and the parent and child relationship may be established under the Uniform Parentage Act.

§ 30.1-04-10 (2-110). *Advancements.*

If a person dies intestate as to all his estate, property which he gave in his lifetime to an heir is treated as an advancement against the latter's share of the estate only if declared in a contemporaneous writing by the decedent or acknowledged in writing by the heir to be an advancement. For this purpose the property advanced is valued as of the time the heir came into possession or enjoyment of the property or as of the time of death of the decedent, whichever first occurs. If the recipient of the property fails to survive the decedent, the property is not taken into account in computing the intestate share to be received by the recipient's issue, unless the declaration or acknowledgment provides otherwise.

§ 30.1-04-11 (2-111). *Debts to decedent.*

A debt owed to the decedent is not charged against the intestate share of any person except the debtor. If the debtor fails to survive the decedent, the debt is not taken into account in computing the intestate share of the debtor's issue.

---

[5] The common law equivalent of this statute was the doctrine of escheat. Under the common law, the definition of "heir" was broad enough that ordinarily every decedent had an heir. Compare § 30.1-04-02, 03 above. Of course, practically speaking, it was/is often difficult to identify a remote collateral heir.

§ 30.1-04-12 (2-112). *Alienage.*

No person is disqualified to take as an heir because he or a person through whom he claims is or has been an alien.

§ 30.1-04-13 (2-113). *Dower and curtesy abolished.*

The estates of dower and curtesy are abolished.[6]

2. Title 47

§ 47-02-05. *Concurrent ownership defined.*

The ownership of property by several persons is either:

> 1. Of joint interests;
>
> 2. Of partnership interests; or
>
> 3. Of interests in common.

§ 47-02-08. *"Interest in common" defined.*

An interest in common is one owned by several persons not in joint ownership or partnership. Every interest created in favor of several persons in their own right is an interest in common, unless acquired by them in partnership for partnership purposes, or unless declared in its creation to be a joint tenancy.

§ 47-02-10. *"Present interest" defined.*

A present interest means that the owner is entitled to the immediate possession of the property.

§ 47-02-15. *Future estates — Classification.*

A future interest is either vested or contingent. It is vested when there is a person in being who would have a right, defeasible or indefeasible, to the immediate possession of the property upon the ceasing of the intermediate or precedent interest. It is contingent while the person in whom or the event upon which it is limited to take effect remains uncertain.

§ 47-02-16. *Alternative contingencies.*

Two or more future interests may be created to take effect in the alternative so that if the first in order fails to vest, the next in succession shall be substituted for it and take effect accordingly.

§ 47-02-18. *Future interests pass.*

Future interests pass by succession, will, and transfer in the same manner as present interests.

§ 47-02-20. *Mere possibility not an interest.*

A mere possibility, such as the expectancy of an heir apparent, is not to be deemed an interest of any kind.

§ 47-02-24. *Illegal conditions void.*

If a condition precedent requires the performance of an act wrong in itself, the instrument containing it is so far void, and the right cannot exist. If it requires the performance of an act not wrong of itself, but otherwise unlawful, the instrument takes effect and the condition is void.

---

[6] These common law estates, created by law in a widow upon the death of her husband and in a man upon marriage, were not within the scope of this guide. However, they provide examples of life estates at common law. *See* 2 R. Powell, *The Law of Real Property* ¶¶ 209-213 (P. Rohan, rev. ed. 1991).

§ 47-02-25. *Restraints upon marriage void — Use until marriage.*

Conditions imposing restraints upon marriage, except upon the marriage of a minor, or of the widow of the person by whom the condition is imposed, are void. This does not affect limitations when the intent was not to forbid marriage but only to give the use until marriage.

§ 47-02-26. *Restraints on alienation — When void.*

Conditions restraining alienation, when repugnant to the interest created, are void.

§ 47-02-27.1. *Statutory rule against perpetuities — Invalidity of certain contingent property interests, general powers of appointment, special powers of appointment, and general testamentary powers of appointment.*

1. A contingent property interest is invalid unless:

    a. When the interest is created, it is certain to vest or terminate no later than twenty-one years after the death of an individual then alive; or

    b. The interest either vests or terminates within ninety years after its creation.

2. A general power of appointment not presently exercisable because of a condition precedent is invalid unless:

    a. When the power is created, the condition precedent is certain to be satisfied or to become impossible to satisfy no later than twenty-one years after the death of an individual then alive; or

    b. The condition precedent either is satisfied or becomes impossible to satisfy within ninety years after its creation.

3. A special power of appointment or a general testamentary power of appointment is invalid unless:

    a. When the power is created, it is certain to be irrevocably exercised or otherwise to terminate no later than twenty-one years after the death of an individual then alive; or

    b. The power is irrevocably exercised or otherwise terminates within ninety years after its creation.

4. In determining whether a contingent property interest or a power of appointment is valid under subdivision a of subsection 1, subdivision a of subsection 2, or subdivision a of subsection 3, the possibility that a child will be born to an individual after the individual's death is disregarded.

5. If, in measuring a period from the creation of a trust or other property arrangement, language in a governing instrument seeks to disallow the vesting or termination of any interest or trust beyond, seeks to postpone the vesting or termination of any interest or trust until, or seeks to operate in effect in any similar fashion upon, the later of the expiration of a period of time not exceeding twenty-one years after the death of the survivor of specified lives in being at the creation of the trust or other property arrangement or the expiration of a period of time that exceeds or might exceed twenty-one years after the death of the survivor of lives in being at the creation of the trust or other property arrangement, that language is inoperative to the extent it produces a period of time that exceeds twenty-one years after the death of the survivor of the specified lives.

§ 47-02-27.2. *When contingent property interest or power of appointment is created.*

1. Except as provided in subsections 2 and 3 of this section and in subsection 1 of section 47-02-27.5, the time of creation of a contingent property interest or a power of appointment is determined under general principles of property law.

2. For purposes of sections 47-02-27.1 through 47-02-27.5, if there is a person who alone can exercise a

power created by a governing instrument to become an unqualified beneficial owner of a contingent property interest or a property interest subject to a power of appointment described in subsection 2 or 3 of section 47-02-27.1, the contingent property interest or power of appointment is created when the power to become the unqualified beneficial owner terminates.

3. For purposes of sections 47-02-27.1 through 47-02-27.5, a contingent property interest or a power of appointment arising from a transfer of property to a previously funded trust or other existing property arrangement is created when the contingent property interest or power of appointment in the original contribution was created.

§ 47-02-27.3. *Reformation.*

Upon the petition of an interested person, a court shall reform a disposition in the manner that most closely approximates the transferor's manifested plan of distribution and is within the ninety years allowed under subdivision b of subsection 1 of section 47-02-27.1, subdivision b of subsection 2 of section 47-02-27.1, and subdivision b of subsection 3 of section 47-02-27.1, if:

1. A contingent property interest or a power of appointment becomes invalid under section 47-02-27.1;

2. A class gift is not but might become invalid under section 47-02-27.1 and the time has arrived when the share of any class member is to take effect in possession or enjoyment; or

3. A contingent property interest that is not validated by subdivision a of subsection 1 of section 47-02-27.1 can vest but not within ninety years after its creation.

§ 47-02-27.4. *Exclusions from statutory rule against perpetuities.*

Section 47-02-27.1 does not apply to:

1. A contingent property interest or a power of appointment arising out of a nondonative transfer, except a contingent property interest or a power of appointment arising out of a premarital or postmarital agreement, a separation or divorce settlement, a spouse's election, a similar arrangement arising out of a prospective, existing, or previous marital relationship between the parties, a contract to make or not to revoke a will or trust, a contract to exercise or not to exercise a power of appointment, a transfer in satisfaction of a duty of support, or a reciprocal transfer.

2. A fiduciary's power relating to the administration or management of assets, including the power of a fiduciary to sell, lease, or mortgage property, and the power of a fiduciary to determine principal and income.

3. A power to appoint a fiduciary.

4. A discretionary power of a trustee to distribute principal before termination of a trust to a beneficiary having an indefeasibly vested interest in the income and principal.

5. A contingent property interest held by a charity, government, or governmental agency or subdivision, if the contingent property interest is preceded by an interest held by another charity, government, or governmental agency or subdivision.

6. A property interest, power of appointment, or arrangement that was not subject to the common-law rule against perpetuities or excluded by another statute of this state.

§ 47-02-27.5. *Prospective application.*

1. Except as extended by subsection 2, sections 47-02-27.1 through 47-02-27.5 apply to a contingent property interest or a power of appointment that is created on or after July 1, 1991. For purposes of this section, a contingent property interest or a power of appointment created by the exercise of a power of appointment is created when the power is irrevocably exercised or when a revocable exercise becomes irrevocable.

2. If a contingent property interest or a power of appointment was created before July 1, 1991, and is determined in a judicial proceeding, commenced on or after July 1, 1991, to violate this state's rule against perpetuities as that rule existed before July 1, 1991, a court upon the petition of an interested person may reform the disposition in the manner that most closely approximates the transferor's manifested plan of distribution and is within the limits of the rule against perpetuities applicable when the contingent property interest or power of appointment was created.

§ 47-02-30. *Future interest — Effect of change of intermediate interest.*

No future interest can be defeated or barred by any alienation or other act of the owner of the intermediate or precedent interest, nor by any destruction of such precedent interest by forfeiture, surrender, merger, or otherwise, except as provided by section 47-02-32, or when a forfeiture is imposed by statute as a penalty for the violation thereof.

§ 47-02-32. *Future interest — Effect of determination of precedent interest Contingent remainders not artificially destructible.*

No future interest, valid in its creation, is defeated by the determination of the precedent interest before the happening of the contingency on which the future interest is limited to take effect, but should such contingency afterwards happen, the future interest takes effect in the same manner and to the same extent as if the precedent interest had continued to the same period.

§ 47-02-33. *Rights of owner of life estate.*

The owner of a life estate may use the land in the same manner as the owner of a fee simple, except that he must do no act to the injury of the inheritance.

§ 47-04-04. *"Estate in fee" defined.*

Every estate of inheritance is a fee, and every such estate, when not defeasible or conditional, is a fee simple or an absolute fee.

§ 47-04-05. *Estates tail abolished — Declared fees.*

Estates tail are abolished and every estate which would be adjudged a fee tail at common law is a fee simple, and if no valid remainder is limited thereon, is a fee simple absolute.

§ 47-04-06. *Fee tail valid as contingent limitation upon a fee.*

Where a remainder in fee is limited upon any estate which, by the common law, would be adjudged a fee tail, such remainder is valid as a contingent limitation upon a fee and vests in possession on the death of the first taker, without issue living at the time of his death.

§ 47-04-07. *Estate for life is freehold.*

An estate during the life of a third person, whether limited to heirs or otherwise, is a freehold.

§ 47-04-09. *"Reversion" defined.*

A reversion is the residue of an estate left by operation of law in the grantor or his successors or in the successors of a testator commencing in possession on the determination of a particular estate granted or devised.

§ 47-04-10. *"Remainder" defined.*

When a future estate, other than a reversion, is dependent on a precedent estate, it may be called a remainder and may be created and transferred by that name.

§ 47-04-20. *Remainder limited to heirs of body of life tenant — Rule in Shelley's Case abolished.*

When a remainder is limited to the heirs, or heirs of the body, of a person to whom a life estate in the same property is given, the persons who, on the termination of the life estate are the successors or heirs of the body of the owner for life, are entitled to take by virtue of the remainder so limited to them and not as mere successors of the owner for life.

§ 47-04-21. *Remainder limited on estate for life or years — When effective.*

When a remainder on an estate for life or for years is not limited on a contingency defeating or avoiding such precedent estate, it shall be deemed intended to take effect only on the death of the first taker or the expiration by lapse of time of such term of years.

§ 47-09-14. *"Without issue" defined.*

When a future interest is limited by a grant to take effect on the death of any person without heirs, or heirs of his body, without issue, or in equivalent words, such words must be taken to mean successors or issue living at the death of the person named as ancestor.

§ 47-09-15. *Words of inheritance or succession unnecessary to fee.*

Words of inheritance or succession shall not be requisite to transfer a fee in real property.

§ 47-10-13. *Grant presumes fee simple title.*

A fee simple title is presumed to be intended to pass by a grant of real property unless it appears from the grant that a lesser estate was intended.

§ 47-10-16. *Reconveyance when estate defeated by non-performance of condition subsequent.*

When a grant is made upon condition subsequent and subsequently is defeated by the nonperformance of the condition, the person otherwise entitled to hold under the grant must reconvey the property to the grantor or his successors by grant duly acknowledged for record.

INDEX

[References are to sections.]

[References are to sections.]